THE
EVERYTHING
NORDIC
COOKBOOK

Dear Reader,

In my youth, I spent a lot of time with my grandparents, who, although native Minnesotans, ultimately settled in South Carolina (theirs was probably the only home in the state where a curling stone decorated the den and Scandinavian plates graced the walls). Still, they clung to the Nordic culinary traditions they had grown up with. We always had wild game, fish, and the freshest of local vegetables. ("Eat your rabbit food!" Grandpa would insist. "I'd rather pay grocery bills than doctor bills.") And we always, no exceptions, sat down around the formal dining table to enjoy our meals together.

After spending my twenties in southern California (learning to cook Chinese, Indian, and Mexican food like a pro), I landed in the Pacific Northwest—a place my grandparents would've loved, with its still-vibrant Scandinavian-American population, its cold waters, its bountiful forests. It was coming full circle . . . it was coming home. The availability of fresh-caught wild salmon, cold-climate root vegetables, and an abundant variety of berries inspired me to return to preparing our meals as my grandparents had: with a focus on freshness, seasonality, and simplicity.

I'm thrilled to be able to share their Nordic legacy with you. *Vær så god! Smaklig måltid!*

Kari Schoening Diehl

Welcome to the EVERYTHING® Series!

These handy, accessible books give you all you need to tackle a difficult project, gain a new hobby, comprehend a fascinating topic, prepare for an exam, or even brush up on something you learned back in school but have since forgotten.

You can choose to read an Everything® book from cover to cover or just pick out the information you want from our four useful boxes: e-questions, e-facts, e-alerts, and e-ssentials.

We give you everything you need to know on the subject, but throw in a lot of fun stuff along the way, too.

We now have more than 400 Everything® books in print, spanning such wide-ranging categories as weddings, pregnancy, cooking, music instruction, foreign language, crafts, pets, New Age, and so much more. When you're done reading them all, you can finally say you know Everything®!

QUESTION

Answers to common questions

FACT

Important snippets of information

ALERT

Urgent warnings

ESSENTIAL

Quick handy tips

PUBLISHER Karen Cooper

MANAGING EDITOR, EVERYTHING® SERIES Lisa Laing

COPY CHIEF Casey Ebert

ASSISTANT PRODUCTION EDITOR Melanie Cordova

ACQUISITIONS EDITOR Lisa Laing

ASSOCIATE DEVELOPMENT EDITOR Hillary Thompson

EDITORIAL ASSISTANT Matthew Kane

EVERYTHING® SERIES COVER DESIGNER Erin Alexander

LAYOUT DESIGNERS Erin Dawson, Michelle Roy Kelly, Elisabeth Lariviere

Visit the entire Everything® series at *www.everything.com*

THE
EVERYTHING®
NORDIC
COOKBOOK

Kari Schoening Diehl

Avon, Massachusetts

This book is dedicated to my parents, Kari Lenning Schoening and Kenneth Stengel Schoening. Thanks for making me your own and for sharing your lives, your love, and your legacy with me.

An Everything® Series Book.
Everything® and everything.com® are registered trademarks of F+W Media, Inc.

Published by Adams Media, a division of F+W Media, Inc.
57 Littlefield Street, Avon, MA 02322 U.S.A.
www.adamsmedia.com

ISBN 10: 1-4405-3186-2
ISBN 13: 978-1-4405-3186-6
eISBN 10: 1-4405-3282-6
eISBN 13: 978-1-4405-3282-5

Printed in the United States of America.

10 9 8 7 6 5 4 3 2 1

This publication is designed to provide accurate and authoritative information with regard to the subject matter covered. It is sold with the understanding that the publisher is not engaged in rendering legal, accounting, or other professional advice. If legal advice or other expert assistance is required, the services of a competent professional person should be sought.

—From a *Declaration of Principles* jointly adopted by a Committee of the American Bar Association and a Committee of Publishers and Associations

Many of the designations used by manufacturers and sellers to distinguish their products are claimed as trademarks. Where those designations appear in this book and Adams Media was aware of a trademark claim, the designations have been printed with initial capital letters.

Always follow safety and commonsense cooking protocol while using kitchen utensils, operating ovens and stoves, and handling uncooked food. If children are assisting in the preparation of any recipe, they should always be supervised by an adult.

Photographs by Susan Whetzel.

*This book is available at quantity discounts for bulk purchases.
For information, please call 1-800-289-0963.*

Contents

Acknowledgments

Family should always come first, and so it is with heartfelt love and gratitude that I thank my best friend and husband, Peter Diehl, and our children, Eric, Anna, and David, for their willingness to play second fiddle while I finished this book. Thanks for taking over the marketing, cooking, and cleaning during the final writing stages, guys! I'll take my apron back now, please, free to prepare all of Eric's "Top 10 Nordic Things—besides me—That Mom's Ever Made."

Many thanks also to my parents, Kari and Kenneth Schoening, to my sister Krista Fox, to Magga Harðardottir, and to Margrit Meinel Diehl for your love, encouragement, cooking advice, and editing support. Barbara Rolek, Ellen Hinds, Hank Shaw, and the late Kevin Weeks—thanks for sharing your professional expertise with me and for talking me through the rough spots. Lynn and Cheyanne Bennett, you rock. So do Shellie Stevens, Susan Amanda Eurich, Laurent Martel, the sisters of Nellie Gerdrum Lodge #41 of the Daughters of Norway, the About.com food guides, and Diehls and Horners all. Ditto to my novelist/writers' group friends Janet Oakley, Sherry Brummel, Heidi Thomas, and also to Deborah Hale (for sending me the Swedish editions of her great stories). Finally, thanks to the wisest and most generous writing manager ever, Jason Reece, for giving me extended leaves of absence so that I could pursue this dream of publication. I'm truly blessed in my family, friends, and associates.

Introduction

SCANDINAVIA, WITH ITS HARSHLY beautiful mountains, deep fjords, isolated islands, thermal hot springs, and, perhaps most of all, the ageless sea that surrounds, feeds, and even today defines its people, has not always been viewed as the most likely candidate to produce a world-class cuisine. Until very recently, if asked to describe typical "Scandinavian" or "Nordic" food, many people—no doubt thinking of all of that polar snow and ice— would think, "Well, it's very . . . fishy and white, isn't it?" White cod. White fish pudding. Bergen white fish soup with white dumplings. White cheeses. White potato soups and *lefse* (soft Norwegian potato flatbread). White horseradish. White Icelandic *skyr* (yogurt). White sauce on white lutefisk. Nordic cuisine—at least as it has been stereotyped—would hardly seem a contender if forced to compete with the vibrant colors and flavors of the foods of warmer regions like Italy, southern France, and Spain.

Fortunately, a cohort of Scandinavia's finest chefs and food journalists, led by Claus Meyer and René Redzepi (founders of Copenhagen's Noma, twice selected as the "Best Restaurant in the World" in *Restaurant Magazine*'s San Pellegrino awards), have spearheaded what amounts to a culinary revolution: the New Nordic Cuisine Movement. Utterly dispelling the stereotype, these chefs demonstrate how the foods native to Denmark, Norway, Sweden, Iceland, and Finland are just as healthy, delicious, and even as colorful as those of Mediterranean climes. Even more important, they emphasize many of the same principles that other advocates of rising culinary and dietary movements have stressed: that our modern generation, threatened by unprecedented levels of obesity, cardiovascular disease, and diabetes, needs to return to the saner methods of food acquisition, preparation, and consumption that our grandparents or great-grandparents practiced.

That's inspiring news for many Americans and Canadians, many of whom live in snowy climates similar to Scandinavia's, and who, given the increasingly publicized cases of food contamination that have resulted from the country's widespread distribution system, are beginning to worry about the safety of foods gathered, processed, and transported by and from unknown sources. As the current generation is beginning to realize, at long last, physical health and emotional welfare can be significantly enhanced when you take an active role in procuring local ingredients in season, cook and prepare your meals from scratch, and take the time to sit down and enjoy them with your favorite people.

So, how does one adapt the tenets espoused by highly trained, professional Nordic chefs to American home kitchens and working conditions? Perhaps it's easiest to remember the one thing that has always characterized the best in Scandinavian food and interior design—simplicity. When you focus upon using the purest and freshest of local root vegetables, berries, meats, and seafood, you don't need to spend a lot of time in the kitchen or worry about possessing the culinary genius of René Redzepi. You simply need to retrain your palate to appreciate the freshness and texture of seasonally gathered foods, to experience the deep sensory pleasure that comes from baking homemade bread or setting a soup to simmer "low and slow," and to discover the pride that comes from cooking with ingredients that you have either foraged for yourself or have acquired directly from the person who has grown them for you.

Simplicity. Seasonality. Sustainability. Social Engagement. This is what the Nordic culinary lifestyle is all about. *Er du sulten*? (In Norwegian, "Are you hungry?")

CHAPTER 1

Introduction to Nordic Food

"New Nordic Cuisine," a concept developed and promoted by Scandinavia's leading chefs, dietitians, and food journalists, is worthy of exploration not only by people who live where it snows, but by anyone interested in learning how to enrich their diet with the freshest of locally procured or foraged foods. While it celebrates the goodness of cold-climate foods native to Denmark, Norway, Sweden, Iceland, and Finland, this exciting food movement is just as much about how one acquires and prepares seasonal, local ingredients. Here's how to embrace not only a cuisine but a healthy lifestyle worthy of emulation.

The New Nordic Cuisine Movement

"New" Nordic cuisine took shape as a movement in 2004, when Claus Meyer and René Redzepi, founders of Copenhagen's now-famous restaurant, Noma, organized a symposium between twelve of Scandinavia's foremost chefs. Their intention? To define nothing less than a comprehensive, uniquely Scandinavian nutritional credo.

Subsequently adopted by the Nordic Council of Ministers in 2005, the results of this historic symposium, "A New Nordic Kitchen Manifesto," is defined by ten key objectives (here paraphrased in brief from Claus Meyer's original statement):

- To prepare fresh, pure, and seasonal food
- To eat foods in season
- To base cooking on local Nordic ingredients to create food that's not only delicious, but healthy
- To promote Nordic products, producers, and culture on a global level
- To ensure that fishing, hunting, and farming processes are safe, organic, and humane
- To reinvent or modernize traditional Nordic recipes
- To welcome the "fusion" of Nordic culinary traditions with inspiration from abroad
- To promote a regional distribution of some food products while still endorsing local self-sufficiency
- To build mutually beneficial, pan-Scandinavian partnerships across the food industry and with consumers, scientists, educators, politicians, and authorities

QUESTION

Where can I learn more about the New Nordic Kitchen Manifesto? For a detailed discussion of the history, principles, and benefits of the New Nordic Cuisine Movement, please visit Claus Meyer's website at: *www.clausmeyer.dk*.

Setting folks on fire faster than Vikings on a spree, Redzepi and Meyer's vision has been embraced across Scandinavia and Great Britain by chefs and home cooks eager to return to the foodways of our grandparents' generation: utilizing the freshest of seasonal, locally procured ingredients to create delicious, nutritionally balanced meals meant to be savored as they are best prepared—slowly and mindfully.

The success and positive outcomes of the movement are tangible: In 2010 and 2011, Noma captured *Restaurant Magazine*'s title of "Best Restaurant in the World." Scandinavian chefs swept the 2011 Bocuse d'Or competition (the Olympics of the international culinary world). And both the beautifully produced public television series *New Scandinavian Cooking*, hosted by Meyer, Andreas Viestad, Tina Nordström, and Sara La Fountain, and two equally beautiful cookbooks by Trina Hahnemann, *The Scandinavian Cookbook* (Andrews McMeel Publishing: 2009) and *The Nordic Diet* (Quadrille Publishing: 2010/Skyhorse Publishing: 2011) have sparked widespread interest in Nordic cooking in the United States.

The desire to promote "Nordic" cuisine wasn't original to Redzepi and Meyer, who stand on the shoulders of a culinary giant. Sweden's most famous restaurateur, Tore Wretman (1916–2003), although trained in French professional kitchens, was passionate about promoting *Husmanskost*, traditional Swedish home cooking. (This is a bit ironic, since Wretman was also responsible for introducing imported avocados and green bell peppers to Scandinavian cuisine.) He revived the tradition of the *smörgåsbord* at his Stockholm restaurants, Riche and the Operakällaren ("Opera Cellar"). He also cofounded Sweden's Gastronomic Academy.

Local Flavors: Scandinavian "Terroir" Principles

One of the primary principles of the New Nordic Cuisine Movement is an emphasis on what the French call *terroir*: the climatic conditions and cultivation practices responsible for those foods that flourish in specific environments. Food that is gathered, farmed, fished, or hunted in Scandinavia has characteristics distinctive to its environmental landscape—what Claus Meyer calls "the 'soul' of the location." The *terroir* of Scandinavia, although it varies from country to country, is generally a harsh one; yet, the plants and animals that have naturally adapted to its alternating seasons of light and darkness, its polar winters, its short summers, and—often—its mountainous soils are just as conducive to good health as those native to warmer climes closer to the equator. The glory of the New Nordic Cuisine Movement is that it showcases the health benefits of basing your diet primarily upon local, organic foods, unaltered by genetic engineering or forced farming, that have been allowed to ripen at their own pace in minimally cultivated ecosystems. Foraging and/or acquiring foods straight from their source—when they are in season—is a primary first step in recovering what many of us have lost in this age of packaged and prepared food transported across vast distances. It's a reminder of our symbiotic connection to our environment and the joy of anticipating foods you can (or at least, should) only experience at specific times of the year.

Although certainly not identical to the Nordic *terroir*, the climates of the northern states and provinces of North America are similar enough to Scandinavia's to enable us to emulate the principals of the Nordic food movement. It isn't a coincidence that more Scandinavian immigrants settled in Minnesota, Wisconsin, Upper Michigan, Iowa, and the Pacific Northwest than in Florida or New Mexico. They wanted to be in places that reminded them of home, and that allowed them to continue to enjoy the cold-climate berries, root vegetables, fish, and wild game of their homelands.

Things that Grow in Snow: Native Fruit, Grains, and Vegetables

Look at any recent top ten list of the healthiest foods you can eat, and you will find that most of the foods mentioned are native to Nordic climes. There is the vast abundance of summer's berries: lingonberries, cloudberries (called "bakeapples" where they grow wild in Alaska and Canada), gooseberries, elderberries, blueberries, and strawberries—all rich in antioxidants vital to nervous system and brain health. The hardy, unrefined, high-fiber grains of Scandinavia—rye, barley, oats, and spelt (now returned to cultivation after a hiatus of a century or two)—are proven to reduce the risk of Type 2 diabetes and cardiovascular disease, and contain amounts of cancer-fighting phytochemicals equal to or greater than fruits and vegetables. These whole grains have the added benefit of being useful for reducing the discomfort of perimenopause and of significantly lowering the risk of colon and breast cancer. And colorful cold-climate root and cruciferous vegetables—beets, rutabagas, onions, kohlrabi, cabbage—are all indispensible superfoods. Even often-vilified potatoes are extremely nutritious when prepared properly (baked, not deep-fried): they are a great source of nervous system–soothing B6.

Fresh from the Fjord: Fish, Seafood, and Shellfish

In water-locked Scandinavia, fish and seafood from the ocean and pristine lakes were traditionally key both to subsistence and to the economy (Norway is still a leading exporter of salt cod). Two to three servings a week of heart-healthy cold-water fish like salmon, cod, herring, and halibut, rich in omega-3 fatty acids, can lower triglycerides and "bad" LDL cholesterol, preventing the metabolic syndrome that leads to heart disease, diabetes, and stroke.

ALERT

Please note that before following any of the dietary suggestions in this book, you should first secure the approval of your physician, especially if you have a pre-existing condition like kidney disease, cancer, diabetes, heart disease, or pregnancy that requires a special diet. People with kidney disease, for example, shouldn't eat venison, which is high in purines and can contribute to kidney stones or gout; neither should they ingest juniper berries (often a flavoring used for wild game). Women who are pregnant or nursing and also young children should limit their consumption of cold-water fish, which may contain mercury. Safety first: check with your doctor.

What Big Antlers You Have: Wild Game and Fowl

In Scandinavia, where a strong hunting culture still predominates, one can find wild game in the supermarket—a distribution practice that Americans should lobby for. Game meat—venison, boar, moose, elk (in America), rabbit, wild fowl—is so lean and succulent when cooked properly that it deserves a much larger place in American cuisine than it now enjoys. If you don't hunt yourself or have hunter friends willing to share their bounty with you, you can order farm-raised game online from several suppliers. It's often fairly expensive, requiring refrigerated shipment from far away, but is worth the cost if that's the only way you can get it. Enjoyed in moderation—as most red meat and pork should be—wild game is the perfect antidote to restore palates and waistlines destroyed by too many fast-food burgers.

Use What You Have: Nordic Seasonal Cooking from Scratch

In 1755, Swedish cookbook author Kasja Warg championed a cooking method that became proverbial for generations: *Man tager hvað man hafver.* Loosely translated, this means "Use what you have on hand," a piece of wisdom that ought to be embroidered and hung in kitchens everywhere, with perhaps the addition of the word "locally" added for clarification. Cooking seasonal foods from scratch isn't difficult—often it calls for little more than a pot of water, some spices, ingenuity in using what you can find in your cupboard . . . and the one thing that's harder than fresh venison for many to find: time. It takes more time to source and select fresh fruit, vegetables, meats, and seafood than it does to order a pizza. It takes more time to cook food from scratch than it does to zap a frozen dinner in the microwave. It takes more time to sit together at a dinner table with your loved ones, enjoying good food and uninterrupted conversation, than it does to gobble a fast-food burger in the car, at your desk, or in front of the television set. Yet the health and emotional benefits of slowing down—even just a little bit—are incalculable.

ESSENTIAL

A key time-saving tip to think about when contemplating baking the Nordic way is that most Scandinavian cookies, cakes, and baked goods freeze magnificently. So do soups, stews, and savory pies. The trick is to make them when you have the leisure and inclination, then freeze them for later use on days when you're too tired to cook or when unexpected company drops by.

One of the greatest things about cooking many of the Nordic recipes in this book is that, while they are often (although not always) slow foods that need time to simmer over low and slow heat or to rest in the refrigerator for a few hours or even days, most of them don't take a lot of effort or advanced cooking skills to make. The only thing they require is some planning ahead. The hallmark of Nordic cooking, past and present, has always been simplicity. If you have your ingredients on hand, the primary time required is for tossing them together before allowing them to cook in the oven, to smoke outdoors (or indoors in a SAVU Smoker Bag), or to cold-cure in the refrigerator.

The Nordic Cupboard

So what are some of the staples you should keep on hand to facilitate cooking like a modern Viking? Here's a checklist:

○ **Whole Grains and Legumes:** rye flour, rye flakes, cracked rye, spelt flour, spelt berries, barley flour, pearl barley, oat flour, steel-cut oats, rolled oats, semolina, Swedish brown beans, dried yellow peas, potato starch flour (Swan brand), all-purpose flour

○ **Canned Seafood:** pickled herring, smoked herring, cod or lumpfish roe (caviar), Kalles roe spread, dried salt cod, Swedish spiced sprats (Swedish "anchovies")

○ **Dairy and Cheeses:** Icelandic *skyr* (Siggi's brand), buttermilk, *Snøfrisk*, Danish blue cheese (like Danablu brand), *gjetost* (Ski Queen brand), *Västerbotten*, *Nøkkelost*, Havarti, *Hushållsost* (farmer's cheese)

○ **Vegetable Bin:** onions, garlic, leeks, beets, rutabagas, cabbage, carrots, celery, celery roots, kohlrabi, potatoes, turnips, broccoli, cauliflower, horseradish

○ **Herbs and Spices:** cardamom pods or seed, dill (fresh and dried), dill seeds, star anise, anise seed, fennel seed, caraway seed, allspice berries, cloves, peppercorns, ground ginger, dried bitter orange peel, curry powder, coriander seed, mustard seed, saffron, bay leaves, juniper berries, rosemary, thyme, sage, tarragon, kosher salt, sea salt, cinnamon sticks, ground cinnamon, white pepper

○ **Dried Fruit:** prunes, cranberries, currants, raisins, rosehips, apples, apricots

○ **Jams and Sweeteners:** lingonberry jam, red currant jam, cloudberry jam, vanilla sugar, Swedish dark syrup (*mörk sirap*), Swedish light syrup (*ljus sirap*), honey, sugar, meringue powder, cocoa powder

○ **Nuts:** walnuts, hazelnuts, almonds

○ **Miscellaneous:** cold-pressed rapeseed oil (a.k.a. canola oil), hornsalt (baker's ammonia), dried mushrooms (morels, chanterelles, porcini), aquavit or potato vodka, vanilla beans, vanilla extract, cardamom extract, almond extract, lingonberry vinegar, rennet liquid or tablets, gravy browning (Kitchen Bouquet brand), unflavored gelatin powder, sheet gelatin, sago or pearl tapioca, active dry yeast, frozen puff pastry, capers, gherkins

Specialty Cooking Equipment

You don't necessarily need fancy cooking equipment to prepare flavorful Nordic recipes. However, if you love to bake, it's really nice to have these items: a *lefse* griddle, a *lefse* stick, a grooved rolling pin, a hob-knobbed rolling pin, a *plattar* (or plett) pan for Swedish pancakes, a Danish *æbleskiver* (or ebleskiver) pan, an almond cake pan, a 3-liter Danish rye bread pan (or a pullman pan), *sandbakkel* tins, a rosette iron, *kransekake* rings, a *krumkake* baker or iron, a waffle iron, and a potato ricer. To ease preparation of cooking in general, it's also great to own a stand mixer, a slow cooker, an outdoor or stovetop smoker (or Finnish SAVU Smoker Bags for use in the oven or on the grill), an immersion blender, a digital thermometer, and an oven thermometer.

Tips for Living a Nordic Culinary Lifestyle

Most of the principals espoused by current fads like the "whole food," "local food," and "slow food" movements apply to Nordic cooking as well—all reasons why this cuisine has attracted so much interest. If you close your eyes and think back to how your grandparents or great-grandparents procured, cooked, and consumed their meals, you'll find that you already know the basics:

- Whenever possible, buy vegetables, meats, and fish from local farmers, fishermen, and butchers—you should be able to shake the hand that picked your cabbage or caught your fish. Patronize farmers markets or become part of a CSA (Community Supported Agriculture)

food box program. Many CSAs allow you to request specific box contents, but it's even more fun—like Christmas every other week—to let yourself be surprised and creatively inspired by whatever they've placed in the box for you.

- Unless it's cheese, whole grains, or local meat or seafood, try to resist the urge to buy any food product packaged in plastic, Styrofoam, or cardboard. You can't smell foods for freshness if they're wrapped in plastic, and you can't control the ingredients of processed mixes or ready-made meals.

- If a food doesn't grow in your area or it's out of season, think twice, and then twice more, before eating it. Yes, there are exceptions to this tip—healthy staples like olive oil, seasonal treats like Christmas oranges, or the imported Scandinavian specialties like lingonberry jam and *matjes* herring you can find at any IKEA marketplace. But let your buying be ruled primarily by what's local and what's in season.

- Instead of going to a smelly gym to work off the results of a sedentary lifestyle, get outside and celebrate the changing seasons by foraging for nettles or elderflowers, picking summer berries, or fishing for lake trout. Plant a container or a hydroponic garden. There's something deeply rewarding about eating natural foods you've foraged or harvested for yourself.

- Avoid big-box stores (except for IKEA, of course, which features Scandinavian products). If you can, leave your car at home and patronize markets or grocery stores that are within walking or biking distance. Never buy more food at one time than you can carry home in two shopping bags. One of the reasons that Europeans are generally more fit than Americans is that many still walk to do their shopping.

- Enjoy sugar and alcohol—but *only* in the presence of others, where three or more are gathered together. Seriously. The Swedes love their *fika* (coffee breaks often accompanied with a sweet yeasted bread or pastry), often two or three times a day, but they generally walk to the coffee shops to meet their friends—they don't sit alone in their work cubicle drinking a double-sized caramel latte. You'll find an abundance of recipes for sweet breads, desserts, and alcoholic beverages in this book, but these are meant to be shared with others, in modest proportions, at special social occasions—not as comfort food pick-me-ups to wolf down in solitude.

Health Benefits of the New Nordic "Diet"

Neither this book nor the New Nordic Cuisine Movement in general are about weight loss. Rather, they're about lifestyle—the choices you make about what you choose to eat, where it comes from, how you get it home, how you prepare it, and how you eat it (hopefully, in the spirit of Danish *hygge*, relaxing with good friends at a cozy and calming dinner table).

Yet the evidence is mounting that following the principles endorsed by the New Nordic Kitchen Manifesto can indeed help to combat obesity and lead to improved health. In 2011, the American Society for Nutrition's *Journal of Nutrition* revealed how scientists from Denmark's Institute of Cancer Epidemiology and Aarhus University investigated the health benefits of a diet based on native Nordic foods, concluding that the consumption of things like root vegetables, healthy seafood, and—especially—whole-grain rye could be directly related to lower mortality among middle-aged Danes, especially men.

FACT

To read these early research findings favoring the Nordic diet, have a look at the abstract of the article "Healthy Aspects of the Nordic Diet Are Related to Lower Total Mortality" by Anja Olsen et al., of the Institute of Cancer Epidemiology, Danish Cancer Society, published in the *Journal of Nutrition* (2011, 141:4), and Claus Meyer's article "The Health Benefits of the Nordic Diet," at *www.clausmeyer.dk/en/the_new_nordic_cuisine*.

Additionally, in collaboration with Claus Meyer, an obesity research team at the University of Copenhagen has been conducting a $20 million, two-year research study investigating the weight-loss potential of a Nordic diet. Preliminary findings of one twenty-six-week study revealed that participants who adhered to a strict diet of native Scandinavian foods had, by week twelve, achieved a weight loss of 3.1 kilos (6.8 pounds) as opposed to the 1.6 kilo loss by participants who ate typical meals of meat, potatoes, and refined grain products.

Now that you know about the health benefits of a Nordic foods diet and lifestyle—let's get started!

CHAPTER 2

Appetizers

Gravlax on Crispbread

Gravlax, Scandinavia's hallmark cold-cured salmon dish, is so easy to make that you will never pay high prices for it in specialty markets again. Its name, translated roughly as "grave salmon," refers to a process dating back to medieval times when the raw fish was buried in sand to cure.

INGREDIENTS | SERVES 12 OR MORE

1 large skinless salmon fillet (3–4 pounds)

1 cup kosher salt

1 cup sugar

1 tablespoon freshly ground white pepper

2 bunches dill, finely chopped

¼ cup aquavit or potato vodka (optional)

Food Safety

If you live on a coast and have access to locally harvested salmon within a day or two of catch, it's fine to use the raw fish to prepare gravlax or salmon tartar. Otherwise, use salmon that has been frozen at −10°F for at least three days, defrosting it before preparation.

1. Rinse the fillet under cold water and pat dry with paper towels. Feel along the surface of the fillet and carefully remove any pin bones with pliers.

2. Mix together the kosher salt, sugar, white pepper, and chopped dill. Scatter half of the mixture across the bottom of a casserole dish just large enough to hold the fish. Place fillet on top, sprinkle with vodka (if using), then cover with remaining dill mixture.

3. Cover dish loosely with plastic wrap, then place a heavy rock or can directly on top of fillet to weight it down. Allow to sit at room temperature for 30 minutes to 1 hour so that the salt and sugar have time to dissolve into the fish.

4. Place the dish, rock and all, into the refrigerator and chill for at least two days (three if the fillet is more than 1½" thick), turning the fish and basting with any accumulated juices every 12 hours.

5. Before serving, rinse most of the curing mixture off the fillet (some dill should remain), and allow to dry out on a rack on the counter for an hour or so. Slice paper-thin and serve with rye crispbread and Dilled Mustard Sauce or Cucumber Horseradish Sauce (see recipes in this chapter).

Dilled Mustard Sauce

Dilled mustard sauce is the traditional accompaniment to Scandinavian gravlax. For best results, use sweet Swedish mustard as your base (available at most Scandinavian food suppliers).

INGREDIENTS | MAKES 1½ CUPS

4 tablespoons sweet Swedish mustard (or substitute 3 tablespoons honey mustard and 1 tablespoon Dijon mustard)

2 tablespoons white vinegar

1 cup finely chopped dill

1 tablespoon sugar

1 cup canola or olive oil

1. Using a large whisk, combine the mustard(s) with the vinegar.

2. Rub the dill and sugar together with a mortar and pestle until the sugar is absorbed, then whisk together with the mustard-vinegar sauce. Gradually stir in the oil until the sauce has the consistency of ketchup.

3. Chill in refrigerator for 1 hour before serving. Store covered and refrigerated for up to 3 weeks.

Curried Mustard Sauce

For a spicier sauce, try adding 2 teaspoons of your favorite curry blend (or more, if you like things hot) to this recipe.

Cucumber Horseradish Sauce

Horseradish sauce, (in Swedish, pepparrotssås) is a popular condiment in Scandinavia. Here, its sharpness is tempered by the subtle sweetness of minced cucumber.

INGREDIENTS | MAKES 1 CUP

1 cup low-fat sour cream

½ cup 1% milk

1 tablespoon prepared horseradish

1 tablespoon dill or parsley, finely chopped

¼ teaspoon freshly ground white pepper

1 medium garden cucumber, peeled, seeded, and finely minced

1. Whisk together sour cream, milk, prepared horseradish, chopped dill (or parsley), and white pepper.

2. Gently fold minced cucumber into sauce.

3. Refrigerate at least 1 hour before serving.

Salmon Roll with Baby Shrimp and Anchovy Sauce

Yogurt cheese provides the base for the creamy filling of this delicious appetizer. Made from low-fat Icelandic skyr, this homemade cream cheese imparts a tanginess that complements seafood perfectly.

INGREDIENTS | SERVES 6

3 cups plain Icelandic yogurt (*skyr*) or nonfat Greek yogurt (or substitute 8 ounces cream cheese)

½ cup precooked baby shrimp (defrosted if frozen)

¼ cup celery, finely diced

1 shallot, finely diced

1 tablespoon lemon juice

¼ teaspoon freshly ground white pepper

¼ teaspoon salt

16 slices gravlax or cold-smoked salmon

¼ cup fresh basil leaves

10 Swedish anchovies (or 1 [2-ounce] can of anchovy fillets)

⅔ cup milk to soak the anchovies

¼ cup parsley, roughly chopped

3 cloves garlic

Juice of 1 large lemon

2 cups extra-virgin olive oil

Icelandic *Skyr*

Thick and tangy *skyr*, a nonfat yogurt made in Iceland since Viking times, is now available in American markets under the Siggi's label. When *skyr* is eaten alone, it's traditional to top it with plenty of milk, sugar, and fresh berries.

1. To make yogurt cheese, place yogurt in a fine-meshed sieve lined with cheesecloth; position sieve over a bowl to drain at room temperature for 2 hours. Transfer to refrigerator to continue draining process overnight.

2. Fold together 1 cup of yogurt cheese, baby shrimp, celery, shallot, lemon juice, white pepper, and salt.

3. On an 8" × 11" piece of plastic wrap, overlap salmon slices in a straight line. Cover with a layer of basil leaves. Pipe or carefully spoon the shrimp mixture just left of the center of the rectangle; fold the left-hand side of the salmon layer over the filling, then continue rolling into a tight cylinder. Pull up the plastic wrap to cover the salmon roll and refrigerate for at least 1 hour before serving.

4. For the anchovy sauce, soak anchovies in milk for 30 minutes. Drain, rinse, and pat dry with paper towels.

5. Purée anchovies, parsley, garlic, and lemon juice in a food processor, about 1 minute. Gradually pour olive oil into the running processor until sauce is smooth.

6. To serve, drizzle anchovy sauce on plates. Cut chilled salmon roll into 6 diagonal slices; place on plates and garnish with additional lemon slices, parsley, or basil.

Salmon Tartar

As sushi-lovers have always known, wild salmon tastes best when served in all of its raw glory, adorned simply with a few well-chosen fresh vegetables.

INGREDIENTS | SERVES 24

1 pound frozen wild salmon fillet (king salmon, also called chinook salmon, is best; if you'd like to use fresh rather than flash-frozen salmon, make sure that you're using it within two or three days of catch)

1 tablespoon red onion, finely diced

1 tablespoon fresh fennel, finely diced

2 green onions, finely diced

1 teaspoon salt

¼ teaspoon sugar

¼ teaspoon freshly ground white pepper

Wasa rye crispbread or toasted rye bread slices

Swedish or Dijon mustard, as needed

1. Defrost salmon fillet and pat dry. Chop into a small, uniform dice.

2. Mix salmon with red onion, fresh fennel, green onions, salt, sugar, and pepper. Cover and refrigerate for at least 30 minutes (and up to 4 hours).

3. To serve, spread crispbread or toasted rye bread with a thin layer of mustard and top with mounds of salmon tartar.

Toast Skagen

Developed by famous Swedish restaurateur Tore Wretman in an attempt—decades before the New Nordic Cuisine Movement—to promote Scandinavian ingredients over imported fare, Toast Skagen showcases the unique baby shrimp harvested by fishermen in Skagen, Denmark.

INGREDIENTS | SERVES 6

2 tablespoons butter

6 slices spelt or rye bread, crusts removed

16 ounces peeled baby shrimp

6 tablespoons mayonnaise

1 teaspoon fresh dill, finely chopped

6 ounces salmon roe or lumpfish roe

Lemon slices, for garnish

1. Butter both sides of each slice of bread and fry in a skillet until golden.

2. In a medium bowl combine baby shrimp, mayonnaise, and chopped dill. Spoon onto toast slices.

3. Drain caviar well in a fine-meshed sieve lined with a paper towel or cheesecloth. Pat gently with paper towel to remove excess water and dye (if using lumpfish roe).

4. Top each toast with dollops of roe. Garnish with additional dill and lemon slices.

Scallop and Shrimp Skewers with Red Beet Mayonnaise

Red beets, the ultimate in cold-weather vegetables, are ubiquitous in Scandinavia. Roasting them brings out their sweetness. Or, when blended into a light mayonnaise sauce, they provide a colorful accompaniment to grilled shellfish.

INGREDIENTS | SERVES 10

1 large beet

2 cloves pressed garlic

½ cup low-fat mayonnaise

½ teaspoon salt

¾ teaspoon freshly ground pepper, divided use

¼ cup cold-pressed rapeseed (canola) oil

2 tablespoons lingonberry or red wine vinegar

2 teaspoons lemon juice

1 pound jumbo shrimp, peeled and deveined

1 pound large scallops

½ pound whole mushrooms

Cold-Pressed Rapeseed Oil

Cold-pressed rapeseed oil (a.k.a. canola oil), developed by Canadian scientists Baldur R. Stefansson and Keith Downey in 1978, is praised by modern Nordic chefs for its local availability and versatility. It is high in omega-3s, has a higher smoking point than olive oil, and is high in monounsaturated fat.

1. Preheat oven to 375°F. Scrub beet well and wrap in aluminum foil; roast in oven for 1 hour. Remove from oven; cool, peel, and roughly chop.

2. In a food processor, blend together roasted beet, pressed garlic, mayonnaise, salt, and ¼ teaspoon pepper. Refrigerate sauce until serving.

3. For your marinade, mix together rapeseed (canola) oil, lingonberry or red wine vinegar, lemon juice, and ½ teaspoon ground pepper.

4. Thread shrimp, scallops, and mushrooms onto skewers, pushing each skewer through the sides—not the middles—of the shellfish (if using bamboo or wood skewers, first presoak the skewers in hot water for 1 hour). Cover with marinade and refrigerate for 30 minutes.

5. Grill over medium heat for 4–5 minutes per side, basting with additional marinade when turning, until the shellfish are firm and lose their translucency. Discard remaining marinade.

6. Serve with roasted beet mayonnaise.

Three-Grain Finnish *Blini* with Forest Mushrooms

Finland, sharing a border with Russia, also shares many of the foods one typically identifies as Russian. These blini, best prepared in a flat cast-iron, 7-hole Scandinavian plattar (also called a "plett") pan, incorporate buckwheat, spelt, and the Finns' favorite flour—rye.

INGREDIENTS | SERVES 30

1½ cups 1% milk

1½ teaspoons active dry yeast

1 cup buckwheat flour

3 tablespoons rye flour

½ cup spelt flour (or substitute all-purpose flour)

1½ teaspoons salt

2 eggs, separated into whites and yolks

8 ounces sour cream

2 tablespoons clarified butter

1 ounce dried chanterelle mushrooms

1 ounce dried morel mushrooms

½ ounce dried porcini mushrooms

1 cup warm water

1 cup finely diced button mushrooms

1 tablespoon shallot, finely minced

1½ tablespoons olive oil

1 teaspoon fresh thyme leaves

1 heaping tablespoon crème fraîche or sour cream

Favorite *Blini* Toppings

Blinis are most commonly served with crème fraîche or sour cream and either caviar or the less expensive salmon or lumpfish roe. They're also lovely topped with gravlax, cold-smoked salmon, or smoked meats like reindeer (caribou), elk, or venison.

1. Heat the milk over a medium burner or in the microwave just until lukewarm (97°F). Stir in yeast until dissolved; gradually add buckwheat flour and mix until all is incorporated. Cover bowl with a clean towel and allow to sit and ferment overnight at room temperature.

2. In the morning, stir in rye flour, spelt flour, salt, egg yolks, and sour cream. Beat egg whites until peaks form, and then gently fold beaten whites into batter.

3. Brush the wells of a *plattar* pan or the bottom of a frying pan with the clarified butter and heat over a medium burner just until the butter begins to sizzle; spoon tablespoons of the batter on the pan and fry until golden, about 1 minute per side. Remove, cover, and keep warm until serving.

4. For forest mushroom topping, soak the dried chanterelle, morel, and porcini mushrooms in warm water for at least 30 minutes. Drain the mushrooms, reserving their water. Sauté diced button mushrooms and minced shallots in olive oil over medium heat for about 10 minutes, until mushrooms begin to exude juices. Stir in forest mushrooms and thyme leaves; sauté for an additional 2 minutes. Remove from heat and add salt and pepper to taste. Cool slightly, then blend with sour cream.

5. To serve, spoon generous dollops on warm *blini* and garnish with fresh parsley or thyme.

Hot-Smoked Salmon *Tarteletter*

These savory two-bite salmon tartlets are given a true Scandinavian flair when their shortcrust pastry is baked in pretty fluted sandbakkel tins.

INGREDIENTS | SERVES 30

½ cup butter

1 cup spelt flour (or substitute all-purpose flour)

5 tablespoons ice-cold water

½ cup half-and-half

1 egg

2 teaspoons fresh thyme or dill, finely minced

1 tablespoon red onion, finely minced

1 tablespoon lemon juice

½ pound hot-smoked salmon, finely chopped

½ teaspoon salt

¼ teaspoon freshly ground white pepper

Cold-Cured and Hot-Smoked Salmon

Cold-smoked salmon, the "lox" used on bagels, is prepared by brining the fish before placing it in indirect smoke; it has a slightly cooked edge but maintains its inner translucency. Gravlax, almost identical to lox, is simply brined under weight. Hot-smoked salmon is brined, air-dried, and then smoked over direct heat; drier than cold-smoked salmon, it flakes beautifully and adds an extra level of flavor and texture to appetizer fillings.

1. For spelt shortcrust pastry, chop butter into a ¼" dice and chill in mixing bowl for 30 minutes to 1 hour.

2. In a food processor, mix chilled butter with spelt flour for about 30 seconds, until dough has the texture of fine bread crumbs.

3. Return dough to chilled bowl and, using a fork, gradually stir in the ice-cold water, 1 tablespoon at a time, until it forms a cohesive ball. Transfer to a lightly floured counter and very lightly knead 2 or 3 times. Return dough to bowl, cover with cling wrap, and refrigerate for 30 minutes.

4. For salmon filling, whisk together half-and-half, egg, thyme, red onion, and lemon juice. Fold in chopped salmon; season with salt and white pepper.

5. Preheat oven to 350°F. After dough has rested, pinch off 1½-tablespoon portions and press into *sandbakkel* tins or other 3-inch tart molds. Spoon tablespoons of salmon into prepared tins. Bake for 15–20 minutes, until centers are set and pastry is golden-brown.

Hard-Boiled Eggs with Lumpfish Roe

Attend any gathering of Scandinavians or Scandinavian-Americans, and you're bound to find a plate of stuffed eggs as a key component of the smörgåsbord table.

INGREDIENTS | SERVES 10

5 eggs

¼ cup sour cream or crème fraîche

2 tablespoons red onion, finely chopped

1 tablespoon chives, finely chopped

1 (2-ounce) jar lumpfish roe (often sold under the "Romanoff" label)

1. Place whole eggs evenly on the bottom of a medium saucepan. Add cold water to cover the eggs by 1". Bring the pot to a strong boil, then immediately remove from heat, cover, and allow to sit for 17 minutes. Transfer eggs to a bowl of cold water and let sit an additional 10 minutes before peeling.

2. Slice eggs in half and remove the yolks. Cream the yolks together with the sour cream, red onion, and chives. Spoon or pipe yolk mixture back into the whites. Refrigerate until ready to serve.

3. Before serving, top with caviar and additional chopped chives, if desired.

New Potatoes with Lumpfish Roe

For a colorful arrangement, use both black and red lumpfish roe to top the season's first potatoes.

INGREDIENTS | SERVES 20

10 new potatoes (red, Yukon Gold, or a combination)

1 (2-ounce) jar lumpfish roe

¼ cup sour cream or crème fraîche

1. Boil potatoes in slightly salted water until tender, about 25 minutes. Rinse well, pat dry, and cut in half.

2. Allow lumpfish roe to drain on paper towels.

3. Arrange potatoes on a serving platter and top with teaspoons of sour cream and roe.

Lamb Meatballs with Lingonberries

Appetizers don't get much more Nordic than tender lamb meatballs crowned with lingonberry jam!

INGREDIENTS | SERVES 12

1 cup milk

1 cup rolled oats

½ cup red onion, minced

2 cloves garlic, minced

1 tablespoon canola or olive oil

1 pound ground lamb

1 egg

½ cup fresh mushrooms, finely diced

1 teaspoon rosemary, finely chopped

1 teaspoon salt

½ teaspoon freshly ground pepper

2 tablespoons cooking oil plus 1 tablespoon butter

⅔ cup lingonberry jam

1. In a medium bowl, pour milk over oats and allow to sit at room temperature until absorbed, about 15 minutes.

2. Meanwhile, sauté onion and garlic in oil over medium-low heat just until translucent. Remove from heat.

3. Gently mix together the ground lamb, oatmeal, sautéed onion and garlic, egg, mushrooms, rosemary, salt, and pepper. Cover and refrigerate for 1 hour.

4. Shape lamb mixture into cocktail-sized meatballs. Melt oil and butter in heavy frying pan over medium-high heat; add meatballs (half as many as the pan will hold) and fry for 10 minutes, shaking the pan frequently to rotate meatballs and ensure even browning. Remove and drain on paper towels.

5. Arrange meatballs on a serving platter and top each one with ¼ teaspoon of lingonberry jam. Serve with toothpicks.

Meatballs in Curry

Meatballs in Curry—Boller i Karry—is to Danish children what macaroni and cheese is to American ones. Extend their appeal to an adult crowd with this appetizer version of a revered classic.

INGREDIENTS | SERVES 16

½ pound ground pork

½ pound lean ground beef

1 cup bread crumbs

1 cup milk

4 cloves garlic, minced, divided use

½ cup plus 1 large onion, finely chopped, divided use

1 egg

1 teaspoon salt

4 quarts water

2 tablespoons curry powder

1 large leek, cleaned and chopped

2 tablespoons butter

3 tablespoons flour

¾ cup half-and-half

2 tablespoons finely chopped parsley or chives

1. In a large bowl or stand mixer, combine the ground pork, beef, bread crumbs, milk, 2 cloves minced garlic, ½ cup chopped onion, egg, and salt. Using a large whisk or whisk attachment, whip mixture vigorously, about 5 minutes, until it is light and airy.

2. Bring water to a boil in a large pot. Use a tablespoon to form small meatballs, then drop into the water. Reduce heat to a steady simmer and boil until the meatballs float, about 20 minutes. Remove with a slotted spoon. Reserve 3½ cups of cooking water.

3. Sauté curry powder, 1 chopped onion, leek, and 2 cloves minced garlic in 2 tablespoons butter over medium-high heat for 5 minutes. Stir in flour and ½ cup of cooking water to thicken sauce, then gradually whisk in remaining 3 cups of water. Add half-and-half and bring to a low boil; reduce heat to medium-low, add the meatballs, and simmer for 10 minutes.

4. Transfer meatballs and curry sauce to a serving bowl and sprinkle with chopped parsley or chives for a tasty appetizer; for a main dish, serve over rice or noodles.

Meatballs with Danish Blue Cheese

Had the moon been made of Danish blue cheese, NASA's lunar missions never would have ended. Creamy, mellow, and richly veined with deep blue cultures, Danish blue cheese is the perfect choice for those who prefer a mild blue.

INGREDIENTS | SERVES 12

8 ounces Danish blue cheese

1 pound ground meat (beef, pork, or a combination)

½ cup cold mashed potatoes or bread crumbs

1 large egg

2 tablespoons onion, finely minced

½ cup whipping cream

Fresh herbs for garnish (chopped dill, thyme, or parsley)

1. Preheat oven to 450°F. Dice blue cheese into ¼" cubes, reserving ¼ of cheese (2 ounces) for use in sauce.

2. Mix together ground meat, mashed potatoes (or bread crumbs), egg, and minced onion. Wet your hands and roll meat into walnut-shaped balls, pressing a cube of blue cheese into the center of each one. Make sure each cube is entirely surrounded by the meatball mixture.

3. Bake on ungreased broiler pan for 15 minutes.

4. For sauce, whisk remaining 2 ounces of blue cheese into whipping cream in a saucepan over medium-low heat until cheese has melted. Remove from heat.

5. Remove baked meatballs from oven; toss with blue cheese sauce.

6. Transfer to serving bowl and garnish with fresh herbs.

Gingersnap Meatballs

While Swedish meatballs often incorporate allspice, a quick and easy way to achieve a similarly delicious result is to use gingersnaps as your filler.

INGREDIENTS | SERVES 16

1½ cups crumbled gingersnaps

⅔ cup milk

½ cup onion, minced

1 tablespoon butter

½ pound lean ground beef

½ pound lean ground pork (or veal)

1 egg

¼ cup parsley, chopped

2 tablespoons canola oil plus 1 tablespoon butter to brown meatballs

3 tablespoons flour

1 cup beef broth or bouillon

¼ teaspoon ground allspice

1 teaspoon salt

The Trick to Tender Meatballs

There's a simple trick to achieving tender, juicy meatballs—use a food processor. Older cooks would often double-grind their meat to achieve the finest texture possible but it's far easier to use a few pulses of the processor to create the ultra-fine consistency that's the hallmark of great Swedish meatballs.

1. In a medium bowl place crumbled gingersnaps in milk to soak for 15 minutes.

2. Sauté the minced onion in butter over medium heat until opaque.

3. Place the ground meats, egg, chopped parsley, and sautéed onion in a food processor and pulse until combined. Add soaked gingersnaps and their milk and pulse a second time.

4. Form 1" meatballs, then refrigerate on a plate for 30 minutes.

5. Heat 2 tablespoons canola oil and 1 tablespoon butter in a heavy frying pan over medium-high heat. Add meatballs and fry until nicely browned on all sides, shaking the pan regularly to prevent sticking. Remove from pan.

6. For brown sauce, remove all but 3 tablespoons of fat from pan. Over medium-high heat, vigorously whisk in flour, scraping up the brown bits, until mixture begins to bubble; gradually whisk in beef broth, ground allspice, and salt. Simmer until gravy thickens and is warmed through (about 5 minutes).

7. Fold meatballs into gravy and serve warm.

Glassblower's Herring

Glasmastarsill—glassblower's herring—is one of the best-loved herring preparations in Scandinavia. Be sure to layer the ingredients in a glass jar to showcase the vibrant colors of the silver herring skin and of the vegetables.

INGREDIENTS | SERVES 10

1 pound salt herring fillets

1½ cups distilled or white wine vinegar

½ cup sugar

½ cup water

5 whole allspice berries

3 bay leaves

2 carrots, thinly sliced

1 large red onion, thinly sliced and separated into rings

1 leek, white part only, thinly sliced

2 teaspoons mustard seed

2 teaspoons multicolored peppercorns

Salt Herring Substitute

Salt herring, a perishable item, is available in specialty markets and online. If you can't find it, you can substitute a 12-ounce jar of marinated herring—simply rinse off the marinade and combine with the vegetables and pickling brine.

1. In a large bowl, cover the salt herring with water and soak for 12 hours or overnight.

2. Rinse the desalinized herring well with fresh cold water and cut into 1" diagonal slices.

3. In a large saucepan, bring vinegar, sugar, ½ cup water, allspice berries, and bay leaves to a boil. Reduce heat and simmer until sugar is dissolved. Cool to room temperature.

4. Layer the herring slices, skin side out, and the vegetables in a large glass jar, sprinkling each layer with a few mustard seeds and peppercorns. Pour cooled vinegar mixture over the layers to the top of the jar. Refrigerate for 48 hours before serving to allow flavors to blend.

5. Serve with rye bread and new potatoes. Glassblower's herring will keep for about a week in the refrigerator.

Seafood *Tunnbröd* Rolls

The smokiness of canned mussels gives just the right depth of flavor to these elegant seafood appetizers. If you can't find Swedish tunnbröd ("thin bread"), substitute your favorite flatbread—but then don't skimp on the ground fennel seed.

INGREDIENTS | SERVES 8

1 cup low-fat sour cream or crème fraîche

1 (3.66-ounce) can smoked mussels

¼ pound baby shrimp, crab, or lobster meat, precooked

3 tablespoons red onion, finely diced

1 tomato, seeded and finely diced

¼ teaspoon ground fennel seed

4 slices tunnbröd (or substitute your favorite flatbread)

1. Fold together the sour cream, seafood, red onion, tomato, and fennel seed.

2. Spread mixture evenly over *tunnbröd* or flatbread.

3. Roll each bread into a cylinder, then cut into 4 diagonal slices.

4. Garnish as desired (fennel fronds or fresh dill work well) and serve.

Curry Herring

Curry powder adds just the right kick of spice to currysill (marinated herring in a very light curry cream sauce).

INGREDIENTS | SERVES 10

1 (12-ounce) jar marinated herring

1 tablespoon canola oil

1 tablespoon sugar

1 cup low-fat sour cream

2 teaspoons hot curry powder

¼ cup finely chopped parsley

1 Granny Smith apple, cored and thinly sliced

1. Rinse the marinated herring with fresh water; pat dry with paper towels.

2. Whisk together the canola oil, sugar, sour cream, curry powder, and chopped parsley. Fold in the herring. Cover and refrigerate for 24 hours.

3. Garnish with green apple slices and serve.

Pickled Herring with Fresh Tomatoes and Dill

A Scandinavian take on Italian Caprese salad, this easy recipe substitutes cholesterol-smashing herring for buffalo mozzarella.

INGREDIENTS | SERVES 10

1 (12-ounce) jar marinated herring

4 green onions, finely chopped

1 tablespoon capers

½ cup ketchup

4 tablespoons white balsamic vinegar or white wine vinegar

1 tablespoon sugar

1 teaspoon white pepper

1 large tomato, seeded and chopped

3 tablespoons fresh dill, roughly chopped

Mixed lettuce (romaine, spinach, arugula), as needed

1. Pour the jar of marinated herring into a colander and allow the liquid to drain off. Pat the herring pieces dry with paper towels, then toss together with chopped green onions and capers.

2. Whisk together the ketchup, vinegar, sugar, and white pepper. Pour over herring.

3. Cover and refrigerate for 4–6 hours.

4. Just before serving, fold chopped tomatoes and dill into herring mixture. Place on a bed of mixed lettuce, garnish with additional dill, and serve.

Pickled Salmon with Horseradish Cream

*Poaching the salmon in its brine and then allowing it to temper overnight
lends a special piquancy to this Swedish pickled salmon.*

INGREDIENTS | SERVES 8–10

1 pound salmon fillet, skin on

⅔ cup distilled or white wine vinegar

2½ cups water

¼ cup sugar

1 tablespoon salt

2 bay leaves

2 teaspoons mustard seeds

2 teaspoons peppercorns

2 yellow onions, peeled and thinly sliced

1 cup low-fat sour cream

1 teaspoon white wine vinegar

1 tablespoon prepared horseradish

1 tablespoon chives, finely chopped

1. Place salmon fillet, skin side down, in a casserole dish. Lightly score the fish with a cross-hatch pattern to allow brine to penetrate.

2. Bring vinegar, water, sugar, salt, bay leaves, mustard seeds, and peppercorns to a boil.

3. Pour boiling brine over salmon, cover with aluminum foil, and allow to sit at room temperature until the brine has cooled. Add onion slices, re-cover, and place in refrigerator for 24 hours.

4. For horseradish cream, combine the sour cream, white wine vinegar, prepared horseradish, and chopped chives. Whip with a large whisk or mixer until light and creamy.

5. To serve salmon, remove from brine and scrape off excess spices. Place on a platter and serve with pickled onions and horseradish cream.

Våsterbotten Cheese Crisps with Fresh Pears

*Sweden's tangy Våsterbotten cheese is even tastier than Parmesan
when used in these crunchy baked crisps.*

INGREDIENTS | SERVES 16

1 cup finely grated Våsterbotten cheese
(or substitute Parmesan)

½ cup finely chopped walnuts

2 pears, cored, quartered, and very
thinly sliced

1 (8.8-ounce) package Snøfrisk cheese
(or substitute a spreadable chèvre)

Walnut halves for garnish

Snøfrisk

Snøfrisk, a tangy, spreadable goat cheese from Norway, was launched by Tine SA, a large Norwegian dairy co-operative, during the 1994 Lillehammer Olympics. Made from a superlative combination of 80 percent goat's milk and 20 percent cow's milk, it comes in a distinctive triangular box and is to ordinary chèvre what champagne is to grape juice.

1. Preheat oven to 350°F. In a small bowl, toss together the grated *Våsterbotten* cheese and chopped walnuts. Line a baking pan with a silicone mat or parchment paper, then carefully spoon 1 tablespoon mounds of the cheese mixture on the pan, separating each by 2–3 inches. Press each mound slightly with the back of a large spoon to level out into an even thickness, about ⅛" thick.

2. Bake 5–6 minutes, watching closely to prevent burning. Remove and transfer to cool on a cookie rack.

3. Once cheese crisps have cooled, top each one with a pear slice. Spread about 1 teaspoon of *Snøfrisk* on each appetizer and top with a walnut half.

Fried *Våsterbotten* Cheese

The unique flavor of Sweden's "King of Cheeses" achieves its full glory when lightly fried with seasoned bread crumbs.

INGREDIENTS | SERVES 24

Canola oil, as needed for frying

1 pound Våsterbotten cheese, cut into ½" cubes

⅔ cup rye or spelt flour

2 large eggs, beaten

1 cup fine rye bread crumbs

1 teaspoon caraway or fennel seed

1. Heat 3" of canola oil in a skillet or fondue pot until temperature reaches 365°F.

2. Toss cheese cubes in flour, then dip in beaten eggs.

3. In a separate bowl mix together rye bread crumbs and caraway (or fennel) seed. Roll cheese cubes in bread crumbs until well coated.

4. Fry in oil until golden, about 4 minutes.

5. Serve on toothpicks.

Bacon-Wrapped Prunes with Danish Blue Cheese

Pork and blue cheese have traditionally been two of Denmark's most lucrative exports. Use a hearty, thick-cut smoked bacon if you don't have access to Danish bacon.

INGREDIENTS | SERVES 12

12 pitted prunes

6 ounces Danish blue cheese

6 thick slices of smoked bacon

1. Preheat oven to 400°F.

2. Pack each prune with as much blue cheese as it can hold.

3. Cut each bacon slice in half, then wrap each half around a prune. Secure bacon with toothpicks.

4. Place on broiler pan and roast in oven, about 20 minutes, until bacon is crisp, turning once during the baking cycle.

Ginger Cookies with Blue Cheese and Apricots

Appetizers don't get easier or more interesting than this—the saltiness of a mild blue cheese and the sweetness of apricots provide the perfect counterpoint to Scandinavia's favorite cookie, Anna's Ginger Thins.

INGREDIENTS | SERVES 12

6 ounces mild blue cheese
12 Anna's Ginger Thins or other thin ginger cookies
¼ cup apricot preserves

1. Thinly slice blue cheese with a cheese knife.

2. Place a slice of cheese on each ginger cookie.

3. Top each appetizer with a teaspoon of apricot preserves.

Anna's Ginger Thins

Swedish housewife Anna Karlsson's thin ginger cookies were so popular in her community that she and her sister opened a bakery in Stockholm in the 1920s. Now the company is global, its bakeries manufacturing 1.95 million delicious cookies each day.

Gjetost and Apples

Gjetost cheese, commonly sold in America under the Ski Queen brand, is a smooth goat's milk cheese with subtle caramel undertones. Norwegians enjoy it not only on apples but sliced thin on hot homemade waffles (where it melts beautifully) and on crispbread.

INGREDIENTS | SERVES 20

1 red apple
1 green apple
1 (8.8-ounce) block Ski Queen gjetost cheese
7 tablespoons lingonberry or currant jam

1. Wash and core apples; quarter and cut into thin slices. Alternate red and green apple slices on serving plate.

2. Using a cheese slicer, cut paper-thin slices of *gjetost*. Place a slice of *gjetost* on each apple wedge.

3. Top each appetizer with a teaspoon of lingonberry jam. Serve immediately.

CHAPTER 3

Soups and Stews

Better than Grandma's Yellow Pea Soup

Yellow pea soup is a long-standing tradition in Sweden, commonly served on Thursdays and accompanied with silver dollar–sized pancakes and lingonberry jam. Improving upon an old favorite, this recipe substitutes star anise for cloves; you can find star anise in most Oriental groceries and in many organic food stores.

INGREDIENTS | SERVES 8

1 pound whole or split dried yellow peas

4 cups water to soak peas plus 8 cups water for soup

3 carrots, peeled and finely chopped

2 large yellow onions, finely chopped

3 smoked ham hocks (or 1½ cups leftover ham, diced)

3 star anise

1 teaspoon dried thyme

1 teaspoon salt

¼ teaspoon ground white pepper

1. Rinse off dried peas in a colander, removing any bad ones or grit. Place in 4 cups water in a bowl to soak overnight on the counter.

2. Drain soaked peas, rinse well, and place in large stock pot with 8 cups fresh water, chopped carrots, chopped onions, and ham hocks. Bring to a boil; cover and reduce heat to low. Cook for 90 minutes, checking occasionally to remove any pea skins rising to the surface.

3. Temporarily remove the ham hocks from the soup. Using an immersion blender, purée soup briefly until some but not all of the peas are liquefied (this will help to thicken the soup). Return the ham hocks to the pot.

4. Simmer at least 20 minutes more (or, like Grandma, you can also leave it to simmer on low for a few hours on a back burner).

5. A half-hour before serving, remove ham hocks. Cut away all fat and chop the remaining meat; return to pot. Use immersion blender again to blend the entire soup into a smooth purée.

6. Stir in star anise, thyme, salt, and pepper; simmer for an additional 15 minutes. Remove anise pods and serve.

Tuesday Soup (*Tisdagssoppa*)

While pea soup is the classic Thursday lunch in Sweden, "Tuesday Soup," a delectable mixture of root vegetables and smoked ham thickened with barley, is often enjoyed earlier in the week. The root vegetables are merely a suggestion—feel free to substitute ones you have readily available.

INGREDIENTS | SERVES 6

½ celeriac (celery root)

2 large potatoes

2 carrots

1 turnip or parsnip

1 rutabaga

1 tablespoon butter

1 tablespoon canola (rapeseed) oil

¼ cup white wine

3 cups vegetable broth

2 cups water

1 cup half-and-half or light cream

¼ cup quick-cooking barley

½ cup chopped ham or smoked pork

Salt and pepper to taste

1 cup Swedish Grevé or Emmentaler cheese, grated

2 tablespoons fresh parsley, finely chopped

1. Peel and chop the root vegetables into a 1" dice. Melt butter and oil together in a large saucepan over medium heat; add chopped vegetables and sauté them until they begin to soften, about 5 minutes.

2. Increase heat to medium-high and add the white wine. Stir the vegetables until the liquid has reduced, about 2 minutes. Add the vegetable broth, water, half-and-half, and barley; bring to a boil. Reduce heat to a simmer and cook, uncovered, until the vegetables and barley are tender, about 20 minutes.

3. Using an immersion or countertop blender, purée soup. Add the chopped ham and simmer for 10 more minutes, until warmed through. Season with salt and pepper to taste.

4. Garnish with grated cheese and chopped parsley to serve.

Celeriac

Although it's a lot of work to clean, celeriac, also called celery root, is a super vegetable to use in soups, salads, and mashed potatoes. A root vegetable that thrives in cold climates, it imparts a mild celery taste to these dishes. Look for roots that are as smooth and unwrinkled as possible in order to minimize the chore of peeling them.

Icelandic Lamb and Pea Soup (*Saltkjöt og Baunir*)

Icelanders prefer to use lamb or mutton rather than pork to flavor their pea soup—not surprising, since there are more sheep in Iceland than there are people. This soup, made in Iceland with salt-dried lamb (Saltkjöt), is served on Shrove Tuesday. This adaptation substitutes roasted lamb; it's both healthier and moister than salt-dried lamb.

INGREDIENTS | SERVES 6

1 pound split dried yellow peas

4 cups water to soak peas plus 8 cups for soup

¼ cup olive oil

2 cloves pressed garlic

8 ounces lamb stew meat, cut in ½" cubes

1 large yellow onion, peeled and coarsely chopped

3 medium potatoes, peeled and coarsely chopped

2 carrots, peeled and coarsely chopped

1 rutabaga, peeled and coarsely chopped

1. Clean and pick through yellow peas, then soak in 4 cups water overnight.

2. Preheat oven to 375°F. Whisk together olive oil and pressed garlic into a marinade; fold in lamb stew meat. Transfer meat to broiler pan and roast for 10 minutes, turning once.

3. Drain peas in a colander. Fill a large stockpot with 8 cups water; add the soaked peas, roasted lamb, and chopped onion. Bring to a boil; reduce heat to medium-low, cover, and simmer for 1 hour.

4. After 1 hour, add potatoes, carrots, and rutabaga. Simmer for 30 more minutes, or until the vegetables are tender.

5. Icelanders enjoy this recipe either as a soup or else they remove the meat and cooked vegetables and eat them separately after the soup course.

Norwegian Lamb and Cabbage Stew (*Fårikål*)

Fårikål, or "Lamb in Cabbage," is the perfect make-ahead dish, since the flavor is best when the dish is allowed to sit, refrigerated, for a day or two. With a sentiment similar to the Finns' love of Karelian Hot Pot, Norwegians have voted Fårikål as their national dish.

INGREDIENTS | SERVES 6

1 large white cabbage

3½ pounds fatty lamb shanks, on the bone

2 teaspoons salt

4 teaspoons mixed peppercorns

2 tablespoons flour

1½ cups boiling water

Slow Cooker Preparation

Fårikål cooks up beautifully in a slow cooker—simply layer the lamb, cabbage, seasonings, and water in your cooker in the morning, cover, and cook on the low setting for 10 hours. Voilà, dinner is served!

1. Wash and slice the cabbage in thick wedges, from the outside through the core, so that the core remains (it will hold the slices together through the lengthy cooking process).

2. Place the fattiest lamb shanks on the bottom of a large stock pot; sprinkle with salt, peppercorns, and flour. Add a layer of cabbage, seasoning again with the spices and flour. Repeat layers, ending with a layer of cabbage.

3. Pour boiling water over contents of pot. Bring to a boil; reduce heat to a simmer. Cover pot and allow to simmer on low heat for 2 hours, until the meat falls off the bone.

4. Serve with boiled potatoes in large soup or pasta bowls, accompanied with thick bread to sop up the rich sauce.

Sailor's Beef (*Sjömansbiff*)

Sailor's beef is one of the classic dishes of Swedish husmanskost—home cooking. For chilled seamen, a warm, oven-baked beef casserole was surely welcome after days of landing, handling, and transporting boatloads of cold fish.

INGREDIENTS | SERVES 4–6

1½ pounds boneless beef round steak, cut into ½"-thick slices.

6 tablespoons butter

1 large red onion, thinly sliced and separated into rings

2 medium yellow onions, thinly sliced and separated into rings

5 medium potatoes, peeled and sliced

Salt and pepper to taste

1½ cups beef stock

12 ounces dark beer

2 bay leaves

1 tablespoon minced chives or parsley for garnish

1. Preheat oven to 375°F. Pound the beef slices between waxed paper until paper-thin. Melt half of the butter in a large frying pan over medium-high heat, then brown meat evenly in butter. Remove from pan.

2. Melt remaining butter in pan and sauté onion rings until lightly browned. Remove from heat.

3. In an oven-proof casserole dish, layer the potatoes, onions, and beef, ending with a layer of potatoes; lightly season each layer with a generous pinch of salt and pepper.

4. Pour beef stock and beer over the layers and top with bay leaves.

5. Cover and bake in oven for 45 minutes. Remove bay leaves; garnish with chives or parsley, and serve.

Karelian Hot Pot (Karjalanpaisti)

Considered by many to be the national dish of Finland, Karelian Hot Pot proves that frugality is indeed a virtue—after slow and steady simmering, cheap cuts of meat become melt-in-your-mouth tender.

INGREDIENTS | SERVES 6

1 pound beef stew meat, cut into 1" cubes

1 pound lamb stew meat, cut into 1" cubes

1 pound boneless pork, cut into 1" cubes

3 large onions, peeled and sliced

1 teaspoon salt

8 whole allspice

3 cups water (or enough to cover meat in pot)

3 cups mashed potatoes

1. Combine meat and layer with onions in a 5- or 6-quart slow cooker, sprinkling salt and a few allspice on each layer.

2. Pour water over meat. Cover with lid; cook on low heat for 6–8 hours.

3. Serve over mashed potatoes, accompanied with lingonberry jam if desired.

Cream of Potato Soup with Smoked Salmon and Dill

The peppery hot-smoked salmon in this potato soup will make everyone ask for seconds. It's best to double the recipe!

INGREDIENTS | SERVES 4

5 medium potatoes, peeled and chopped

2 large leeks, peeled and chopped

4 cups vegetable stock

1 cup cream

⅓ pound hot-smoked salmon, finely chopped

3 tablespoons fresh dill, finely chopped

1. In a stockpot, combine potatoes, leeks, and vegetable stock. Bring to a boil; reduce heat and simmer, uncovered, for 20 minutes until potatoes are tender.

2. Purée the soup with an immersion blender (or transfer to a traditional blender); stir in cream, smoked salmon, and chopped dill.

3. Return pot to medium heat and cook for 5 more minutes. Garnish as desired and serve.

Icelandic Lamb Stew (*Kjötsúpa*)

Warm and rich, Kjötsúpa provides energy and comfort to Icelanders during cold, dark Nordic winters.

INGREDIENTS | SERVES 6–8

1 medium onion, peeled and sliced

3 cloves garlic, finely minced

2 tablespoons canola oil

3 pounds cheap, fatty lamb cuts, on the bone

6 cups water

½ cup brown rice or rolled oats

2 bay leaves

½ white cabbage, coarsely chopped

3 carrots, coarsely chopped

1 rutabaga, peeled and coarsely chopped

4 Yukon Gold potatoes, skins on, coarsely chopped

1 teaspoon dried oregano

1 teaspoon dried thyme

1. In a large soup pot, lightly sauté the onion and garlic in oil over medium heat just until translucent (about 3 minutes). Add the lamb and brown on all sides.

2. Add the water and brown rice (or rolled oats). Bring contents of the pot to a steady boil, and allow to boil for 5 minutes, skimming off all froth.

3. Lower heat to medium, add bay leaves, cover pot, and simmer for 40 minutes.

4. Add the chopped vegetables and dried herbs. Cook, covered, for 20 more minutes, until the vegetables are tender.

5. Remove meat, bones, and bay leaves from the pot; coarsely chop meat and return to pot. Keep soup warm until serving.

Dilled Beef Stew (Tilliliha)

Dill is to the Finns what basil is to the Italians or tarragon is to the French. It is a colorful, integral part of most Finnish meat and fish stews.

INGREDIENTS | SERVES 6

3 pounds boneless chuck roast

3 tablespoons butter

4 cups beef broth

1 large onion, peeled and chopped

2 carrots, peeled and chopped

1 teaspoon whole allspice

1 tablespoon coarsely ground pepper

2 bay leaves

2 teaspoons salt

¼ cup flour

2 tablespoons water

1 tablespoon sugar

1 tablespoon red wine vinegar

½ cup half-and-half or cream

½ cup dill, finely minced

1. In a large pot, brown all sides of the chuck roast in butter over medium-high heat, about 8 minutes.

2. Add beef broth and bring to a boil; reduce heat to low. Add onion, carrots, allspice, pepper, bay leaves, and salt.

3. Cover and simmer for 2–3 hours, occasionally skimming off any foam that rises.

4. When meat is cooked, remove from broth and cut into 1" pieces. Strain the broth, then return 2½ cups to the pot and bring to a boil.

5. Whisk together flour, water, sugar, and red wine vinegar; stir into the boiling broth to thicken. Reduce heat to medium-low. Add half-and-half, chopped meat, and dill; allow to simmer an additional 10 minutes.

6. Transfer to bowls, garnish with additional dill, and serve.

Scandinavian Dill

Dill is ubiquitous in Scandinavian cooking, baking, and curing (it's a key ingredient of cold-cured gravlax). It's always good to have some on hand—you can freeze or dry the fresh fronds for later use as last-minute seasoning for stews, or use dill seeds in dishes that require slow cooking times. Substitute 1 tablespoon of dill seeds for 3 heads of dill in pickling preparations. If adding to stews, sprinkle the dill in with the meat at the beginning of the cooking process rather than adding it at the end.

Finnish Salmon Soup (Lohikeitto)

Fresh dill and salmon are showcased in this velvety soup from Finland.

INGREDIENTS | SERVES 6

2 tablespoons butter

1 large onion, peeled and finely chopped

2 celery stalks, finely chopped

5 cups fish stock

5 Yukon Gold potatoes, peeled and chopped into a 1" dice

1 small salmon fillet (about 1¼ pounds), chopped into a 1" dice

1 cup half-and-half or whipping cream

2 teaspoons salt

½ teaspoon pepper

1 cup fresh dill, finely chopped

1. Melt butter in a large stockpot over medium heat; sauté onions and celery in butter until soft.

2. Pour in fish stock, add potatoes, and bring to a boil. Reduce to a simmer, cover pot and cook 15 minutes, until the potatoes are tender.

3. Add salmon; cook for an additional 5 minutes.

4. Incorporate half-and-half or cream, season with salt and pepper, and cook until warmed through, about 10 minutes.

5. Stir in dill and serve with dense rye bread.

Bergen Fish Soup with Dumplings

One of the hallmark soups of Norway, creamy Bergen Fish Soup with Dumplings is the ideal antidote to the endless rain and sharp winds of dark polar nights.

INGREDIENTS | SERVES 8

3 quarts fish stock

2 large carrots, chopped into a ½" dice

1 parsnip, chopped into a ½" dice

2 celery stalks, chopped into a ½" dice

1 tablespoon potato starch flour or cornstarch plus 1 additional tablespoon for dumplings

1 cup half-and-half or cream

¼ cup red wine vinegar

1 heaping tablespoon sugar

1½ pounds skinned, boneless saltwater white fish (cod, halibut, monkfish, or a combination), chopped into a 1" dice, plus 1 additional pound boneless white fish for dumplings, also chopped into a 1" dice

1 egg

1 tablespoon chopped chives

Salt and pepper to taste

1 (8-ounce) container sour cream (optional)

1. In a large stockpot, bring fish stock to a boil. Add carrots, parsnips, and celery; reduce heat to medium-low and simmer until vegetables are tender (about 8 minutes).

2. Whisk 1 tablespoon potato starch flour into 1 cup half-and-half. Stir into soup and bring to a low boil. Add red wine vinegar and sugar (to give the soup its characteristic sweet-sour tang). Add 1½ pounds chopped fish, bring to a boil, then reduce heat again to medium-low.

3. To make fish dumplings, in a large bowl combine the remaining 1 pound of diced fish with 1 tablespoon potato starch flour, 1 egg, chopped chives, and about ½ teaspoon each of salt and pepper. Process the mixture twice in a food processor or else run it through a food grinder or fine-meshed sieve to make it as fine as possible.

4. Drop generous teaspoons of fish dumpling batter into the simmering soup. Simmer for an additional 8 minutes, until the dumplings float to the top.

5. To serve, transfer to bowls. Stir dollops of sour cream across the surface of each bowl (if desired).

Spring Nettle Soup

Foraging for fresh ingredients doesn't get more exciting than this—pull on your leather gloves this spring, walk out into the woods with a knowledgeable guide, and celebrate the bounty of tender young nettle leaves.

INGREDIENTS | SERVES 4–6

2 tablespoons butter

1 large onion, peeled and chopped

2 cloves garlic, minced

2 large baking potatoes, peeled and chopped

6 cups chicken or vegetable broth

1 pound stinging nettles (or substitute fresh spinach)

½ cup heavy cream

½ teaspoon ground nutmeg

1 teaspoon salt

½ teaspoon freshly ground white pepper

2 hard-boiled eggs, sliced

Nettle Harvest

Nettle season is short, since only the top, tender new shoots of the plant should be used for cooking. Schedule a picking date in April or early May, pull on your gloves, and forage one of the riches of spring. If you pick extra, you can either dry the leaves or, after blanching to remove the sting, freeze them for future use.

1. Melt butter in a large stockpot. Add chopped onion, garlic, and potatoes; brown until onion is transparent.

2. Pour in broth and bring to a boil; reduce heat to a simmer. Allow to simmer for 15–20 minutes, until potatoes are tender.

3. Wearing gloves, coarsely chop the nettles, then add them (or substitute fresh spinach) to the pot. Simmer for an additional 5 minutes.

4. Using an immersion blender, purée the soup in the pot until smooth.

5. Stir in cream, nutmeg, salt, and white pepper. Simmer 5 more minutes, until soup is warmed through.

6. Transfer soup into bowls, float slices of hard-boiled egg on top, and serve.

Root Vegetable Soup

Who needs pumpkin pie? The flavors of autumn marry together in this nutritious and warming soup, flavored with ginger and nutmeg.

INGREDIENTS | SERVES 6

2 large sweet potatoes, peeled

2 small rutabagas, peeled

2 carrots, peeled

3 small red potatoes

1 large onion

2 tablespoons butter

3 cloves garlic, finely minced

6 cups water

½ cup half-and-half or cream

2 teaspoons fresh ginger, grated

1 teaspoon grated nutmeg

1 tablespoon brown sugar

Root Vegetables

Root vegetables have always been a saving grace in Scandinavia, where the short growing season yields all-too-few heat-loving crops like tomatoes or corn. Beets, rutabagas, potatoes, carrots, garlic, and celeriac not only adore cold weather, they also store well over the winter, providing excellent nutrition in tasty soups and stews.

1. Finely dice the sweet potatoes, rutabagas, carrots, red potatoes, and onion. Melt the butter in the bottom of a soup pot; add the chopped vegetables and garlic, and sauté over medium heat just until garlic is golden (about 5 minutes).

2. Add water and bring to a boil. Reduce heat and simmer, uncovered, for 20 minutes until root vegetables are tender.

3. Purée the soup with an immersion blender (or in batches in a traditional blender); stir in half-and-half, ginger, nutmeg, and sugar.

4. Simmer for 5 more minutes over medium-low heat. Garnish and serve.

Cauliflower Soup

Puréed cauliflower is jazzed up here with just enough richly veined Danish blue cheese and crunchy bacon.

INGREDIENTS | SERVES 6

1 leek, cleaned and finely chopped

2 garlic cloves, finely minced

1 tablespoon butter

1 quart vegetable broth

1 large head cauliflower, divided into florets

2 tablespoons potato starch flour or cornstarch

½ cup crumbled Danish blue cheese

2 tablespoons chopped parsley

4 slices thick-cut bacon, fried and crumbled

Potato Starch Flour

Potato starch flour is the same thing as potato starch. Not to be confused with potato flour, it is a fabulous, gluten-free thickener for soups. Look for the Swan's variety in the baking section of your grocery store. You can substitute cornstarch in equal proportions when recipes call for potato starch flour as a thickener for soups, stews, or gravies.

1. In the bottom of a large stockpot, lightly sauté the chopped leek and garlic in butter until opaque. Pour in the vegetable broth; add the cauliflower florets. Bring soup to a boil; reduce heat to medium-low, cover, and allow to cook until cauliflower is crisp-tender, 10–15 minutes.

2. Transfer 1 cup of broth to a mixing bowl; whisk in potato starch flour to make a slurry. Set aside.

3. Using an immersion blender (or regular blender), purée the soup in the pot until creamy. Whisk the slurry into the purée to thicken; fold in the blue cheese and parsley. Simmer for an additional 5–10 minutes.

4. Garnish with crumbled bacon and additional blue cheese to serve.

Spring Soup

The cheerful color of Spring Soup echoes the outdoors as the white Nordic landscape greens with the lengthening days.

INGREDIENTS | SERVES 4–6

1 tablespoon butter

1 tablespoon canola or olive oil

1 pound fresh spinach (or substitute 1 pound of nettles, if you can get them)

1 leek, cleaned and roughly chopped

½ teaspoon salt

¼ teaspoon pepper

1 tablespoon flour or potato starch flour

5 cups vegetable stock

1 bunch tender asparagus spears, diced

1 egg yolk, at room temperature

1 cup light cream, at room temperature

1 bunch radishes, cleaned and sliced

1. Melt the butter and olive oil in a large saucepan over medium heat. Add the spinach and chopped leek, season with salt and pepper, and sauté until the spinach softens.

2. Stir in the flour and 1 cup of the broth; raise to a boil. Immediately add the rest of the stock and the asparagus, and simmer for 10 minutes until the asparagus is tender.

3. Beat together the egg yolk and cream. Remove the pot from heat and vigorously stir the egg mixture into the soup. Add the sliced radishes and serve.

Chilled Cucumber Soup

This chilled cucumber soup, enriched with fresh dill, is the perfect starter for a summer crayfish party.

INGREDIENTS | SERVES 4–6

2 large cucumbers, peeled, seeded, and finely chopped

½ cup finely chopped dill

1 ripe avocado, peeled and finely chopped

5 cups vegetable stock

Juice and zest of 1 lime

3 cloves garlic, pressed

2 cups skyr (or low-fat Greek yogurt)

Salt to taste

6 crayfish tails

1. In a large bowl, stir together cucumbers, dill, avocado, vegetable stock, lime juice and zest, pressed garlic, and *skyr* (or Greek yogurt). Use an immersion blender to purée the mixture (or purée in batches in a blender or food processor).

2. Season to taste with salt, and refrigerate for at least 1 hour.

3. Garnish with crayfish tails and additional dill or lime zest to serve.

The Rite of August

Late summer is crayfish season in Scandinavia and people partake with gusto. Simply prepared by boiling in water with dill in large pots, August's crayfish are the center of parties devoted to them—accompanied with generous amounts of schnapps.

CHAPTER 4

Fresh, Marinated, and Pickled Salads

Pickled Beets

If your only experience with pickled beets is of the canned variety, you owe it to yourself to make them from scratch—you'll soon see why they are such a favorite in Scandinavia! Wear an apron and rubber gloves, and line your work surface with paper towels to avoid beet stains.

INGREDIENTS | SERVES 12

6 large beets

Cold water, as needed

2 cups vinegar

1 cup sugar

1 cup water

5 white peppercorns

8 whole cloves

1½ tablespoons fresh horseradish, minced

Preserving Beets

To preserve pickled beets, place cooked beet slices in hot sterilized jars. Bring the pickling mixture to a boil, then pour over beets to almost the top of each jar. Seal jars and store in a cupboard.

1. Rinse and scrub the beets well to remove any dirt, then cut off their stalks, leaving 1" of stalk on each beet. Place in a nonreactive pot, add enough cold water to cover, and bring to a boil. Reduce heat to medium-low and simmer until beets are tender (1 hour or more, depending on the size of your beets).

2. When beets are cooked, plunge into cold water to cool, then use a vegetable scrubber or your gloved hands to rub off the skins under running water. Allow to cool completely, then cut into paper-thin slices, discarding the stalks.

3. Place the beet slices in a large glass bowl or other nonreactive container. In a separate bowl or large measuring cup, whisk together the remaining ingredients; pour over the beets, stirring slightly so that the marinade is evenly distributed.

4. Cover with cling wrap and refrigerate for at least 48 hours before serving.

Norwegian Cucumber Salad (Agurksalat)

As ubiquitous as lefse and krumkake among Norwegians and Norwegian-Americans, this crispy cucumber salad is great to have on hand in your refrigerator for those days when you don't have the time, inclination, or fresh ingredients to make a tossed salad.

INGREDIENTS | SERVES 4–6

1 European cucumber
1 teaspoon salt
2 tablespoons distilled or white wine vinegar
2 tablespoons water
1 tablespoon sugar
⅛ teaspoon white pepper
1 teaspoon celery seed
2 tablespoons onion, finely minced
1 tablespoon fresh parsley, finely minced

1. Wash the cucumber, then use a sharp knife or vegetable peeler to cut paper-thin slices. Arrange the slices on a plate, sprinkle with salt, and cover with a second plate. Allow to sit for 30 minutes to draw off the moisture.

2. After 30 minutes, drain the liquid from the cucumbers. In a nonreactive bowl, whisk together the vinegar, water, sugar, white pepper, celery seed, minced onion, and parsley. Fold in the cucumbers; cover with cling wrap and refrigerate for at least 1 hour to allow the flavors to meld.

3. Serve chilled as a side dish for fish or meat.

Wild Mushroom Salad

The fruits of Finland's forests come into their own in this creamy salad. It also makes a wonderful topping for baked potatoes.

INGREDIENTS | SERVES 6

1 cup whipping cream
¼ cup sour cream
1 tablespoon white wine vinegar
½ teaspoon sugar
½ teaspoon salt
¼ teaspoon dried thyme
Pinch pepper
1 pound fresh wild mushrooms (chanterelles, morels, porcini)
½ red onion, finely minced
2 tablespoons chives, finely minced

1. Whip the cream until stiff peaks form. In a small bowl, whisk together the sour cream, vinegar, sugar, salt, thyme, and pepper, then stir this gently into the whipped cream.

2. Fold the mushrooms, minced red onion, and chives into the whipped cream.

3. Cover and chill for at least 1 hour before serving in dollops on rye bread, lettuce leaves, or halved avocados.

Pickled Mushrooms

This recipes also works well when substituting small button mushrooms or other fresh varieties (morels, porcini, shitake) for the chanterelles. Experiment with different combinations!

INGREDIENTS | SERVES 10

2 pounds fresh chanterelles
3 cups water
2 cups white vinegar
½ cup sugar
¼ teaspoon salt
5 whole allspice
3 dried cloves
1 star anise
1 cinnamon stick

1. Clean the chanterelles, cutting any large ones in half.

2. Combine all of the ingredients in a large saucepan and bring the mixture to a low boil. Boil for 10–15 minutes until the mushrooms are tender.

3. Transfer the mushrooms to canning jars, covering with their warm brine. Seal, cool, and allow to marinate in the refrigerator for at least 2 days before serving. The mushrooms can also be processed in a water bath, then stored at room temperature.

Multicolor Cabbage Salad

To achieve its ideal flavor and texture, this vinegar-based coleslaw should sit in the refrigerator for 2 days before serving.

INGREDIENTS | SERVES 6

½ white cabbage
½ red cabbage
1 medium onion, peeled
1 cup white balsamic or white wine vinegar
¾ cup canola oil
½ cup sugar
1 teaspoon mustard seed
1 teaspoon dill seed
1 teaspoon celery salt
1 teaspoon salt

1. Finely shred the white and red cabbages and the onion.

2. Whisk together the remaining ingredients to form a dressing, then toss together with the shredded cabbage and onion.

3. Weigh the cabbage down with a small plate and place in the refrigerator. Allow to chill for 2 days, draining off accumulated water and stirring twice a day.

4. Serve chilled.

Pickled Winter Vegetables

Cruciferous and root vegetables, easily stored over the winter,
are tangy and refreshing when pickled in a spicy brine.

INGREDIENTS | SERVES 8

5 cups water, divided use

4 cups ice water

12 pearl onions

1 head cauliflower, divided into florets

1 head broccoli, divided into florets

12 baby carrots, thinly sliced

½ fennel bulb, thinly sliced

6 sprigs fresh dill, finely minced

¾ cup white wine vinegar or distilled vinegar

½ cup sugar

3 whole star anise or 1½ tablespoons anise seed

1 teaspoon fennel seed

¼ teaspoon salt

1. Bring 4 cups of water to boil in a large saucepan. Add the onions, cauliflowers, broccoli, carrots, and fennel; blanch for 1 minute. Drain and plunge into ice water. Peel the onions.

2. Toss the vegetables with the minced dill, then divide into canning jars.

3. Whisk together the remaining 1 cup water, vinegar, sugar, anise, fennel seed, and salt in a saucepan and bring to a boil, stirring until sugar is dissolved. Remove from heat, cover, and allow to sit for 1 hour.

4. Return the pan to a rapid boil. Pour the brine over the vegetables, leaving ½" at the top of the jars. Tighten the lids and store in the refrigerator for at least 2 days before using; keep refrigerated. (Alternatively, you can seal the jars and process them in a hot water bath for 15 minutes, then store them in the cupboard. Again, allow the jars to sit at least 48 hours before serving.)

Pickled Rhubarb

Use the reddest rhubarb stalks you can find when making Pickled Rhubarb—the rosy color of the pickles, when added to "white" Scandinavian dishes like Spring Chicken Salad with New Asparagus and Pickled Rhubarb (see recipe in this chapter), really makes the dishes pop!

INGREDIENTS | MAKES ABOUT 1 POUND

5 rhubarb stalks

4 cups water

4 cups ice water for chilled water bath

1 cup sugar

1 cup apple cider vinegar

1 teaspoon whole cloves

1 teaspoon whole allspice

2 star anise

How to Sterilize Canning Jars

Set the jars in your canner, right side up, then add cold water to fill the canner up to an inch over the jars. Bring the water to a boil and maintain a boil for 10 minutes. Reduce heat to a steady simmer, leaving jars in the hot water until ready to use.

1. Clean the rhubarb stalks well, discarding any tough fibers. Chop into ½" pieces. In a large pot, bring 4 cups of water to a rolling boil, then blanche the rhubarb for exactly 1 minute. Remove rhubarb from the pot and plunge immediately into the 4-cup ice-water bath. Drain the rhubarb slices, spread out on paper towels, and allow to cool.

2. Clean and sterilize 2 (1-pint) jars and their lids in a hot water bath; keep jars and lids warm in simmering water until you're ready to fill them.

3. In a nonreactive saucepan, whisk together the sugar, vinegar, cloves, and allspice; bring to a strong boil over medium-high heat.

4. Use tongs to remove the sterilized jars from the hot water bath, shaking out any excess water. Place a star anise in each jar and then pack with the rhubarb up to the fill line.

5. Carefully pour the boiling brine over the rhubarb, leaving ½" of space at the top of the jars to allow contents to expand. Seal with the lids and allow to sit at room temperature for 24 hours, then store in the refrigerator for up to a month. These pickles are best when served chilled.

Carrot Salad with Currants

*Scandinavia's cold climate is perfect for growing all sorts of berries,
including the currants that stud this colorful carrot salad.*

INGREDIENTS | SERVES 4

⅔ cup dried currants

Hot water, as needed

¼ cup slivered almonds

5 large carrots

1 cup canola oil

1 tablespoon lemon juice

1 tablespoon honey

1 teaspoon cardamom, freshly ground

½ teaspoon ground ginger

1 teaspoon black pepper, coarsely ground

1. Place the dried currants in a small bowl, cover with hot water, and allow to plump for 10 minutes. Drain and pat dry with a paper towel.

2. Place the almonds in a single layer in a frying pan and toast over medium heat until golden, about 8 minutes. Remove from burner and allow to cool.

3. Peel and coarsely grate the carrots, then toss them together with the currants.

4. Whisk together the oil, lemon juice, honey, cardamom, ground ginger, and pepper, then stir this dressing into the carrots. Sprinkle toasted almonds on top to garnish and serve.

Danish Summer Salad with Smoked Cheese

*This one-of-a-kind salad, held together with smoke-infused Danish Rygeost cheese,
is also often enjoyed as a spread on toasted rye open-faced sandwiches.*

INGREDIENTS | SERVES 4

8 ounces Danish *Rygeost* (smoked cheese) or smoked ricotta

3 generous tablespoons sour cream or crème fraîche

1 seedless cucumber, peeled and chopped into a ¼" dice

6 radishes, chopped into a ¼" dice

2 green onions, finely chopped

2 tablespoons chives, finely chopped

½ teaspoon salt

¼ teaspoon pepper

2 large tomatoes

1. In a large bowl, cream together the smoked cheese and sour cream.

2. Stir the chopped vegetables and chives into the cheese, and season with salt and pepper. Chill for at least 1 hour.

3. To serve, halve and scoop out the centers of the tomatoes to make "bowls," removing all seeds. Fill each tomato with the salad and serve.

Spring Chicken Salad with New Asparagus and Pickled Rhubarb

Rhubarb is as sure a harbinger of spring in Scandinavia as tender young asparagus. Its arrival is celebrated widely, especially at rhubarb festivals such as the annual May rhubarb event in the Swedish county of Sörmland, just south of Stockholm.

INGREDIENTS | SERVES 4

2 rhubarb stalks, cleaned and thinly sliced

½ cup water

2 tablespoons lingonberry, red wine, or balsamic vinegar

2 tablespoons honey

Zest and juice of 1 lemon

1 teaspoon Swedish or Dijon mustard

½ cup canola oil

Salt and pepper to taste

½ pound white asparagus (or substitute green)

4 cups ice water for chilled water bath

1 roasted chicken

4 cups baby spinach leaves

⅓ cup Pickled Rhubarb (see recipe in this chapter)

Cleaning Rhubarb

If you're new to rhubarb, keep in mind that the leaves are highly toxic to humans. To use the stalks, cut away all leaves and roots, wash well, and remove any tough fibers.

1. For rhubarb vinaigrette, place sliced rhubarb stalks in ½ cup water in a small saucepan. Bring to a low boil over medium-high heat and cook for 5 minutes. Strain and transfer to a food processor or blender; add the vinegar, honey, lemon zest and juice, and mustard. Pulse until smooth. Then add the oil to the vinaigrette in a steady stream, processing into a smooth dressing. Season with salt and pepper to taste.

2. Clean the asparagus stalks, place them in a frying pan, and add enough water to cover. Bring the water to a steady simmer and blanche the stalks until tender, about 8 minutes. Immerse the blanched stalks in the ice-water bath, pat dry with a paper towel, and cut into 1" slices.

3. Debone and roughly chop the meat of the roasted chicken. Toss it with the asparagus, baby spinach, and pickled rhubarb in a salad bowl, stirring in enough vinaigrette to moisten.

4. Serve with additional dressing on the side.

Herring Salad

Herring salad lends itself to experimentation. Love pickled beets? Toss a few in. Prefer marinated cucumbers? Their crisp texture will provide a pleasing crunch. Have fun switching out the vegetables you add to the herring according to your taste and what you have available.

INGREDIENTS | SERVES 6

1 (12-ounce) jar pickled herring tidbits in wine sauce

3 green onions, thinly sliced

½ cup chopped celery, green bell pepper, or marinated cucumbers

1 apple, peel on, cored and coarsely chopped

½ cup mayonnaise

1 cup sour cream

1 tablespoon celery seed

1 tablespoon sugar

½ teaspoon salt

¼ teaspoon white pepper

3 cups mixed salad greens

1. Drain the herring tidbits, then toss with the green onions, chopped vegetables, and apple.

2. Whisk together the mayonnaise, sour cream, celery seed, sugar, salt, and white pepper; fold this mixture together with the herring.

3. Chill for at least 1 hour before serving on a bed of lettuce.

Crab Salad

Serve this colorful crab salad either on large lettuce leaves or as a superlative topping for open-faced sandwiches on toasted rye bread.

INGREDIENTS | SERVES 6

2 tablespoons mayonnaise

1 tablespoon sour cream or crème fraîche

Zest and juice of one small lemon

2 shallots, peeled and finely minced

2 garlic cloves, peeled and finely minced

¼ cup chopped celery

1 teaspoon salt

¼ teaspoon white pepper

1½ tablespoons fresh cilantro or dill, finely chopped

2 cups cooked lump crab meat

12 cherry tomatoes, halved

1 avocado, chopped into a ½" dice

1. Mix together the mayonnaise, sour cream, lemon zest and juice, minced shallots and garlic, celery, salt, white pepper, and dill (or cilantro).

2. Toss the crab meat with the chopped tomatoes and avocado, then fold into the mayonnaise mixture.

3. Serve well chilled.

Shrimp Salad

Adding just a smidgeon of tomato paste and paprika gives a bright tint and zing to this zesty shrimp salad.

INGREDIENTS | SERVES 4

¼ cup sour cream or crème fraîche

2 tablespoons mayonnaise

1 tablespoon lemon juice

1 tablespoon tomato paste

2 teaspoons sweet paprika

1 teaspoon Swedish or Dijon mustard

1 pound baby (bay) shrimp, peeled, and cooked

1 English cucumber, peeled and chopped into a ½" dice

½ cup fresh, uncooked peas

¼ cup fresh dill, finely chopped

1. Combine the sour cream, mayonnaise, lemon juice, tomato paste, sweet paprika, and mustard. Fold the shrimp into the dressing; refrigerate for 1 hour.

2. Before serving, lightly toss the shrimp salad with the chopped cucumber, peas, and dill.

3. Serve on a bed of lettuce or as a sandwich spread.

New Potato Salad

Use a generous hand when sprinkling caraway seed into the tiny new potatoes of this early summer salad. It goes beautifully with cold sliced meats like lamb or pork.

INGREDIENTS | SERVES 6

4 cups new potatoes

3 eggs

1 cup mayonnaise

1 tablespoon finely chopped onion

1 tablespoon finely chopped celery

1 heaping tablespoon caraway seed

1 teaspoon salt

1. Cover the potatoes and eggs with water in a pot; bring to a boil over high heat. Reduce heat to low and simmer for 20 minutes or just until potatoes are fork-tender. Drain potatoes and eggs, then plunge into cold water to cool.

2. Cut potatoes into halves; peel and coarsely chop the hard-boiled eggs.

3. Whisk together the mayonnaise, onion, celery, caraway seed, and salt. Fold in the potatoes and eggs.

4. Chill for at least 1 hour before serving.

Lobster Salad with Nobis Dressing

Tore Wretman, Sweden's world-famous restaurateur, created Nobis dressing as an accompaniment to both warm and cold shellfish and vegetable dishes.

INGREDIENTS | SERVES 4

1 egg

2 cups canola oil

1 tablespoon white wine vinegar

1 teaspoon Swedish or Dijon mustard

1 teaspoon crushed garlic

½ teaspoon salt

¼ teaspoon white pepper

1 tablespoon shallots, finely minced

1 tablespoon chives, finely minced

2 cups cooked lobster meat

2 hard-boiled eggs, sliced

1 English cucumber, peeled, seeded, and chopped into a fine dice

½ sweet red pepper, chopped into a fine dice

¼ cup fennel bulb or celery, chopped into a fine dice

1. In a small saucepan, bring 3 cups of water to a rapid boil. Add the egg and boil for precisely 2 minutes. Immediately remove the egg and immerse in a bowl of cold water; crack and scrape the coddled egg into a mixing bowl or food processor.

2. Blend half of the oil, then the vinegar, then the rest of the oil into the egg in a steady stream, until mixture is the consistency of a light mayonnaise.

3. Stir the mustard, crushed garlic, salt, white pepper, shallots, and chives into the sauce, then cover and chill in the refrigerator for 15 minutes.

4. Gently toss together the lobster meat, hard-boiled egg slices, cucumber, sweet red pepper, and chopped fennel bulb.

5. Serve lobster salad topped with dollops of Nobis dressing.

Tore Wretman

Tore Wretman (1916–2003) was Sweden's most famous restaurateur, ultimately leading operations of Stockholm's historic Operakällaren. Passionate about celebrating Swedish "home" cooking (*husmanskost*), Wretman modernized and reintroduced the concept of the smörgåsbord to the Swedish dining scene. A few of the hallmark recipes he created or popularized: Toast Skagen, Småland potato dumplings (*Småländska kroppkakor*), salmon pudding (*laxpudding*), Swedish meatballs (*köttbullar*), and cabbage rolls (*kåldolmar*).

Smoked Potato Salad

Smoked potatoes are a popular addition to open-faced sandwiches in Denmark. Here they are partnered with crispy bacon and just the right amount of grated horseradish to create a scrumptious side salad.

INGREDIENTS | SERVES 6

2 cups hardwood chips
6 slices hickory-smoked bacon
6 large red potatoes, unpeeled
½ cup kosher salt
½ cup finely diced red onion
6 hard-boiled eggs, coarsely chopped
1 cup mayonnaise
1 heaping tablespoon horseradish

Stovetop Smokers

Smoking meat, fish, vegetables, and cheese has never been easier than with the advent of stovetop smokers—they're a godsend for those of us who want to embrace our Nordic heritage but secretly prefer not to mess with carcinogenic coals and nasty lighter fluid outdoors in a rainstorm! Camerons Products' stovetop smokers are reliable products.

1. Cover the hardwood chips with water and soak for 30 minutes. Fry the bacon until crisp; cool and crumble. Reserve the bacon fat.

2. Wash the potatoes, prick all over with a fork, and place in a large pot with enough water to cover. Bring to a low boil and cook for 15 minutes, just until potatoes are crisp-tender.

3. Cut the potatoes in half. Spear them with a fork and rub both sides lightly in the reserved bacon fat, then rub them all over with the kosher salt.

4. Heat the coals of your grill to medium-high, then drain and scatter the soaked woodchips on the coals. Place the potatoes on the grill rack, close the lid, and smoke for 15 minutes, turning once, until potatoes are golden (you can also use a stovetop smoker for this step, following the manufacturer's directions).

5. Coarsely chop the potatoes and toss with the red onion, hard-boiled eggs, and crumbled bacon. In a separate bowl, mix the horseradish into the mayonnaise; fold the dressing into the potatoes. Garnish and serve.

CHAPTER 5

Homemade Breads

Swedish Limpa Bread

Swedish limpa bread is also known as vörtlimpa ("wort loaf"), because it was traditionally made with brewer's malt. This recipe substitutes dark beer; while the flavor is not as intense as when using brewer's malt, it still provides a quite tasty loaf.

INGREDIENTS | MAKES 2 LOAVES

1 (12-ounce) bottle of dark beer (porter)
¼ cup butter
⅓ cup dark molasses
2½ teaspoons salt
¼ cup dark brown sugar
1 teaspoon fennel seeds
1 teaspoon caraway seeds
1 teaspoon anise seeds
2 packages active dry yeast (4½ teaspoons)
2 tablespoons freshly grated orange peel
2½ cups rye flour
2 cups all-purpose flour
¾ cup cold coffee

1. In a small saucepan, combine the beer, butter, molasses, salt, brown sugar, fennel seeds, caraway seeds, and anise seeds. Bring to a low boil and cook for 5 minutes, stirring occasionally to dissolve the sugar. Cool until the mixture is lukewarm.

2. Sift the dry yeast, orange peel, and rye flour into the bowl of a large mixer equipped with a paddle.

3. Set the mixer on low and gradually incorporate the liquid into the flour. Scrape down the sides of the mixer bowl and exchange the paddle for the dough hook.

4. At low speed, incorporate the all-purpose flour into the dough; increase speed to medium-high and beat for 7 minutes or so, until the dough begins to pull away from the sides of the bowl. Allow the dough to rest in the bowl for 20 minutes. As the dough rests, preheat oven to 300°F, then turn it off immediately.

5. After the dough has rested, knead it lightly, either with the dough hook or your hands, until it is stiff and smooth, about 5 minutes.

6. Place dough in a lightly buttered bowl, flipping once to coat with butter. Cover with a clean tea towel, place in the warmed oven, and let rise until doubled in size, anywhere from 1 to 2 hours.

7. Punch down the dough, divide it into even halves, and shape each half into a round loaf. Place on a lightly floured baking pan or wooden paddle (if you use a bread stone in your oven). Cover with the tea towel and let the loaves rise until doubled in size, 1–1½ hours.

8. Preheat oven to 375°F. Place a cake pan on the lowest shelf in the oven; position the bread stone (if using) on the shelf above.

9. Slash each loaf 2 or 3 times diagonally, then brush with cold coffee. Transfer to the oven and place 2 or 3 ice cubes in the lower pan, shutting the door immediately. Bake for 30 minutes, or until a toothpick inserted in the center comes away clean (the loaves should sound hollow when you tap them on the bottom with a knife). Brush with coffee and allow to rest until cooled before serving.

Spelt Bread

The secret to making the perfect loaf of spelt bread is to treat it very gently—the complete mixing and kneading cycle should take no longer than five minutes. Be sure to "proof" your yeast to test that it's still active as well (make sure it bubbles after being stirred into the recipe's warm liquid), and always use a warmed mixing bowl.

INGREDIENTS | MAKES 1 LOAF

1 package active dry yeast (2¼ teaspoons)

1½ cups "finger-warm" water (105°F to 110°F).

2 tablespoons honey

2 tablespoons melted butter

2 teaspoons salt

4½ cups spelt flour

1 tablespoon additional butter

A Saintly Grain

"The spelt is the best of grains. It is rich and nourishing and milder than other grain. It produces a strong body and healthy blood to those who eat it and it makes the spirit of man light and cheerful."—Saint Hildegard von Bingen (1098–1179)

1. Warm the mixing bowl of a stand mixer with hot water, then pat dry. Mix the yeast, water, and honey in the bowl and allow the yeast to proof for 15 minutes until the mixture's surface becomes foamy. Stir in the melted butter and salt.

2. Place 2 cups of the flour in the bowl, equip the mixer with its paddle, and mix on medium-low speed for 1 minute. Exchange the paddle for the dough hook, add the remaining flour, and mix for 1 more minute, until all of the flour is incorporated. Increase the speed to medium and knead for 2½ minutes, just until the dough clings to the hook.

3. Turn the dough out into a bowl greased with butter, rolling once to cover completely with butter. Cover dough with a clean tea towel and allow to rise in a warm place for 1½ hours.

4. Punch the dough down, form it into a loaf, and transfer it to a greased 9" × 5" bread pan (or an ungreased stoneware pan). Cover and allow to rise for 1 hour, until doubled.

5. Preheat oven to 425°F. Place the bread in the oven and bake for 35–40 minutes, or until the loaf is firm and a toothpick inserted in the middle comes out clean. Then turn the bread out onto a rack, rub the remaining tablespoon of butter over the top and sides, and allow to cool.

Norwegian Flatbread

Norwegians have traditionally used cold-climate barley or oat flours in their flatbread.
Look for these in health-food stores or community co-ops.

INGREDIENTS | SERVES 20

2 cups barley or oat flour

2 cups all-purpose flour

1 cup oat bran

½ cup sugar

1 teaspoon salt

1 teaspoon hornsalt (baker's ammonia) or baking soda

1 tablespoon chopped fresh herbs (thyme or rosemary) or caraway seed (optional)

¾ cup butter, diced and chilled

1½ cups buttermilk

1. Preheat oven to 350°F. Combine the flours, oat bran, sugar, salt, hornsalt (or baking soda), and herbs or caraway seed (if using) in a mixing bowl. Use a pastry blender or two knives to cut the butter into the flour until the mixture has the consistency of coarse crumbs. Add the buttermilk and mix well with a fork to form a soft dough.

2. Turn the dough out onto a lightly floured counter and knead until smooth. Pinch off golf ball–sized pieces of dough and roll them out thinly into 8"-diameter circles.

3. Transfer the flatbread to ungreased baking sheets, prick well with a fork, and cook for 10–12 minutes. Cool on a wire rack, then store in an airtight container.

Lefse Bowls

You can use lefse, the Nordic "tortilla," in any way that you would use other wraps.
Here they are baked into crispy bowls perfect for holding Scandinavian stews or salads
or for serving smörgåsbord appetizers like pickled herring.

INGREDIENTS | SERVES 4

4 pieces prepared Potato *Lefse* (see recipe in this chapter)

Tortilla bowl molds or oven-proof bowls

1. Preheat oven to 375°F.

2. Grease the inside of tortilla bowl molds, then press a piece of *lefse* into each mold. Alternatively, you can grease the outside of oven-proof bowls, invert them on a baking sheet, and mold the *lefse* over the bowls. Or, you can use large biscuit cutters to cut smaller circles out of the softened *lefse* and then press them into greased muffin tins.

3. Bake the bowls in the oven for 15 minutes, until browned and crispy.

Swedish *Tunnbröd*

Tunnbröd *is Sweden's premier flatbread; it's wafer thin, and often flavored with fennel and/or anise. For best results, use a knobbed rolling pin.*

INGREDIENTS | SERVES 12

¼ cup butter

2½ cups milk, room temperature

2 packages active dry yeast (4½ teaspoons)

½ teaspoon salt

¼ cup sugar

1 tablespoon Swedish light syrup or Lyle's Golden Syrup

1 cup rye flour

4 cups all-purpose flour (or substitute 2 cups spelt flour plus 2 cups all-purpose)

½ teaspoon hornsalt (baker's ammonia), optional

1 teaspoon ground fennel seeds

1 teaspoon ground anise seeds

1. In a medium saucepan heat the butter and milk together over medium heat just until the butter melts. Transfer to a mixing bowl and cool until lukewarm (105°F to 110°F). Stir in the yeast, salt, sugar, and syrup; allow to sit for 15 minutes.

2. Whisk together the flours, hornsalt (if using), ground fennel, and ground anise, then mix into the liquid until all of the flour is incorporated. Knead by hand or with the dough hook of a mixer until the dough is smooth and glossy. Place dough into a greased bowl, turning to coat, cover with a towel, and allow to rise in a warm place for 30 minutes–1 hour (the dough doesn't need to double in size, it just needs to rest).

3. Divide the dough into 12 equal portions, then use a knobbed or grooved rolling pin to roll out each piece until it is paper-thin (it's your choice as to whether you prefer to roll it into a circle or a rectangle).

4. Set a *lefse* or a pancake griddle to medium heat. Prick the flatbread well with a fork, then transfer to the griddle. Bake for 2 minutes on each side.

5. Alternatively, you can bake the flatbread on baking sheets in a 400°F oven, 3 minutes per side.

6. Allow the flatbread to cool between moist towels, then store in an airtight container.

Danish Rye Bread

As you make this bread the first time, be sure to save some of the starter—you'll find yourself craving it once the loaf is gone, and having starter on hand will reduce the preparation time so significantly that you won't think twice about starting a new batch.

INGREDIENTS | SERVES 12

1¼ cup buttermilk

4½ cups rye flour, divided use

4 teaspoons plus 1 tablespoon sea salt, divided use

1 (12-ounce) bottle light ale, room temperature

1½ cups "finger-warm" water (105°F to 110 °F)

2 tablespoons honey

2½ cups all-purpose flour

¾ pound cracked rye grain

1 cup warm water

¼ cup raw sunflower seeds or flaxseeds

Danish Bread Pans

The Danes use a special 3-liter, nonstick, straight-sided bread pan for making their beloved rye bread, available from Eva Solo in Denmark if you have Danish connections. If not, order a nonstick pullman pan from any one of numerous U.S. suppliers. They're also great to use for another Danish favorite: leverpostej (liver paste).

1. For the bread starter, stir together the buttermilk, 1½ cups rye flour, and 1 teaspoon of the sea salt. Sprinkle the remaining 1 teaspoon of sea salt over the top of the starter. Cover with a lid or aluminum foil and allow to sit in a warm space (at least 78°F) for 4 days.

2. To prepare the bread dough, place the starter in the bowl of a stand mixer equipped with the paddle attachment. Stir in the ale, 1½ cups finger-warm water, honey, 1 tablespoon sea salt, 3 cups rye flour, and all-purpose flour, beating at medium speed until combined (about 5 minutes).

3. Remove ¼ cup of the dough to use as a starter for your next batch. Place in a container, sprinkle with 1 teaspoon of salt, cover, and store in the refrigerator for up to 2 months.

4. Add the cracked rye and remaining cup of warm water to the batter, stirring to combine. Transfer to a nonstick pullman pan, cover with a tea towel, and allow to rise in a warm place for 6 hours or until the dough has risen to the top of the pan.

5. Preheat oven to 350°F. Bake the bread for 1 hour and 45 minutes. Remove from the oven, turn out the loaf onto a rack, and allow to cool completely.

Sourdough Rye Muffins

These "English" muffins, made from a sourdough rye starter, are perfect when toasted and topped with gjetost cheese or when used as part of a Nordic-style eggs Benedict.

INGREDIENTS | SERVES 12

⅔ cup buttermilk

¾ cup plus 1½–2 cups rye flour, divided

1¾ teaspoons salt, divided use

1 cup warm water

2 tablespoons honey

1 cup all-purpose flour

2 tablespoons instant nonfat dry milk powder

1½ teaspoons caraway seeds

¼ cup cornmeal

1. For your sourdough starter, stir together the buttermilk, ¾ cup rye flour, and 1 teaspoon salt in a lidded container. Cover and allow to sit in a warm place (at least 78°F) for 4 days.

2. Stir the starter together with the warm water, honey, all-purpose flour, and 1 cup of the rye flour. Cover again and let stand at room temperature overnight.

3. Whisk together the milk powder, ¾ teaspoon salt, and ½ cup of the remaining rye flour. Stir into the sourdough mixture, then turn the dough out onto a floured counter. Flour your hands well, then knead the dough, adding enough of the remaining rye flour to make a dough that is smooth and no longer sticky.

4. Roll the dough to a ½" thickness, then use a 3" round cutter to cut out the muffins. Dust a greased or parchment-lined cookie sheet with half of the cornmeal, then place the muffins on top. Sprinkle the tops with the remaining cornmeal and the caraway seeds. Cover with a tea towel and allow to rise in a warm place for 45 minutes or until doubled.

5. Heat a *lefse* griddle or pancake griddle to 275°F. Slide the muffins onto the griddle and cook for 10 minutes; flip and cook for 15 additional minutes or until browned.

Potato *Lefse*

All good Norwegian-Americans (and their descendants!) should know how to make lefse, *the thin potato "wrap" traditionally prepared as a much-loved holiday bread. For best results, use the grooved rolling pin specifically designed for* lefse-making.

Lefse Supplies

Want to make lefse just like Grandma did . . . but someone else inherited her rolling pin? Three quality sources of lefse griddles, rolling pins, and pastry boards are Lefse Time (*www.lefsetime.com*); Bethany Housewares (*www.bethanyhousewares.com*); and Inge-bretsen's (*http://ingebretsens.com*).

1. Preheat oven to 175°F. Peel the potatoes, coarsely chop them into 1" pieces, then boil just until tender. Drain boiled potatoes well, then place in the warm oven for 15 minutes to dry further.

2. Press the potatoes through a ricer twice, then combine with the salt, cream, butter, and sugar. Cover and chill for 8 hours or overnight.

3. Preheat *lefse* griddle to 425°F. Cut the flour into the chilled potato mixture, then use an ice-cream scoop to form balls about the size of a racquetball.

4. With a grooved *lefse* rolling pin in a well-floured sleeve, roll out each ball on a floured pastry cloth into a circle the size of a dinner plate.

5. Carefully lift the circle with a *lefse* stick and transfer quickly to the griddle. Bake until brown spots begin to appear; flip and bake the other side for a minute or two more, until it begins to brown.

6. Cool between clean cloths, then serve with butter and sugar. *Lefse* can also be frozen for up to 6 months.

Hardanger *Lefse*

Hardanger lefse is probably similar to what the Vikings carried along on their journeys. Like hardtack, it can last for months without refrigeration, needing only to be softened by steaming before use.

INGREDIENTS | SERVES 30

3 eggs

¾ cup sugar

1½ cups buttermilk

¾ cup butter, melted then cooled

¾ cup Swedish light syrup or Lyle's Golden Syrup (if necessary, substitute light corn syrup)

9 cups all-purpose flour

2 teaspoons hartshorn (also called hornsalt, or baker's ammonia) or substitute baking powder

1 teaspoon baking soda

1 teaspoon salt

1. In a large bowl cream together the eggs and sugar, then stir in the buttermilk, melted butter, and light syrup.

2. Use a balloon whisk to toss together the dry ingredients in a separate bowl, then stir them into the liquid to form a soft dough.

3. Pinch off racquetball-sized portions of the dough (about ⅓ cup), then use a grooved rolling pin to roll out the dough into thin rounds, 10" in diameter.

4. Heat a *lefse* griddle to 450°F and heat the rounds until small brown spots begin to appear, flipping once (about 2-4 minutes per side). Or, preheat oven to 400°F and bake on cookie sheets for 4 minutes.

5. Cool on racks and store in an airtight container until needed. To serve, spray with water and place between warmed tea towels for 30 minutes–1 hour.

Norwegian Thick *Lefse* (*Tyukklefse*)

Unlike most Norwegian lefse, tyukklefse is, as its name implies, "thick"—it's almost like a pancake and is normally served in the place of coffeecake. For your next party, slice four tyukklefse in half, as you would layer cake, spread seven of the layers with Cinnamon-Butter Kling (see below), then stack them into an eight-layer cake.

INGREDIENTS | MAKES 10 PIECES

2½ cups buttermilk, kefir, or Siggi's Probiotics (drinkable nonfat yogurt)

2 eggs

1 cup Swedish light syrup, Lyle's Golden Syrup, or light Karo syrup

1 cup sugar

1 cup melted butter

2 teaspoons hornsalt (or substitute baking powder)

8–9 cups all-purpose flour

Cinnamon-Butter *Kling*

To make kling, cinnamon-butter spread, whip together 2 cups softened butter, 5 cups powdered sugar, 3 cups crème fraîche or sour cream, 1 tablespoon vanilla sugar, and cinnamon to taste (start with 2 teaspoons, adding more until the kling is as spicy as you like it). Use as a spread for lefse or as a frosting for coffeecakes.

1. The day before baking, combine the buttermilk, eggs, light syrup, sugar, and melted butter.

2. Stir in the hornsalt and enough of the flour to make a soft, slightly sticky dough. Cover and refrigerate overnight.

3. Lightly flour a counter, then divide the dough into 8 pieces. Roll or pat out each piece into 1"-thick circles, about 8" in diameter.

4. Bring a *lefse* griddle or pancake griddle to medium heat, then fry the *lefse* until puffed and golden, flipping once (4-5 minutes per side).

5. Serve with Cinnamon-Butter *Kling* (see sidebar recipe).

Møsbrømlefsa

Møsbrømlefsa—*flour lefse that is spread with a sweet mixture of melted brown cheese (brunost) and buttermilk—is unique to the Salten region of the Norwegian county of Nordland. If you have a passion for gjetost cheese, you owe it to yourself to try this!*

INGREDIENTS | SERVES 20

6 cups all-purpose flour

2 cups rye flour

2 teaspoons hornsalt (or substitute baking powder)

4 cups whole milk, divided use

3 cups buttermilk, divided use

1 (8.8-ounce) block Ski Queen or other brunost, grated

¼ cup all-purpose flour

1 tablespoon sugar

1 teaspoon vanilla sugar

Sour cream and butter to taste

1. Whisk together the flours and hornsalt, then combine with 2 cups milk and 2 cups buttermilk to make a soft dough. Cover and chill in the refrigerator for at least 2 hours.

2. Pinch off egg-sized pieces of the dough, then roll them out into 12"-diameter circles on a floured counter or board, using a grooved rolling pin equipped with a floured sleeve.

3. Bake on a *lefse* pan or pancake griddle at medium heat until the bottom of each lefse is browned. Do not flip; transfer and stack between warm, moist towels while you prepare the cheese sauce.

4. For the *møsbrøm* sauce, combine the grated cheese, 2 cups milk, and 1 cup buttermilk in a saucepan and bring to a steady simmer, stirring until the cheese melts completely. Gradually stir in enough of the flour so that the sauce thickens to the consistency of a thick "nacho" cheese sauce. Sweeten to taste with the sugar and vanilla sugar.

5. To serve, ladle the cheese sauce onto the warmed *lefse*, then top each one with a tablespoon of sour cream and a teaspoon of butter. Fold into quarters and serve immediately.

Lingonberry Archipelago Bread

Finnish archipelago bread is characterized by its use of rye malt, an ingredient that's not always readily available in the United States. This recipe substitutes malted wheat flakes and barley malt syrup, which you can order online from sources such as King Arthur Flour (www.kingarthurflour.com).

INGREDIENTS | SERVES 16

½ cup buttermilk

¼ cup barley malt syrup

½ cup Swedish dark syrup or molasses

1 packet (2¼ teaspoons) active dry yeast

1 teaspoon salt

1½ cups malted wheat flakes

1 cup rye flour

2–2½ cups wheat or spelt flour

½ cup Lingonberry Jam (see Chapter 7)

3 tablespoons molasses plus 3 tablespoons water to glaze

1. In a small saucepan, heat the buttermilk just until finger-warm. Remove from heat, transfer to a mixing bowl, and stir in the barley malt syrup, dark syrup, dry yeast, and salt. Allow to sit for 15 minutes.

2. In a large bowl, whisk together the malted wheat flakes, rye flour, and wheat flour. Stir the Lingonberry Jam into the buttermilk texture, then gradually add the dry ingredients, mixing to form a loose, sticky batter. This will look like a quick bread batter.

3. Grease two 9" × 5" loaf pans, then divide the batter evenly between them. Cover with a moist tea towel and allow to rise in a warm place for 2 hours or until doubled in size.

4. Preheat oven to 350°F. Bake the loaves for 30 minutes, then glaze with the combined molasses and water. Reduce the temperature to 325°F. Bake for an additional 60–90 minutes, basting with the molasses glaze every 30 minutes, until the loaves are firm and a toothpick inserted in the middle comes out clean.

5. Remove the loaves from oven, baste one last time with the glaze, then cool completely before serving (overnight is best).

Icelandic Thunder Bread

Even if you don't live beside a geothermal spring, as many Icelanders do,
you can make this steamed rye bread using a slow cooker.

INGREDIENTS | MAKES 2 LOAVES

3 cups rye flour
1 cup all-purpose flour
1 tablespoon baking powder
1 teaspoon baking soda
1 cup molasses
1½ cups warm scalded milk

1. Combine the dry ingredients in the bowl of a stand mixer.

2. Stir the molasses into the warm scalded milk until it dissolves, then beat the milk into the flour. Once it is combined, knead it by hand or with your mixer's dough hook until it is smooth and glossy. Divide the dough into 2 equal halves.

3. Grease the insides of 2½-cup ramekins or sanitized tin cans. Place the dough inside; it shouldn't quite reach the top of the ramekins. Cover the ramekins with aluminum foil, leaving an inch of air space to allow for rising; secure the foil tightly around the edges of the ramekins with cooking string.

4. Place two canning-jar lids in the bottom of your slow cooker, then set the ramekins on top of these. Pour in enough boiling water to cover the lower half of the molds.

5. Place the lid on the slow cooker, set the temperature on low, and allow to steam-cook for 12 hours or overnight.

Icelandic Rye Flatbread (*Flatbrauð*)

Forced in the past, because of limited fuel, to cook flat, quickly prepared breads rather than oven-baked loaves, Icelanders still enjoy making rye flatbread to use as "wraps" for meats and cheeses.

INGREDIENTS | SERVES 10

3 cups rye flour (or combine 2 cups rye with 1 cup spelt flour)

1 teaspoon baking powder

½ teaspoon salt

1 cup boiling water

1 pan warm water

How to Eat Like an Icelander

What's the second-best way (if you can't actually visit Iceland) to experience the best food Iceland has to offer? Order a "used" copy of Nanna Rögnvaldardóttir's outstanding cookbook, *Icelandic Food & Cookery* (Hippocrene Books, 2002) from an online bookstore (available—often actually in new condition even if listed as used—for around $25.00). This beautifully written book not only provides superior recipes, it also offers an intriguing look at the history of the preparation techniques and foods that the Icelanders developed over the years in response to their harsh but breathtakingly beautiful terrain.

1. Combine the flour, baking powder, and salt in the bowl of a stand mixer equipped with a paddle. Turn the mixer on to its lowest setting, then pour in the boiling water in a steady stream, gradually increasing the speed to medium as the water is incorporated.

2. Once the flour has been worked into a stiff dough, replace the paddle with the dough hook, increase the speed to a high setting, and knead for 7 minutes or so until the dough pulls away from the sides of the bowl and is smooth and glossy.

3. Pinch off a racquetball-sized piece of dough and roll it into a thin circle, 8" in diameter. Prick it well all over with a fork.

4. Heat a dry *lefse* griddle or nonstick frying pan on medium until a drop of water sizzles on the surface. Place the flatbread on the griddle and cook until black circles begin to form. Flip and cook the other side until browned.

5. Remove the bread from the griddle, dunk in the pan of warm water, shake off any excess water, and place on a plate. Cover with a moistened towel, then proceed to the next flatbread to add to the stack. (If you don't allow the bread to cool in a moist, warm environment, it will dry out too much to eat easily.)

Westfjord Wheatcakes (*Vestfirskar Hveitikökur*)

Although they look and are prepared like pancakes, Iceland's Westfjord Wheatcakes are enjoyed like flatbread, topped with meats like smoked lamb or salmon. Traditionally made directly on the stovetop, they are best cooked on a lefse griddle or a pancake griddle set on medium heat.

INGREDIENTS | SERVES 16

½ cup butter, softened

1 cup sugar

1 egg, beaten

4 cups all-purpose flour

4 cups spelt flour (or substitute all-purpose, wheat, or barley flour)

6 teaspoons baking powder

½ teaspoon baking soda

1 teaspoon hornsalt (optional)

4 cups buttermilk

1. In a large mixing bowl, cream together the butter and sugar, then stir in the egg.

2. In a separate bowl, combine the flours, baking powder, baking soda, and hornsalt, then use a balloon whisk to toss them all together.

3. Stir the buttermilk and the flours into the batter in alternating 1-cup increments to form a soft dough.

4. Lightly knead the dough 2–3 times on a floured counter, then divide into 16 equal portions. Roll each portion into a "pancake," 7"–8" in diameter. Prick each cake well with a fork.

5. Transfer each pancake to a *lefse* or pancake griddle and cook over medium heat until baked through, puffed, and golden, flipping once.

Icelandic Scones (*Skonsur*)

Skonsur, Icelandic scones, like Westfjord Wheatcakes, are pancake-like,
½"-thick griddle cakes enjoyed in place of bread. They're incredible served right out of the pan,
spread with butter, and with a fast-melting cheese or cold cuts on top.

INGREDIENTS | SERVES 6

2 cups all-purpose flour
2 tablespoons sugar
2 teaspoons baking powder
½ teaspoon baking soda
1 teaspoon salt
2 eggs
2 cups milk
3 tablespoons butter

1. In a large bowl, whisk together the dry ingredients. Beat the eggs into the milk, then pour into the dry ingredients and stir until incorporated.

2. Melt the butter in a pancake pan or frying pan over low heat. Use a soup ladle to transfer the batter to the pan, forming ½"-thick pancakes the size of dinner plates. Cook until the *skonsur* develop open bubbles across the top.

3. Flip and cook for 2 more minutes.

4. Serve warm or cool. Wrap any leftovers, and save to use in place of bread for sandwiches.

CHAPTER 6

Specialty Sandwiches and Spreads

Smørrebrød: Danish Open-Faced Sandwiches

Of all of their wonderful foods, the Danes are perhaps best known for their stunning open-faced smørrebrød—sandwiches so complex in structure and design that people take special training courses to learn how to prepare them properly.

INGREDIENTS | SERVES 20

A selection of rye bread, rye crispbread, sourdough bread, and French bread

5 cups of butter, softened

2 heads of Bibb lettuce

½-1 pound each of smoked and pickled herring

½-1 pound each of cooked baby shrimp, cooked large shrimp, sardines, fried sole or flounder, smoked salmon, and gravlax (marinated salmon)

Hard-boiled egg slices, tomato wedges, cucumber slices, red onion rings, grated fresh horseradish, pickled beets, and sweet pickles

½-1 pound each of sliced chicken breast, roast beef, ham, lamb roll, meatballs, bacon, and liver pâté

¼-½ pound each of Danish blue cheese, and Camembert, Samsø, and Emmentaler cheeses

Grapes, strawberries, cherry tomatoes

Danish Remoulade Sauce, mayonnaise, cream cheese, brown mustard

1. Butter a piece of bread generously (this keeps the bread from becoming soggy from the toppings) and place it on a plate.

2. Cover the bread completely with a lettuce leaf so that none of the bread shows.

3. Generously pile your choice of herring, seafood, meat, and/or cheese, along with vegetables and garnishes, on the bread (returning for a new plate with each consecutive "sandwich" course: a herring sandwich comes first, then one with seafood, the third sandwich with meat, then a final "dessert" sandwich with cheese).

4. Name your creations after yourself, toast your companions, and eat with a knife and fork.

Create a *Smørrebrød* Buffet

It's fun to throw a smørrebrød buffet, where you provide various ingredients and allow your guests to design their own special variations of the four basic smørrebrød courses (herring, seafood, meat, and cheese, in that order) they would enjoy at a good restaurant in Copenhagen. Be sure to have good Danish beer and aquavit on hand to heighten the enjoyment!

Fried Sole *Smørrebrød* with Asparagus

European plaice, a white-fleshed flatfish, is often prepared in Denmark as the topping for seafood smørrebrød. Here, sole (or flounder) is used as a flavorful substitute.

INGREDIENTS | SERVES 6

1 cup all-purpose, rye, or spelt flour

1 teaspoon salt

½ teaspoon pepper

6 sole or flounder fillets

2 tablespoons butter

3 tablespoons canola oil

½ cup low-fat yogurt

½ cup cooked baby shrimp

1 teaspoon lemon zest

2 teaspoons fresh dill, finely chopped

6 leaves Bibb lettuce

6 young asparagus stalks, blanched until tender

6 slices rye or French bread, buttered on top

6 lemon slices

1. Mix together the flour, salt, and pepper. Debone and then rinse the fish fillets, patting gently with paper towels to remove excess water. Toss fish in the flour.

2. In a heavy frying pan, melt together butter and canola oil over medium heat. Fry fish until done, about 3–5 minutes per side, depending on the thickness of the fish. Remove and drain on paper towels.

3. Whisk together the yogurt, shrimp, lemon zest, and dill.

4. To assemble *smørrebrød*, place a lettuce leaf on each piece of bread. Top with a fried fish fillet, then place a generous spoonful of the shrimp yogurt on the fish. Angle the asparagus stalks on one side of the yogurt to give height to the presentation; complete with a twisted slice of lemon on the opposite side.

Restaurant Ida Davidsen's *Smørrebrød*

Copenhagen's most famous smørrebrød restaurant is Restaurant Ida Davidsen, now located at Store Kongensgade 70. First opened in 1888 at a different location as a wine bar by Ida's great-grandfather, Oskar Davidsen, by 1901 the restaurant had developed a list of 178 open-faced sandwich selections—a Guinness World Record. Many of the classic "named" open-faced sandwiches now served by other Danish smørrebrød restaurants (such as the "Victor Borge" smørrebrød and "Hans Christian Andersen" smørrebrød) were first developed by the Davidsen family.

"Sun over Gudhjem" Smoked Herring *Smørrebrød*

One of Denmark's most famous open-faced sandwiches, "Sun over Gudhjem" celebrates the ocean riches of Gudhjem, a fishing town on the island of Bornholm in the Baltic Sea. Smoked herring—Gudhjem's major claim to fame—co-stars here with a raw egg yolk (the sun) presented on top of the herring in half an egg shell.

INGREDIENTS | SERVES 6

Butter, as needed

6 pieces dense rye bread

6 pieces Bibb lettuce

6 smoked herring

12 red radishes, grated or chopped in small matchsticks

¼ cup chives, finely chopped

6 pasteurized eggs

Raw Egg Yolk Substitute

Raw egg yolks are nature's perfect sauce, but unfortunately, because of the salmonella risk, they are unsafe to consume raw unless pasteurized. If you can't find pasteurized eggs (such as Davidson's Safest Choice Eggs, which are safe to eat raw) in your supermarket, you can lightly poach the egg yolks in their shells to sterilize them (although to be 100 percent safe, please don't serve these to children, the elderly, pregnant women, or people with compromised immune systems).

1. Butter the entire surface of the rye bread to seal the bread and enhance the flavor of the toppings.

2. Cover the entire surface of the bread with a piece of Bibb lettuce.

3. Scrape off the skins of the smoked herring, if present. Split each herring in half and lay the 2 halves side-by-side on the buttered bread.

4. Sprinkle the radishes and chives liberally over the herring.

5. Carefully crack the pasteurized eggs and separate the yolks from the whites; reserve the whites for other uses. Place one yolk, in half of its shell, on top of each sandwich.

Shrimp *Smørrebrød* with Caviar Mayonnaise

Precision is everything when constructing eye-catching smørrebrød—as important as creating a still-life work of art (which in fact you are!). Take a page out of Ida Davidsen's book and arrange the shrimp on this sandwich evenly across the bread, with heads and tails all in the same direction.

INGREDIENTS | SERVES 6

½ pound cooked shrimp

¼ cup lemon juice

2 teaspoons fresh dill, finely chopped

1 ounce red lumpfish caviar

½ cup olive oil mayonnaise

Butter, as needed

6 pieces dense rye, French, or sourdough bread, or crispbread

6 lettuce leaves

Lemon slices and additional fresh dill to garnish

1. Toss together the shrimp, lemon juice, and fresh dill; allow to marinate for 30 minutes.

2. Rinse and pat the lumpfish caviar dry with a paper towel, then fold into the mayonnaise. Cover and refrigerate for 30 minutes.

3. Butter the bread thickly and cover each slice with a lettuce leaf. Line the shrimp in two neat rows down the center of the bread. Top with a dollop of caviar mayonnaise, then garnish with additional dill and lemon slices.

Danish Remoulade Sauce

The Danes' version of French remoulade sauce is unique in that it includes curry powder to add color and spice. Be careful with the curry; use just enough to give the remoulade a light yellow tint.

INGREDIENTS | MAKE 1 CUP

1 cup olive oil mayonnaise

1 tablespoon fresh parsley, finely chopped

2 tablespoons green onions, both white and green parts, finely chopped

2 cornichon (gherkin) pickles, finely chopped

1 teaspoon capers, finely chopped

1 tablespoon lemon juice

1 teaspoon Dijon mustard

½–1 teaspoon curry powder

Salt and pepper to taste

1. Combine all ingredients except the curry powder, salt, and pepper. Sample the mixture, adding additional chopped cornichons, capers, lemon juice, or mustard to taste.

2. Stir in curry powder in ¼-teaspoon increments until remoulade is light yellow in color. Taste again, adding a bit more curry if you prefer a sharper edge. Season with salt and pepper.

3. Refrigerate for at least 1 hour (overnight is better) to allow time for the flavors to meld.

Fish Cakes (*Fiskefrikadeller*) *Smørrebrød*

*Crunchy fish cakes and Denmark's own unique curried remoulade sauce
give this open-faced sandwich its special bite.*

INGREDIENTS | SERVES 6

1½ pounds cod or other white fish fillets

¼ cup green onions, finely chopped

3 tablespoons parsley, finely chopped

1 tablespoon chives, finely chopped

2 eggs

¼ cup Icelandic skyr or Greek-style plain
low-fat yogurt

1 teaspoon pepper

½ teaspoon salt

10 pieces dense rye bread

2 tablespoons butter

2 tablespoons canola or olive oil

Fresh dill, lemon slices, Danish
Remoulade Sauce (see recipe in this
chapter), and additional chopped
chives to garnish

Use Your Fork

Danish smørrebrød aren't intended to
serve as finger food—the buttered bread,
like medieval bread trenchers, is simply the
"plate" upon which fresh meats, cheeses,
and vegetables are intricately arranged
(ideally so that the surface of the bread is
covered completely). It's thus necessary to
use a knife and fork when eating these
generously loaded sandwiches.

1. Finely chop the fish fillets, then mix with the green onions, parsley, chives, eggs, yogurt, pepper, and salt. Refrigerate for 1 hour.

2. Toast 4 slices of the rye bread, then process into fine bread crumbs.

3. Shape the fish mixture into 12 small patties and roll them in toasted rye bread crumbs.

4. Melt the butter and oil together in a frying pan over medium heat; fry the fish cakes, turning once, until nicely browned, about 5 minutes per side.

5. To assemble the sandwiches, butter the tops of the 6 remaining pieces of rye bread. Arrange 2 fish cakes on each piece of bread, tucking the dill and lemon slices around them. Top each cake with a dollop of Danish Remoulade Sauce; sprinkle with chopped chives.

Roast Beef *Smörgåstårta* (Sandwich Cake)

*Creamy layers of roast beef spread, liver sausage spread,
and pimento blue cheese alternate in this hearty* smörgåstårta.

INGREDIENTS | SERVES 30

16 ounces Danish Liver Pâté (see recipe in this chapter) (*Leverpostej*) or liver sausage (*liverwurst*) spread

16 ounces low-fat cream cheese

2 heaping tablespoons minced onion

1 tablespoon lemon juice

3 tablespoons dill pickle relish

2 pounds roast beef, cooked and coarsely chopped

¼ cup celery, chopped

1 cup light mayonnaise

2 teaspoons prepared horseradish sauce

½ teaspoon salt

¼ teaspoon pepper

72 slices dense rye bread, crusts removed

4 cups Pimento Blue Cheese Spread (see recipe in this chapter)

Cucumber slices, red onions, hard-boiled eggs slices, cheese slices, cornichons (gherkins), tomato slices, and additional roast beef to garnish

Smörgåstårta Garnishes

Garnishes are key when preparing a grand smörgåstårta as both the centerpiece and the *piéce de rèsistance* of a party buffet table. Choose edible vegetable, herb, and fruit garnishes that are fresh and seasonal, representing a rich variety of colors. Then artistically arrange these garnishes with curls of meat, sliced eggs, or generous amounts of seafood so that the top and sides of the *smörgåstårta* are completely covered.

1. One day before serving, make your liver sausage spread by whipping together liver sausage, cream cheese, minced onion, lemon juice, and pickle relish.

2. Next, for the roast beef spread, fold chopped roast beef and celery into the mayonnaise, then mix in horseradish sauce, salt, and pepper.

3. On a large serving platter, lay out 12 of the bread slices edge to edge in a 3 × 4 grid. Spread half of the liver sausage spread over this bottom layer of bread, then top with 12 more pieces of bread.

4. Spread half of the roast beef spread on this layer, topping again with 12 pieces of bread. Use 1½–2 cups of the Pimento Blue Cheese Spread to frost this middle layer. Cover with 12 more bread slices.

5. Use the remaining roast beef spread for the next layer, add a bread layer, then use the remaining liver sausage spread for your top layer. Crown with the remaining bread; lightly frost the sides and top of the sandwich cake with the remaining Pimento Blue Cheese Spread (focus on getting the sides covered and don't worry if you run out of spread on the top, since you can hide any bare spots with garnishes).

6. If possible, allow the sandwich cake to sit overnight in the refrigerator so that the flavors can meld together.

7. Before serving, garnish the top and sides of the cake with bright vegetable slices, roast beef curls, cheese slices, and/or hard-boiled egg slices, with an eye for creating pleasing contrasts of color, texture, and height.

Meatballs (*Frikadeller*) *Smørrebrød*

In most people's homes in Denmark, smørrebrød are prepared with whatever one has on hand—in many cases, the previous evening's leftovers—and tucked into four-compartment boxes for lunches. It's worth making extra meatballs at night if one is guaranteed these superlative sandwiches the following day!

INGREDIENTS | SERVES 6

1 pound ground pork

1 pound ground turkey

1 medium onion, roughly chopped

2 cups soda water

½ cup rye or all-purpose flour

2 eggs

¼ cup parsley, finely chopped

2 teaspoons salt

2 teaspoons pepper

1 teaspoon nutmeg

Butter or canola oil for frying

6 slices buttered rye bread

1 cup Danish Red Cabbage (Rødkål) for Smørrebrød (see recipe in this chapter)

French-fried onion rings for garnish

1. Grind the pork, turkey, and onion together in a food processor (or run through a meat grinder 2–3 times) until mixture is very fine.

2. Mix in the soda water, flour, eggs, parsley, salt, pepper, and nutmeg (the mixture will be very loose and watery).

3. Heat butter or oil in a sturdy frying pan (cast-iron is best) over medium-high heat. Using two large spoons, shape meatballs (about the size of an apricot) and place them in the pan, leaving a few inches of space around each meatball. Fry until browned, turning once (about 5 minutes on each side). Remove from heat and drain on paper towels.

4. For open-faced sandwiches, slice the *frikadeller* and then place them in a row on buttered slices of rye bread (use enough to cover the bread). Top with a mound of Danish Red Cabbage (*Rødkål*) mixture crowned with a few French-fried onion rings.

"Hans Christian Andersen" *Smørrebrød*

Ida Davidsen's grandfather, savvy restaurateur Vagn Aage Davidsen, originated the idea of "themed" open-faced sandwiches that celebrated Danish cultural and historical figures. His "Hans Christian Andersen" sandwich, now imitated by others as a classic smørrebrød, incorporates ingredients mentioned in Andersen's diaries.

INGREDIENTS | SERVES 1

1 large leaf of Bibb lettuce
1 slice of buttered rye bread
5 strips crispy bacon
1 triangular slice liver pâté
3 tomato wedges
1 thin, triangular slice Beef Consommé Aspic (see recipe in this chapter)
1 tablespoon freshly grated horseradish
½ teaspoon fresh chives, finely chopped

1. Place the lettuce on the buttered rye bread, then lay the bacon diagonally down the middle of the bread, from corner to corner.

2. Place the liver pâté on one side of the bacon and line the tomato wedges along the other.

3. Top the liver pate with the slice of aspic; tuck the horseradish in with the tomatoes.

4. Sprinkle with chives and serve.

Beef Consommé Aspic

Shimmering, jewel-toned aspic is seldom seen these days on American tables, but it deserves to be revived. At Ida Davidsen's and other smørrebrød shops in Denmark, aspic is often used as part of the elaborate construction of open-faced sandwiches.

INGREDIENTS | SERVES 16

4 cups beef consommé
4½ tablespoons unflavored gelatin
½ cup port wine

1. Place 1 cup of the beef consommé in a small saucepan and sprinkle with the gelatin. Allow to rest for 10 minutes, then place on the stove and warm over medium heat until the gelatin has melted.

2. In a second saucepan, heat the remaining 3 cups of beef consommé and the port wine until boiling. Turn off the heat, remove the pan from the burner, and pour in the gelatin mixture, stirring to combine.

3. Pour the liquid into a loaf pan and chill in the refrigerator until it's quite firm.

4. To serve, cut into thin slices and use on open-faced sandwiches.

Danish Red Cabbage (*Rødkål*) for *Smørrebrød*

Danes serve red cabbage in many different ways—a highly spiced version is always included on a Christmas table, but less labor-intensive variations often accompany evening meals and then add color to leftover lunchtime sandwiches.

INGREDIENTS | SERVES 6

1 head red cabbage
3 tablespoons butter
3 tablespoons red wine vinegar
¼ cup water or orange juice
4 tablespoons currant or lingonberry jam
½ teaspoon salt
¼ teaspoon pepper
3 apples

How to Cook Red Cabbage

Like so many Nordic foods, the flavor of slow-cooked red cabbage really improves with age. Always make cooked red cabbage a day ahead of time and let it sit in the refrigerator so that its flavors can marry; chilled, it keeps up to 10 days.

1. Wash the cabbage well and chop into a fine julienne dice.

2. In a heavy saucepan, melt butter over medium heat. Add the cabbage and stir until it is well coated with the butter.

3. Add the red wine vinegar, water (or orange juice), jam, salt, and pepper, tossing well. Reduce heat to low, cover, and allow to simmer for 30 minutes.

4. Meanwhile, peel, core, and dice the apples into matchsticks. Add to the cabbage, checking to make sure there is water in the bottom of the pot. Cover and simmer for 1–1½ more hours, checking occasionally and adding more water (if necessary) throughout the cooking process.

5. Remove from heat, cool, and refrigerate overnight. Reheat prior to serving.

Danish Liver Pâté (*Leverpostej*)

Although not health food, homemade liver pâté, when enjoyed sparingly, is a justifiable indulgence (especially if you follow the Danes' example and ride your bike daily as your primary means of transportation).

INGREDIENTS | SERVES 30

1½ pounds pork or beef liver, chopped

1 pound fatty pork or bacon, coarsely chopped

½ onion, coarsely chopped

6 anchovies, soaked in milk then chopped

2 eggs

1 cup light cream

¼ cup all-purpose flour

1 teaspoon salt

½ teaspoon pepper

¼ teaspoon allspice

¼ teaspoon ground cloves

8 bacon slices, uncooked

Liver Pâté *Smørrebrød*

For a classic Danish open-faced sandwich, lightly butter a piece of rye bread and top with a leaf of butter lettuce. Place 2 thin slices of liver pâté on the lettuce, then top with sautéed mushrooms and crispy fried onions.

1. Preheat oven to 325°F. In a food processor, grind together the liver, pork (or bacon), onion, and anchovies into a very fine paste.

2. Separate the eggs and beat the whites to firm peaks.

3. Beat the egg yolks together with the cream, then stir in the flour, seasonings, and spices. Vigorously beat the meat and egg mixtures together (the whip attachment on a stand mixer works well for this); fold in the egg whites just until incorporated.

4. Line a loaf pan with the bacon slices, then pour in the batter, smoothing the top so that it's even. Cover with foil, then place in a larger roasting pan filled with 1" of water.

5. Place on center rack of preheated oven and cook for 1½ hours, or until an inserted skewer comes out clean. Cool and chill until ready to serve in thin slices on rye bread; *leverpostej* can also be frozen for later use.

Spicy Lamb Roll (Norwegian *Rullepølse*)

Rullepølse, a favorite on Norwegian-American Christmas tables, is sliced thin and served as a savory topping for open-faced sandwiches. While traditional recipes called for saltpeter, it's far safer and no less effective to use a salt-and-sugar brine.

INGREDIENTS | SERVES 16

1 pound lamb flank steak (or substitute beef)

½ pound boneless pork butt

1 onion, finely chopped

½ teaspoon allspice

½ teaspoon cloves

½ teaspoon powdered ginger

½ teaspoon pepper

2 quarts water

1½ cups rock salt

¼ cup sugar

2 bay leaves, crushed

Rullepølse Press

Rullepølse needs to be pressed after it is cooked so that it will hold together when sliced. To improvise a press, either clamp the roll between two pieces of wood with C-clamps or, more simply, place the roll in a bread pan and weigh it down with a brick wrapped in cheesecloth.

1. Lay flank steak on the counter and pound with a meat mallet on both sides. Trim edges, if necessary, to form a perfect rectangle; place skin side down on the work surface.

2. Carefully slice the pork butt into ⅛"-thick slices, then place slices, slightly overlapping, on top of the flank steak. Sprinkle chopped onion and spices evenly over the pork.

3. Tightly roll the steak, then sew the side and ends of the roll with strong thread or cooking string to secure.

4. Combine water, rock salt, sugar, and crushed bay leaves in a pot and bring to a boil, stirring until the salt and sugar are dissolved. Remove from heat and cool thoroughly in the refrigerator before adding the meat. When brine has cooled, immerse the meat so that it is completely covered. Return to the refrigerator and let sit for 10 days (or up to a month).

5. After 10 days, remove meat from brine and rinse thoroughly. Prick the roll several times with a fork, then place in a pot with enough fresh water to cover by 1". Simmer at a medium boil until tender, about 2 hours.

6. Remove cooked roll from the water and place in a *rullepølse* press. Refrigerate overnight.

7. Slice paper-thin and serve on open-faced sandwiches.

Pimento Blue Cheese Spread

Give a Southern favorite a Nordic twist by using Danish blue cheese (also called "Danablu") for pimento cheese spread. This spread is great as a base for open-faced sandwiches or as a savory filling for a meat-filled sandwich cake (smörgåstårta).

INGREDIENTS | MAKES 4 CUPS

16 ounces Danablu cheese

16 ounces cream cheese

6 tablespoons mayonnaise

1 tablespoon Worcestershire sauce

4 cloves garlic, minced through a garlic press

1 tablespoon salt

2 jars pimentos

1 cup walnuts, finely chopped

2 tablespoons chives, finely chopped

1. Using the whip attachment on a stand mixer or a strong whisk, beat together the Danablu cheese, cream cheese, mayonnaise, and Worcestershire sauce until light and creamy.

2. Add the garlic, salt, pimentos, walnuts, and chives. Fold the mixture together until well blended.

3. Chill for a few hours or overnight before eating.

"Victor Borge" *Smørrebrød*

At Ida Davidsen's in Copenhagen, sandwiches are often christened after famous patrons. When pianist and showman Victor Borge, the "Danish Clown Prince," visited the restaurant, he ordered his bread piled high with gravlax, tiny shrimp, caviar, and crayfish tails. This adaptation substitutes dungeness crab claws for the crayfish tails.

INGREDIENTS | SERVES 6

12 slices of gravlax (or substitute lox)

6 buttered slices of French or rye bread

3 ounces black lumpfish roe or caviar

30 large shrimp, cleaned, cooked, and chilled

12 shelled dungeness crab claws (or 12 cooked crayfish tails, if you can get them)

Lemon slices to garnish

½ cup olive oil mayonnaise

2 tablespoons finely chopped dill

½ teaspoon lemon zest

1. Place 2 slices of gravlax on the buttered bread (use more, if necessary, to cover the bread surface completely).

2. Lay a line of caviar down the center of the bread, then arrange 5 shrimp on one side of the caviar and the crab claws (or crayfish tails) on the other. Garnish with dill and lemon slices.

3. Combine the mayonnaise, dill, and lemon zest to serve as a saucy spread alongside the sandwiches.

Seafood *Smörgåstårta* (Sandwich Cake)

The trick to an outstanding Smörgåstårta is to be generous with colorful garnishes that complement the fillings of the sandwich cake. For a seafood cake, reserve plenty of baby shrimp, cucumber and lemon slices, and fresh dill to decorate the top and sides of what will become the most talked-about dish on your table.

INGREDIENTS | SERVES 15–20

3 cups light cream cheese

1½ cups low-fat sour cream

1½ cups mayonnaise

1 cup fresh dill, very finely chopped

½ pound smoked salmon

¼ cup red onion, finely chopped

1 tablespoon capers, finely chopped

2 avocadoes, peeled and pitted

1 tablespoon lemon juice

1 cucumber, peeled, seeded, and chopped

2 cups cooked baby shrimp

1 tablespoon lemon zest

¼ cup mixed colored sweet peppers, finely chopped

16 slices dense French or artisan bread

Additional lemon and cucumber slices, dill, capers, multiple colors of cod roe (caviar), cucumbers, and tomato wedges to garnish.

Best Bread for *Smörgåstårta*

The bread used for smörgåstårta needs to have a texture firm enough to absorb the complementary flavors of the separate spreads without becoming mushy. Use either homemade rye or spelt bread, or dense, chewy artisan loaves from your favorite bakery, for best results.

1. Beat together the cream cheese, sour cream, mayonnaise, and chopped dill.

2. Crumble the smoked salmon and fold together with 1 cup of the dilled cream cheese spread, chopped red onion, and capers.

3. For the avocado spread, in a separate bowl lightly mash the avocadoes together with the lemon juice, then fold into ½ cup of the dilled cream cheese; add the chopped cucumbers.

4. In a third bowl, combine baby shrimp with 1 cup of the dilled cream cheese spread, lemon zest, and chopped sweet peppers.

5. Slice the crusts off the bread. On a serving plate, arrange 4 slices of bread in a square and cover with all of the smoked spread. Top with 4 more bread slices.

6. Spread all of the avocado mixture on the bread as your middle layer. Top with 4 bread slices.

7. Evenly cover the bread with the shrimp spread as your top layer. Cover with remaining bread slices.

8. Use the remaining dilled sour cream spread to frost the sides and top of the cake, then decorate all surfaces with patterns of baby shrimp, lemon slices, tomato wedges, and other garnishes.

9. Serve immediately or refrigerate overnight (the flavors will intensify and be even better the second day).

CHAPTER 7

Pancakes and Preserves

Swedish Pancakes (Plättar)

Swedish pancakes, or plättar, are probably the origin of American "silver dollar" pancakes. Thin and delicate, plättar are best prepared with a special plett pan, although you can certainly use a griddle or frying pan for equally tasty results.

INGREDIENTS | SERVES 10

4 cups milk

2 eggs

2 cups all-purpose or spelt flour

½ teaspoon salt

1 teaspoon vanilla extract

3 tablespoons melted butter

1. Whisk together all ingredients except for the butter. Cover and refrigerate for 30 minutes.

2. Heat a cast-iron plett pan over medium heat until a drop of water sizzles on the surface. Using a pastry brush, grease each well of the pan with the melted butter; whisk remaining butter into the pancake batter.

3. Pour batter by tablespoons into each well. Fry until golden, flipping once.

4. Serve with lingonberry preserves and whipped cream.

Finnish Oven-Baked Pancake (Pannakakku)

Try making pancakes the way the Finns do: baked in the oven. The basic batter requires an easy ratio of 1 egg to ¼ cup flour to ¼ cup milk; you can make the pancake sweet or savory by adding things like diced ham, chicken, blanched vegetables, fruit, lemon zest, or vanilla.

INGREDIENTS | SERVES 6

6 eggs

1½ cups milk

1½ cups flour

1 tablespoon sugar

1 teaspoon salt

3 tablespoons melted butter

1. Whisk together the eggs, milk, flour, sugar, and salt. Allow to rest at room temperature for 30 minutes.

2. Meanwhile, place butter in a large oven-proof frying pan. Place in a cold oven, then preheat oven to 450°F. Once oven reaches heat, remove frying pan and swirl gently so that the melted butter covers all surfaces.

3. Pour batter in prepared frying pan and return it to the oven. Cook 15–20 minutes, until pancake is puffed and golden.

4. Serve with plum jam, fresh berries, or fruit compote with whipped cream on the side.

Åland Semolina Pancake

Åland, an autonomous archipelago off the coast of Finland, is famous for this pancake. It's commonly served with whipped cream and Åland Prune Cream (see recipe in this chapter).

INGREDIENTS | SERVES 8

4 cups milk

1½ cups semolina (cream of wheat)

4 eggs

½ cup sugar

1 teaspoon vanilla

1 cup flour

¼ teaspoon salt

2 teaspoons freshly ground cardamom

Whipped cream to taste

Rice Porridge

Leftover rice porridge is also sometimes used as the base for the Åland pancake. If you prefer rice, substitute 1 cup of pearl rice for the semolina and increase the cooking time for the porridge to 30 minutes, or until the rice is tender.

1. In a large saucepan, bring milk to a simmer; add semolina in a thin stream, whisking steadily to remove all lumps. Cook over medium heat, stirring constantly until porridge thickens, about 15 minutes. Remove from heat and allow to cool completely.

2. Preheat oven to 395°F. Beat together the eggs, sugar, and vanilla until they're frothy. Stir in the flour, salt, cardamom, and cooled porridge.

3. Pour batter into a 12" × 9" greased baking dish and bake until firm and golden brown, about 40 minutes. Remove from oven and allow to cool slightly.

4. Slice pancake into individual servings and top with whipped cream to taste, or with Åland Prune Cream.

Åland Prune Cream

*Prunes—dried plums—are a favorite accompaniment for Scandinavian cakes and pancakes.
Here they come into their own in a rich, cinnamon-scented "cream."*

INGREDIENTS | MAKES 3 CUPS

15 pitted prunes (dried plums), cut in quarters

4 cups water

1 cup prune juice

1 cinnamon stick

½ cup sugar

2 tablespoons potato starch flour or cornstarch plus 3 tablespoons water

1. Soak chopped prunes in water for 1 hour. After soaking, transfer to a large saucepan, add prune juice and cinnamon stick, and bring mixture to a low boil. Add sugar, stirring until it dissolves. Temporarily remove pot from heat.

2. Whisk together flour and water, then stir into the prune mixture. Return the pot to the burner and bring to a boil once again, stirring constantly. As soon as mixture begins to thicken, turn off the heat.

3. Remove from burner, discard cinnamon stick, and allow to cool before serving with Åland Semolina Pancake (see recipe in this chapter).

Rhubarb Jam

*Rhubarb jam is a staple in Icelandic households, where it doubles as a fabulous filling
for the secret to family bliss, "happy marriage cake" (hjónabandssæla).*

INGREDIENTS | MAKES 3 CUPS

6 cups bright red rhubarb stalks

3 cups sugar

1. Clean the rhubarb stalks of all toxic leaves and cut into a ¼" dice. Place in a glass bowl or measuring cup, stir in sugar, and place bowl in the refrigerator overnight so the sugar can draw out the rhubarb's natural juices.

2. In the morning, transfer the rhubarb and its juices to a large nonreactive saucepan (stainless steel or enamel). Bring the rhubarb to a boil over high heat, then immediately reduce the heat to low and simmer for 1 hour, stirring every so often to prevent sticking.

3. Cool and either preserve in hot jars or refrigerate for up to 3 weeks.

Gotland Saffron Pancake (*Saffranspannkaka*)

*Actually more of a baked porridge casserole than a "pancake,"
Gotland's saffranspannkaka is lovely when served with blackberry or marionberry jam.*

INGREDIENTS | SERVES 4

1½ cups water

1 tablespoon butter

½ teaspoon salt

1 cup sweet, short-grain rice (Jasmine or pearl)

4½ cups milk

¼ teaspoon saffron threads (or ⅛ teaspoon powdered saffron)

2 tablespoons sugar

½ cup blanched almonds, chopped

5 eggs

1. In a medium saucepan, mix water, butter, and salt and bring to a boil over high heat. Steadily pour in rice, stirring constantly. Reduce to low, cover pot, and simmer for 15 minutes, or until most of the water has been absorbed (at this point, stir occasionally to prevent sticking).

2. Whisk milk into the porridge, bring to a boil, then reduce heat again to low. Cover pot and simmer, undisturbed, for 30 minutes.

3. Preheat oven to 400°F. Using a mortar and pestle, muddle the saffron into the sugar, then stir the mixture, along with the chopped almonds, into the rice porridge.

4. Beat eggs together, then stir into porridge. Pour into a 12" × 9" greased baking dish, place in oven, and cook for 40 minutes. Serve warm.

Danish *Aebleskiver*

Prepared in a special aebleskiver pan, Denmark's spherical pancake balls are the popcorn of the pancake spectrum. One great source for aebleskiver pans and for an excellent prepared mix is Aunt Else's Æbleskiver; check out the website, www.auntelse.com, to watch a detailed video on how to do the tricky aebleskiver flip.

INGREDIENTS | SERVES 6

2 eggs

1 tablespoon sugar

2 cups flour

1 teaspoon cinnamon (optional)

1 teaspoon baking powder

1½ cups buttermilk

Canola oil, as needed

Danish Apple Slices

The word aebleskiver means "apple slice," since it's common to insert a small piece of apple into the center of each pancake ball. If using apples, dice them coarsely and simply drop them on top of the batter before you first turn each pancake ball; the apple chunks will sink into the centers and bake quite happily there.

1. Separate the eggs and beat the whites until stiff peaks form. Whisk together the egg yolks and sugar, then in a separate bowl sift together the flour, cinnamon, and baking powder.

2. Gradually mix the flour mixture and buttermilk, in alternating ½-cup additions, into the egg yolks. Then, using a light hand, fold the egg whites into the batter.

3. Pour about ½ teaspoon oil into each well of your *aebleskiver* pan, then place over a medium burner. Heat pan for 15 minutes, then use a pastry brush to spread the oil across the wells and top surface of the pan.

4. Spoon the batter into the wells, filling to just below the top of each well (the pastries will expand).

5. You'll need to make 3 one-quarter turns to form the balls into perfect spheres. After the edges of each ball have begun to brown and pull away from the sides, use a knitting needle or skewer to gently slide the *aebleskiver* up in a quarter-turn. After a minute or two, push the needle into the top corner you've created and slide it around in a 90-degree quarter-turn. Finally, stick the needle into the back of the cooked part and flip it completely over. You'll know it's done when you insert the needle into the center of the pastry and it comes out clean.

6. Remove from pan and serve warm with raspberry jam and powdered sugar.

Icelandic Crepes (*Pönnukaka*)

Paper-thin Icelandic pönnukaka, filled with jam and cream and folded into quarters, are often served as a treat with late-afternoon coffee.

INGREDIENTS | SERVES 8

¼ cup butter

3 eggs

3 cups milk

2 tablespoons sugar

2 cups flour

½ teaspoon baking powder

¼ teaspoon baking soda

¼ teaspoon salt

2 teaspoons freshly ground cardamom

Lingonberry Jam or Rhubarb Jam (see recipes in this chapter) or blueberry jam to taste

Whipped cream to taste

Scandinavian Pancake Pans

In Scandinavia, every pancake has its own special pan. The Swedes have the flat plett pan, the Danes use aebelskiver pans, and the Icelanders swear by their own particular crepe pan—a heavy, 7½" flat pan with a raised ⅛" edge.

1. Place butter in a large crepe pan or 8" skillet and melt over medium heat, swirling the pan to make sure all surfaces are greased. Remove from burner and allow butter to cool.

2. In a large bowl, vigorously whisk together the eggs, milk, and sugar. Sift together the dry ingredients in a separate bowl, then slowly incorporate them into the batter until it has the consistency of heavy cream. Stir in the cooled butter.

3. Return greased crepe pan to the burner and heat at medium-high until a drop of water sizzles on the surface.

4. Place a generous tablespoon of batter on the pan, rotating the pan back and forth until the batter covers the surface evenly. When the bottom of the crepe has browned, use a spatula to flip the crepe over. Cook just until the underside is browned (about 1 minute); remove from pan.

5. If your first crepe is too dark, breathe deeply and sacrifice it to the Norse gods; the first crepe is often overdone because it absorbs any excess butter on the pan. With the pan thus readied, the rest of your crepes should be fine.

6. To serve, spread crepes with jam, spoon a dollop of cream in one quarter, then fold twice into triangles.

Swedish Potato Pancakes with Pork (*Raggmunk med Fläsk*)

When cooking dishes like potato pancakes or potato bread (lefse), it's best to use the oldest, mealiest potatoes you can find; fresh young potatoes contain too much water to work well. The Swedes serve potato pancakes as a comforting evening meal, with fried pork and sweetened lingonberries.

INGREDIENTS | SERVES 6

12 slices thick bacon (preferably unsmoked) or salt pork

2 pounds Idaho russet potatoes

1 cup milk

1 egg

½ cup flour

2 teaspoons salt

1. Fry the bacon in a heavy skillet until crisp. Remove to a warm plate, and pour off all but 1 tablespoon of bacon fat.

2. Peel and coarsely grate the potatoes, then place them in a sturdy paper towel and squeeze out any excess water.

3. Whisk together the milk, egg, flour, and salt; fold the grated potatoes into the batter.

4. Increase the burner under the frying pan to medium-high heat. Use a ⅓-cup measuring scoop to transfer batter to the pan; use the bottom of the cup to flatten each pancake slightly to a 3" diameter. Fry until both sides are golden, a few minutes on each side.

5. Serve with bacon and with fresh or frozen lingonberries sweetened with a little sugar.

Blueberry Spelt Pancakes

Blueberries thrive in Nordic climes, and are a valuable source of antioxidants, vitamin C, manganese, and dietary fiber. Combine them with equally nutritious spelt flour to create what just may be the healthiest pancakes on the planet.

INGREDIENTS | SERVES 4–6

3 eggs

1¾ cups buttermilk

1 cup all-purpose flour

2 cups spelt flour

1 teaspoon baking powder

½ teaspoon baking soda

½ teaspoon salt

1½ cups blueberries (wild ones if available)

1. In a medium bowl, whisk together the eggs and buttermilk. In a separate bowl, sift together the flours, baking powder, baking soda, and salt; combine with the buttermilk mixture into a thick batter. Fold in blueberries.

2. Prepare a griddle or frying pan with cooking spray; bring to heat over a medium burner. Use a serving spoon to drop generous dollops of batter onto the griddle. Cook, turning only once (turning pancakes more than once makes them tough).

3. Serve warm, accompanied with additional blueberries and powdered sugar.

Waffles with *Gjetost* and Lingonberry Jam

Norway's own gjetost cheese melts beautifully on freshly baked cardamom waffles. For the prettiest results, use a heart-shaped Scandinavian waffle iron.

INGREDIENTS | SERVES 10

2 eggs

1½ cups milk

¼ cup sugar

1 teaspoon freshly ground cardamom

2 cups flour

1 teaspoon baking powder

½ teaspoon baking soda

½ teaspoon melted butter

1 block Ski Queen gjetost cheese

½ cup lingonberry jam

1. In a medium bowl, combine the eggs with the milk, sugar, and cardamom. Sift together the dry ingredients in a separate bowl, then add them to the mixture, stirring strongly until the batter is smooth. Allow the batter to sit and swell at room temperature for at least 30 minutes (overnight in the refrigerator is even better).

2. Coat your waffle iron with cooking spray and bring it to heat. Bake waffles according to your iron's specifications.

3. Use a cheese slicer to shave thin curls of *gjetost* cheese. Place the cheese immediately on top of each waffle and crown with a spoonful of lingonberry jam.

Savory Potato Waffles

A popular concession at soccer games in the Norwegian county of Østfold is potetvafler med pølse—potato waffles with sausage. Long, grilled hot dog–style sausages are tucked into potato waffles and topped with ketchup, mustard, and relish.

INGREDIENTS | SERVES 10

4 eggs

2 cups milk

3 tablespoons melted butter, at room temperature

5 dry, mealy baking potatoes (Idaho potatoes work beautifully)

2½ cups all-purpose flour

1 teaspoon salt

1 teaspoon baking powder

Potato Waffle Starters

If you have a heart-shaped waffle iron, separate the fried potato waffles into individual hearts and use them as you would buckwheat blini—topped with sour cream and caviar. Other suggestions: serve them as Norwegians often do, topped with salad greens and crispy bacon, or draw your inspiration from your favorite baked-potato toppers.

1. In a medium bowl, whisk together the eggs, milk, and melted butter.

2. Peel and finely grate the potatoes (or use a food processor to grind them finely). Place them in a colander lined with a paper towel and press all excess water out of them; transfer them to the mixing bowl.

3. Stir the flour, salt, and baking powder into the batter. Allow to sit on the counter at room temperature for at least 20 minutes.

4. Grease your waffle iron and fry waffles as directed by the manufacturer, flipping once.

5. Serve warm with bacon, or save and use as a wrap for Norwegian *pølse* (hot dogs).

Barley Nut Waffle Bread

*Savory and heartier than sweet dessert waffles, barley-nut waffle bread provides
a delicious and unique base for open-faced sandwiches.*

INGREDIENTS | SERVES 8

4 cups milk

3 eggs

2 tablespoons melted butter, at room
temperature

1½ cups all-purpose flour

2½ cups barley flour

1 cup cooked barley

½ cup walnuts, finely chopped

½ teaspoon salt

½ teaspoon baking powder

1. In a large mixing bowl, beat together the milk, eggs, and melted butter. Stir in the all-purpose and barley flours, cooked barley, walnuts, salt, and baking powder. Allow to sit at room temperature for 30 minutes.

2. Grease and heat your waffle iron according to the manufacturer's directions. Bake the waffles until well browned, flipping once (keep in mind that the barley batter may take longer to cook than batters made from all-purpose flour).

3. Serve topped with your favorite spreads, cheese, or cold cuts.

Chocolate Waffles

Dessert waffles are never better than when made using a high-quality European cocoa!

INGREDIENTS | SERVES 10

2 cups milk

2 eggs

3 tablespoons melted butter, at room
temperature

3 teaspoons confectioner's sugar

3 teaspoons vanilla sugar

1½ cups flour

2 teaspoons baking powder

½ teaspoon salt

3 tablespoons European cocoa powder

1. In a large bowl, cream together the milk, eggs, melted butter, confectioner's sugar, and vanilla sugar.

2. In a separate bowl, sift together the flour, baking powder, salt, and cocoa powder. Add to the waffle batter in ½-cup increments, beating well with each addition. Allow batter to sit at room temperature for 30 minutes.

3. Grease and preheat your waffle iron. Pour batter by tablespoons into each well. Fry until the waffles are baked through, flipping once.

4. Dust with additional confectioner's sugar and serve warm with whipped cream and fruit.

Lingonberry Jam

Lingonberries are a true delight. Less than half the size of cranberries, they possess a delicate, refreshing tartness that's ideal for making jam that pair remarkably well with both baked goods and meats.

INGREDIENTS | MAKES 2½ CUPS

4 cups fresh or frozen lingonberries
1 cup water
1 cup sugar

1. Rinse off the lingonberries and drain them, then transfer them to a medium saucepan filled with 1 cup water.

2. Bring the berries to a boil, lower heat to medium-low, and simmer for around 15 minutes. Once the berries begin to pop, remove from heat.

3. Stir in up to 1 cup of sugar, to your preference for sweetness.

4. Store jam in the refrigerator (where it will keep for months).

Gooseberry Jam

Gooseberry bushes adore cold weather and rocky soil, and thus are easy to find in Scandinavia. Use the jam not only on toast and baked goods but also as a unique topping for ice cream.

INGREDIENTS | MAKES 2 CUPS

1½ pounds gooseberries
1 cup water
3 tablespoons lemon juice
2 cups sugar

1. Wash the gooseberries well and pick through them, removing all flower tops and stems.

2. Place gooseberries with water and lemon juice in a large nonreactive saucepan. Bring to a simmer and cook for 15 minutes, until the berries start to burst.

3. Stir in sugar, bring the pot to a steady boil, and, stirring constantly, cook the jam for 5 more minutes until it gels. Remove from heat and either preserve in hot jars or store in the refrigerator.

CHAPTER 8

Scandinavian Cheese, Milk, and Yogurt

Icelandic *Skyr*

Icelandic skyr, much smoother and thicker than American yogurt, is also extremely healthy as far as dairy products go. Created by incubating nonfat milk with live active probiotic cultures, skyr contains three times the protein of regular yogurts.

INGREDIENTS | MAKES APPROXIMATELY 1 QUART

4 quarts nonfat milk

4 tablespoons unflavored *skyr* (look for Siggi's brand)

7 drops liquid rennet (available in the baking aisle of most groceries)

1. Make sure, throughout the *skyr*-making process, that all of your equipment (bowls, whisks, colander, pots, cheesecloth) is sanitized (rinsed with boiling water or removed directly from a hot dishwasher) immediately before using.

2. Heat the milk in a large pot over medium heat to scalding (185°F–190°F), stirring often to prevent scorching. Turn off heat immediately when it reaches the scalding point. Cover, and allow to cool to 110°F.

3. Combine 2 cups of the cooled milk with the *skyr*, then return the mixture to the pot, stirring to incorporate. Stir in the liquid rennet.

4. Cover and keep the mixture in a warm place at around 110°F for 12 hours. (To maintain this temperature, you can try placing the pot in an insulated cooler, wrap it in towels, or place it in an oven with two tealights burning at the bottom of the oven.)

5. Line a sanitized strainer with cheesecloth, place it over a large bowl, and spoon the *skyr* curds into the strainer. Allow to drain in a cool room or in the refrigerator to your desired thickness (it should be thicker than American yogurt, but not as thick as cream cheese).

6. *Skyr* will keep for 3–4 weeks, covered, in the refrigerator.

Danish *Tykmælk*

Tykmælk, "thick milk," is a natural yogurt that is much sweeter and less tangy than many other yogurts.

INGREDIENTS | SERVES 4

4 cups whole milk

5 tablespoons buttermilk or 2 tablespoons all-natural (no preservatives or gelatin) yogurt

1. In a large pot, heat the milk to the scalding point (185°F–190°F). Turn off the heat, insert a thermometer, and allow it to cool to 112°F.

2. When it reaches 112°F, stir in the buttermilk or yogurt. Transfer to sanitized bowls (rinsed with boiling water), cover, and allow to sit overnight in a warm place (like an insulated cooler), to curdle.

3. Transfer to refrigerator and allow to cool for 8 hours before serving.

4. Top with brown sugar and serve as a breakfast or snack.

Danish Buttermilk *Koldskål*

On warm summer evenings, Danes enjoy koldskål, a chilled buttermilk drink they offer with twice-baked kammerjunker cookies, similar to biscotti.

INGREDIENTS | SERVES 4

2 cups buttermilk

1 cup plain nonfat yogurt or *skyr*

4 tablespoons sugar

1 tablespoon vanilla sugar

Juice of 1 lemon

1. Stir all of the ingredients together in a large bowl.

2. Using an egg beater or the whisk attachment of a mixer, strongly whip the mixture until it is smooth, about the consistency of thick cream.

3. Allow to cool for at least 1 hour in the refrigerator before serving.

4. Serve with twice-baked Almond Rusks (see Chapter 18) or biscotti and fresh summer berries.

Homemade Butter

Homemade butter, infinitely superior to the store-bought variety, can be made in a mere 15 minutes in a stand mixer. Mold it into either traditional butter molds or decorative sandbakkel tins for a special finishing touch.

INGREDIENTS | MAKES ABOUT 2 CUPS

1 quart cream or whipping cream
½ teaspoon salt (optional)

Honey Butter

To make honey butter, place 1 pound of homemade butter, slightly softened, in a mixer and beat together with ¼ cup honey until butter is creamy and smooth and the honey is fully incorporated.

1. Pour the cream into a mixing bowl equipped with a splash guard (alternately, cut a 4"-wide strip of aluminum foil and tent it around the top of the mixing bowl).

2. Using the whip attachment of your mixer, beat the cream on low, then gradually increase the speed as the cream begins to thicken.

3. Once the cream has been whipped to the "firm" peak stage, increase the mixer speed to "high" and whip for 10 minutes, or until the butter separates from the buttermilk (it will look like scrambled eggs).

4. Place a fine-meshed colander over a large bowl and strain the buttermilk from the butter through it, pressing down on the butter to release as much liquid as possible.

5. "Wash" the butter by placing it in a bowl of cold water and kneading it. Pour off the water, replace with clean water, and repeat the process until the water remains clear after kneading.

6. Press the butter into molds, wrap tightly, and store in the refrigerator for up to 2 weeks (homemade butter can also be frozen).

Finnish "Squeaky" Cheese (*Leipäjuusto*)

Finnish "bread cheese," leipäjuusto, is as popular among Finnish Americans in northern Wisconsin as it is in Finland. Although it is now packaged and distributed by Trader Joe's, it's fun to make from scratch and to enjoy the distinctive "squeak" when you bite into a piece.

INGREDIENTS | SERVES 12

2½ gallons whole milk

½ rennet tablet or ½ teaspoon liquid rennet

1 tablespoon warm water

1 tablespoon cornstarch

1 tablespoon salt

1 teaspoon sugar

1. Heat the milk to scalding (185°F) in a large pot.

2. Dissolve the rennet in the warm water, then combine with 1 cup of the scalded milk, along with the cornstarch and salt. Pour this mixture back into the pot in a steady stream, stirring steadily to combine.

3. Turn off the heat, cover the pot, and allow to rest until the curds rise to the top of the pot, about 1 hour. They are ready when you can cut through the mass of curds with a knife.

4. Line a strainer with a double thickness of cheesecloth, place it over a bowl, and use a slotted spoon to transfer the curds to the strainer. Allow to drain, then pull up the sides of the cheesecloth and squeeze tightly to remove all excess whey.

5. Preheat oven to 400°F. Press the curds into a 9" cake pan and sprinkle with ½ teaspoon sugar. Broil the cheese on the top rack for 15 minutes or until golden on top. Remove from the heat, invert into a second cake pan, sprinkle with ½ teaspoon sugar, and return to the oven. Broil for 15 minutes more or until golden. Serve immediately, or refrigerate or freeze for later use.

Danish Smoked Cheese (*Rygeost*)

Creamy Rygeost is well worth the effort it takes to make. If you don't have a smoker, you can heat 3 or 4 coals in the bottom of a barbecue grill, placing an aluminum pan (filled ⅔ with water) on top of the hot coals. Put your pans of cheese on the top rack of the grill, close the lid, open the vents, and smoke for 15 minutes or so.

INGREDIENTS | MAKES ½ POUND

2 quarts organic whole milk

1 cup active cultured buttermilk

5 drops liquid rennet

1 tablespoon warm water

1 teaspoon salt

2 tablespoons caraway

A few large handfuls of straw and fresh or dried nettles (optional; you can substitute hickory chips)

How to Dry Nettles

The easiest way to quickly dry nettles is to place them in a dehydrator at 95°F until dry. In dry climates, you can also spread the freshly harvested nettles on old window screens set on bricks outdoors (to allow for air flow); then place them in a non-breezy location or cover them with an additional screen. They'll be dry—and safe to touch!—in a day or two.

1. Sanitize all of your equipment in boiling water.

2. Stir together the milk and buttermilk in a large bowl.

3. Whisk the rennet in the warm water, then stir into the milk. Cover the bowl with clean cheesecloth and place in a warm place (71°F) for 48 hours (an insulated cooler, on top of the refrigerator, or in the oven with two lit tealights).

4. Line a colander or sieve with cheesecloth, place on top of a large sanitized bowl, pour the milk into the colander, and allow to drain for 2–3 hours. Transfer to the refrigerator and continue to drain overnight.

5. Mix the cheese with the salt and 1 tablespoon caraway. Spread in shallow 10" aluminum foil pans, sprinkle with the remaining tablespoon of caraway, and place in the refrigerator (or outdoors if it's cold) for 1 hour.

6. To smoke the cheese, soak the straw and nettles (or the hickory chips) in a bucket with just enough water to moisten thoroughly, for 30 minutes–1 hour. Completely encase one of your smoker racks in heavy aluminum foil. Place 3 empty tin cans on the bottom of the smoker, surround them with the dampened straw/nettles or hickory chips, then place the rack directly on the cans. Fill two metal bread pans with ice cubes, then place these on top of the rack. Place the top rack of the smoker at the highest level in your smoker, then place the pans of cheese on top of it. Cover the smoker, open the vents, and turn it on at the lowest heat possible. Smoke the cheese for 30–45 minutes, checking at 20-minute intervals to make sure it isn't melting/bubbling.

7. Serve immediately or refrigerate, covered, for later use.

Norwegian Cream Porridge (*Rømmegrøt*)

Norwegian grandmothers of days past spent hours stirring rømmegrøt until it reached creamy, velvety perfection. Today, microwaves make the process less labor-intensive.

INGREDIENTS | SERVES 8

3 cups half-and-half

8 ounces unsalted European-style butter (1 stick), plus 4 ounces

½ cup flour

4 tablespoons sugar

½ teaspoon salt

Cinnamon-sugar, to taste

European Butter

To make holiday baked goods as rich as possible (they should be, after all, once-a-year treats), use a European-style butter like Plugra or Kerrygold. These contain twice the butterfat of American butter, and you can truly taste the difference.

1. Pour the half-and-half into a large Pyrex measuring cup and heat in microwave on high just until warm (1 minute–1 minute, 15 seconds, depending on your microwave).

2. Place 8 ounces (1 stick) of butter in a second measuring cup or bowl and heat in the microwave until melted, about 30 seconds.

3. Whisk the flour into the melted butter until it is creamy and smooth.

4. Whisk the heated half-and-half into the butter-and-flour mixture. Stir in the sugar and salt.

5. Place in microwave, uncovered, and heat on high for 4 minutes, removing to stir every minute, until the porridge is thick (repeat for another minute if needed, depending on the strength of your microwave).

6. In a separate bowl, melt the remaining 4 ounces of butter in the microwave.

7. To serve, spoon the porridge into dessert dishes, pour a layer of the melted butter on top, and sprinkle with cinnamon-sugar to taste.

Norwegian *Gomme*

Gomme, a sweet milk product similar to cottage cheese, used to be quite common in Norway, where every region had its own version. Labor-intensive, gomme was a "special occasion" dessert served at weddings and holidays. It is a superlative topping for pancakes and waffles.

INGREDIENTS | MAKES APPROXIMATELY 3 CUPS

2 quarts whole milk

3 cups kefir, Siggi's Probiotics drinkable yogurt, or active cultured buttermilk

2 tablespoons flour

½ cup whole milk

¼ cup sugar

½ teaspoon cinnamon

½ teaspoon cardamom

1. In a heavy-bottomed pot, slowly bring the milk to the scalding point (185°F–190°F) over medium-low heat, stirring constantly. Remove from heat and whisk in the kefir.

2. Return the pan to the heat and continue to whisk steadily until the milk separates into curds.

3. Cover the pot, reduce heat to low, and simmer for 2–2½ hours, stirring every 15 minutes, until the water has cooked off and the *gomme* has thickened.

4. Whisk together the flour and milk, and slowly stir into the curds. Stir in the sugar, cinnamon, and cardamom.

5. Continue to cook at low heat, uncovered, until the curds are lightly browned. Serve warm in bowls in this "porridge" form, sprinkled with brown sugar, or beat the *gomme* smooth in an electric mixer and then chill for use as a topping for pancakes or waffles.

Norwegian *Pultost*

Flavored with caraway (also called Persian cumin) that grows wild in Norway, spreadable Norwegian pultost will be appreciated by those who love very sharp, pungent cheeses. Don't worry—this extraordinary cheese tastes nothing like it smells!

INGREDIENTS | MAKES APPROXIMATELY 1 POUND

5 liters active cultured buttermilk
1 tablespoon caraway seeds
1 tablespoon salt

1. Sanitize all of your equipment (bowls, whisks, pots, cheesecloth) in boiling water before using.

2. Bring the buttermilk to the scalding point (185°F–190°F) over medium-low heat, whisking constantly.

3. Reduce heat to low and continue to cook, whisking occasionally, until the buttermilk separates into curds.

4. Line a large bowl with an 18" × 18" piece of cheesecloth or clean muslin. Use a slotted spoon to transfer the curds from the pot to the bowl. Draw up and knot the ends of the cheesecloth together, then suspend from a broomstick placed across two chairs. Place the bowl underneath to catch the liquid.

5. Squeeze the cheesecloth bag every so often to help release the liquid (you want the cheese to be quite dry).

6. Crumble the cheese into a bowl, stir in the caraway seeds and salt, cover with a clean tea towel, and allow to sit in a warm place (on top of the refrigerator or in an oven with two lit tea lights) for at least 24 hours and up to 3 days. Stir and taste the cheese every 12 hours or so. When it reaches the depth of tanginess you prefer, transfer it to covered containers and refrigerate until ready to use.

Norwegian Egg Cheese (*Eggost*)

Enjoy egg cheese as you would cottage cheese, or—better yet—spread it on rye crispbread and top it with a teaspoon of Lingonberry Jam (see Chapter 7) for a savory-sweet treat.

INGREDIENTS | MAKES APPROXIMATELY 1 POUND

1 quart whole milk
1½ cups skyr, quark (curd), or nonfat Greek yogurt
¼ cup sugar
3 eggs
Cinnamon-sugar to taste

1. Bring the milk to the scalding point (185°F–190°F) over medium heat, stirring constantly.

2. Whisk together the yogurt, sugar, and eggs.

3. Slowly pour the yogurt mixture into the milk in a steady stream, stirring constantly. Reduce heat to medium-low and allow to simmer, stirring occasionally, until the milk curdles on top and the whey is translucent.

4. Line a colander with cheesecloth and strain the mixture through it until the cheese is dry.

5. Transfer the egg cheese to bowls and serve sprinkled with cinnamon-sugar to taste.

Våsterbotten Pie

Swedish Våsterbotten Pie is a popular side dish served at August crayfish parties in Scandinavia. Simplify the preparation by using a ready-made pie crust.

INGREDIENTS | SERVES 6

1 ready-made pie crust
3 eggs
1 cup cream or half-and-half
8 ounces *Våsterbotten* cheese, grated
1 teaspoon salt
½ teaspoon white pepper

1. Preheat oven to 375°F. Press the pie crust into a pie pan, prick well with a fork, and prebake for 10 minutes.

2. Whisk together the remaining ingredients, then pour into the pie shell.

3. Bake for 25–30 minutes, or until the middle of the pie is set and the top is golden brown.

Savory Havarti Cheese Snaps

Feel free to experiment with different varieties of Denmark's Havarti cheese when baking these savory cheese snaps.

INGREDIENTS | MAKES 40 CHEESE SNAPS

1 cup Havarti cheese, grated

3 cups self-rising flour (White Lily is preferred)

½ teaspoon salt

1 cup unsalted butter, chilled and cut into ½" cubes

3 tablespoons ice water

1 egg white

Havarti Cheese Varieties

Of the many varieties of Havarti cheeses produced in Denmark, the following are becoming more and more available in American groceries: garlic, dill, red pepper, caraway, and jalapeño.

1. In a large bowl, lightly toss together the grated Havarti, flour, and salt.

2. Use a pastry blender or two forks to cut the butter into the flour until the mixture is crumbly, the size of lentils.

3. Use a fork to stir the ice water into the flour, 1 tablespoon at a time, to form a soft dough.

4. Transfer dough to a floured counter and knead as lightly as possible, about 3 times. Wrap in cling wrap and refrigerate for 30 minutes.

5. Preheat oven to 325°F. Roll dough out into ⅛"-thickness, then cut with a 1"-diameter cookie or biscuit cutter. Place on a greased baking sheet and brush with the egg white.

6. Bake for 20 minutes or until golden.

Macaroni Casserole with *Nøkkelost* Cheese

This is a creamy macaroni casserole featuring Norway's caraway-studded Nøkkelost cheese.

INGREDIENTS | SERVES 6

⅔ cup yellow onion, chopped

1 teaspoon canola or olive oil

3 cups whipping cream

1½ cups *Nøkkelost* cheese, grated

1 pound elbow macaroni, cooked until al dente

½ cup smoked ham or bacon, cooked and diced

¼ cup melted butter

⅔ cup rye bread crumbs

½ cup *Våsterbotten* cheese, grated (or substitute Parmesan)

1. Preheat oven to 375°F. Sauté the chopped onion in the oil over medium heat until translucent.

2. In a separate saucepan, bring the cream to a steady simmer over medium heat, then stir in the grated *Nøkkelost*. Whisk steadily until the cheese has melted into the sauce. Remove from heat and stir in the macaroni, ham, and sautéed onions.

3. Transfer the macaroni to a greased 12" × 9" casserole dish.

4. Whisk together the melted butter, rye bread crumbs, and grated *Våsterbotten*. Sprinkle the mixture over the casserole.

5. Bake for 30 minutes or until golden.

Nøkkelost Fondue

Caraway-studded Nøkkelost cheese melts beautifully in this beer fondue. Serve with chunks of rye bread, small roasted potatoes, and slices of fried or grilled sausage for dipping.

INGREDIENTS | SERVES 6

1 pound *Nøkkelost* cheese, grated

1 tablespoon flour

1 cup Danish beer (your preference: lager, pilsner, or dark)

2 teaspoons Worcestershire sauce

2 tablespoons Swedish mustard (or substitute Dijon)

1. In a large bowl, toss together the cheese and flour.

2. In a fondue pot, stir together the beer and Worcestershire sauce. Heat at 375°F until bubbling.

3. Gradually add the cheese, stirring until it melts. Stir in the mustard.

4. Reduce temperature to 200°F and serve with rye bread, grilled sausages, and roasted potatoes.

Homemade Quark

Although most common in Germany and Russia, quark—an unripened cheese similar to cream cheese—is also readily available in Scandinavia, especially in Finland, where it is used in rich desserts like Karelian Cheese Torte (Rahkatorttu) (see recipe in this chapter).

INGREDIENTS | MAKES APPROXIMATELY 1 CUP

1 quart whole milk

½ cup active cultured buttermilk (or unpasteurized buttermilk)

Quark Substitutes

No time to make your own quark? You can substitute mascarpone cheese, ricotta cheese, yogurt cheese, or sometimes cream cheese in many Scandinavian recipes calling for quark.

1. Make sure, throughout the quark-making process, that all of your equipment (bowls, whisks, colander, pots, cheesecloth) is sanitized (rinsed with boiling water or removed directly from a hot dishwasher) immediately before using.

2. Bring the milk to the scalding point (185°F–190°F) and allow to simmer for 30 seconds. Remove from the burner, cover with a tight-fitting lid, and allow to cool to room temperature (about 75°F).

3. Use a whisk to stir the buttermilk into the milk. Cover again and allow to sit in a warm place for 24 hours, until the milk curdles.

4. Line a metal colander with cheesecloth and place it over a bowl; pour the clabbered milk into the colander and allow to drain in the refrigerator, stirring occasionally, for 12 hours.

5. Transfer to a covered container and store in the refrigerator for up to 2 weeks.

Karelian Cheese Torte (*Rahkatorttu*)

Quark gives just the right amount of tanginess to this classic Finnish cheesecake.

INGREDIENTS | SERVES 12

½ cup butter, softened to room temperature

3 eggs, divided use

¾ cup Superfine® sugar, divided use

1 teaspoon lemon zest

2 cups all-purpose flour

1 teaspoon baking powder

1 cup Homemade Quark (see recipe in this chapter)

½ cup cream

2 tablespoons lemon juice

2 teaspoons vanilla extract

½ cup raisins or currants (optional)

1. Preheat oven to 400°F. Cream together the butter, 1 egg, ¼ cup of the sugar, and the lemon zest. In a separate bowl, whisk together the flour and baking powder, then gradually stir into the batter to form a soft dough.

2. Grease and flour the bottom and sides of a 9" springform pan. Press the dough evenly over the bottom and up the sides of the pan.

3. For the filling, beat together the quark, cream, remaining 2 eggs, remaining ½ cup sugar, lemon juice, vanilla extract, and raisins (if using). Pour into the prepared crust.

4. Bake for 30 minutes, or until cake is golden and a toothpick inserted in the middle comes out clean. Chill before serving.

CHAPTER 9

Savory Pies and Egg Dishes

Spelt Pie Crust

The renewed popularity of spelt flour across Scandinavia has resulted in the widespread description of anything that uses a spelt crust—be it savory quiches or sweet dessert pies—as a dinkelpaj, "spelt pie."

INGREDIENTS | MAKES 2 CRUSTS

2 cups spelt flour
1 teaspoon salt
⅔ cup unsalted butter, chilled
Ice water, as needed

1. In a large bowl, use a balloon whisk to mix the flour with salt.

2. With a pastry blender or two knives, cut butter into the flour, just until the mixture resembles coarse crumbs (don't overwork it). Add up to 7 tablespoons of ice water in 2-tablespoon increments, until the dough pulls away from the sides of the bowl.

3. Allow the dough to chill for 30 minutes in the refrigerator, then divide and roll into 2 pie crusts. The crusts can be frozen for later use.

Mushroom and Onion *Dinkelpaj*

The nutty flavor of the spelt crust marries beautifully with "earthy" fillings like mushrooms and onions.

INGREDIENTS | SERVES 6

1 Spelt Pie Crust (see recipe in this chapter)
1 tablespoon canola oil
1 teaspoon butter
1 cup onion, thinly sliced
2 cups fresh mushrooms (use a variety of button and wild), sliced thickly
½ teaspoon salt
3 eggs, beaten
1 cup sour cream
⅛ teaspoon white pepper
2 teaspoons dried thyme

1. Preheat oven to 425°F. Line a pie pan with the spelt crust, prick well with a fork, and then bake in oven until light golden, about 10 minutes. Remove and reduce heat to 300°F.

2. Melt the oil and butter together in a frying pan over medium heat, then add the onion and mushrooms. Sprinkle with the salt and sauté until tender, 10–15 minutes.

3. Combine the eggs, sour cream, pepper, and thyme in a mixing bowl, then stir in the sautéed vegetables. Pour into the baked spelt crust.

4. Bake for 30 minutes or until the middle of the pie has set and the surface is lightly browned.

Root Vegetable *Dinkelpaj*

Here's a sneaky but sure-fire way to get kids to eat their root vegetables—hide them in a pie!

INGREDIENTS | SERVES 6

2 Spelt Pie Crusts (see recipe in this chapter)

1 rutabaga

2 parsnips

3 carrots

1 red onion

1 large leek

3 cloves garlic

1½ cups mushrooms, halved or quartered

2 baking potatoes, peeled and cubed

3 tablespoons olive or canola oil

1 teaspoon salt

¼ teaspoon pepper

2 teaspoons fresh thyme, chopped

2 teaspoons fresh sage, chopped

2 teaspoons fresh rosemary, chopped

1 tablespoon parsley, chopped

1½ tablespoons milk or half-and-half

1½ tablespoons butter, softened

Additional milk to glaze the top crust

1. Preheat oven to 425°F. Peel and chop all of the vegetables into a 1"–2" dice, varying the sizes and shapes between the different types of vegetables (slice the carrots into rounds, cut the onions into wedges, cube the rutabaga and potatoes).

2. Toss together all of the vegetables except the potatoes, then place them in a layer covering two-thirds of a large roasting pan. Place the potatoes by themselves in the remaining third.

3. In a small bowl, whisk together the oil, salt, pepper, and herbs, then drizzle over all of the vegetables. Use a spatula to gently turn the vegetables over so they are covered with the oil (but still keeping the potatoes separated).

4. Roast the vegetables in the oven for 40–45 minutes, or until they are tender and begin to caramelize. Remove from oven and cool while you prepare the pie crust. Reduce the heat to 400°F.

5. Line a large pie dish with the bottom crust. Place the roasted potatoes in a large bowl, then mash together with the milk and softened butter until creamy. Fold the rest of the roasted vegetables into the mashed potatoes, then transfer to the prepared pie dish.

6. Position the second crust over the pie; seal, flute, and cut a few vents into the top of the crust. Brush the top of the pie with milk. Place aluminum foil or a pie shield around the edge of the crust.

7. Bake the pie in the oven for 15 minutes, then reduce the temperature to 350°F. Remove the foil/pie shield and bake for 30 minutes more, or until the crust is golden brown.

Crispy Salmon Skin *Dinkelpaj*

Fried salmon skin replaces the bacon in this Scandinavian quiche lorraine. To fry skin quickly, line a baking sheet with foil. Scrape the flesh from the salmon skin, examine the outside to ensure that no scales remain, and place the skin flesh-side down on the pan. Broil on the top rack of your oven until the skin is crispy, about 10 minutes.

INGREDIENTS | SERVES 6

1 Spelt Pie Crust (see recipe in this chapter)

1 tablespoon butter

½ red onion, thinly sliced

3 eggs, beaten

1½ cups milk

¼ teaspoon salt

⅛ teaspoon pepper

1 teaspoon fresh dill, finely minced

¾ cup fried salmon skin, crumbled

1½ cups Havarti cheese, shredded

1 tablespoon spelt or all-purpose flour

1. Preheat oven to 425°F. Line a pie dish with the spelt crust, cover with aluminum foil and pie weights, and cook for 15 minutes. Lift out the aluminum foil and the pie weights; reduce heat to 325°F.

2. Melt the butter in a frying pan and sauté the onion over medium heat until opaque, about 10 minutes.

3. In a large bowl whisk together the eggs, milk, sautéed onion, salt, pepper, dill, and crumbled salmon skin. Toss the cheese and flour together, then fold into the eggs.

4. Pour the mixture into the warm pie crust, return to oven, and bake for 40 minutes, or until the center has set and a toothpick inserted in the middle comes out clean.

Shirred Eggs with Smoked Salmon

How many eggs you use in this recipe will depend entirely on the size of your ramekins—smaller ramekins will use only a single egg, whereas larger ones may require two. The eggs should fill the ramekins at least three-quarters of the way up.

INGREDIENTS | SERVES 1

3–4 slices gravlax or lox

1 or 2 eggs

1 tablespoon plain skyr or low-fat Greek yogurt, drained

⅛ teaspoon garlic, finely minced

¼ teaspoon chives, finely minced

2 tablespoons hard cheese, grated (*Västerbotten* or Pecorino Toscano)

Boiling water for the water bath

1. Preheat oven to 350°F. Butter a ramekin and line it fully with slices of gravlax (the slices should overlap the edge slightly).

2. Carefully crack 1 or 2 eggs into the ramekin.

3. Whisk together the yogurt, garlic, and chives separately, then spoon over the top of the eggs to cover. Sprinkle with the grated cheese.

4. Place the ramekin in a slightly larger casserole dish and add enough boiling water to surround the ramekin half of the way up. Bake for 25 minutes or until the eggs are set and the top is browned.

Jarlsberg Omelette

There's no better way to make an omelette, if you're cooking for more than a single person, than to bake it in the oven. It's all done at once, and everyone can sit down to eat together while it's still warm.

INGREDIENTS | SERVES 6

1 tablespoon olive oil
1 teaspoon butter
½ red onion, thinly sliced
1 clove garlic, minced
½ teaspoon salt
1 teaspoon caraway seeds
2 cups Jarlsberg cheese, shredded
1 tablespoon flour
8 eggs
¼ cup water
1 cup fried bacon or diced ham, crumbled

1. Preheat oven to 400°F. Melt the olive oil and butter in an oven-proof skillet over medium-low heat, using a pastry brush to thoroughly coat the bottom and sides of the pan. Add the sliced onion and garlic, sprinkling them with the salt and caraway seeds. Allow to sauté slowly, 10 to 15 minutes, until the onions begin to brown.

2. Toss the cheese with the flour. Whisk together the eggs and water, then fold in the cheese and bacon until combined.

3. Pour the egg mixture into the frying pan, stirring to combine with the onions. Increase heat to medium and cook for 3 more minutes, without stirring, to brown the bottom of the omelette.

4. Place the frying pan on the upper rack of the oven and cook until evenly browned, 15 to 20 minutes. Use a pot holder to remove the pan from the oven; slice and serve.

Danish "Dirty Eggs" (*Skidne Aeg*)

Danish "dirty eggs," served in a light mustard sauce, earned their name from the fact that they were an easy-to-prepare meal on Easter Saturday, one of the biggest cleaning days of the year in Denmark.

INGREDIENTS | SERVES 4–6

8 hard-boiled eggs (not overcooked—the yolks should still be moist)

3 tablespoons butter

3 tablespoons flour

1⅔ cups half-and-half

¼ cup onion, grated

2 tablespoons Dijon mustard

Salt and white pepper to taste

2 teaspoons chives, finely minced

1. Melt the butter in a saucepan over medium heat until frothy. Stir in the flour to make a roux; allow to bubble for 1–2 minutes, then stir in the half-and-half in a steady stream, stirring vigorously.

2. Stir the onion and mustard into the thickened sauce, then season to taste with salt and white pepper.

3. Peel the eggs and cut in half.

4. Pour the sauce in a large serving dish, arrange the eggs on top, and sprinkle with chives. Serve with a hearty homemade rye bread to soak up the extra sauce.

Green Eggs

Do you like green eggs? Use the Creamed Kale (Grønlangkål) recipe from Chapter 11 to stuff these eggs. Ham optional.

INGREDIENTS | SERVES 12

12 hard-boiled eggs

1 cup Creamed Kale (Grønlangkål) (see Chapter 11) or creamed spinach

1 shallot, minced

⅓ cup grated *Våsterbotten* cheese (or Parmesan)

½ cup mayonnaise

1 tablespoon Swedish or Dijon mustard

1. Slice open the hard-boiled eggs and remove the yolks.

2. Use a fork to mash together the egg yolks, kale or spinach, shallot, and cheese.

3. In a separate bowl, combine the mayonnaise and mustard, then fold it into the kale mixture.

4. Stuff the egg halves generously with the kale.

5. Chill for 1 hour before serving.

Old Man's Mix

Spoon this Swedish classic onto toasted rye bread or on crispbread for an appetizer, chill a few beers, and you're ready for your next football party in the man cave.

INGREDIENTS | SERVES 6–8

6 hard-boiled eggs

5 whole pickled herring fillets or 5 spice-cured sprats (Swedish anchovies)

½ red onion, peeled and diced

1 teaspoon capers

1 tablespoon dill, finely chopped

1 tablespoon chives, finely chopped

1 heaping tablespoon mayonnaise

1 heaping tablespoon crème fraîche or sour cream

1. Peel and dice the hard-boiled eggs; evenly dice the herring or anchovies.

2. In a large bowl, fold all of the ingredients together; chill for at least 1 hour.

3. Serve spread on rye toast, as a dip for chips or celery sticks, or even as a filling for hard-boiled egg halves.

Double Fish Egg Poppers

Spoonfuls of colorful fish eggs crown these delicious poppers. You'll love the contrasting textures as the flavors meld on your tongue!

INGREDIENTS | SERVES 6

24 hard-boiled quail eggs (or 6 hard-boiled chicken eggs), peeled

⅓ cup oil-packed tuna, drained

3 tablespoons mayonnaise

½ teaspoon dry ground mustard

⅛ teaspoon salt

6 teaspoons cod roe or caviar

1. Thinly slice off the pointed end of the eggs so that they can stand upright. Cut off the top fourth of the other broad end of the eggs.

2. Carefully spoon out the yolks from the eggs, taking care not to rip the white shells. Place the yolks in the processor, along with the drained tuna, mayonnaise, ground mustard, and salt. Pulse until combined into a smooth paste. Transfer to a pastry bag, then fill the eggs.

3. Chill for at least 1 hour, then top with a dollop of caviar to serve.

Danish *Æggekage* ("Egg Cake") with Bacon and Tomatoes

Danish Æggekage can be compared to a frittata, an omelette, or an oven-baked pancake, depending on how you choose to make it. This oven-baked version is great fun to make—like an oven-baked pancake, it rises like a soufflé as it cooks. It's a fast and light summer meal. Use the ripest tomatoes you can find.

INGREDIENTS | SERVES 4

12 thick slices bacon or pancetta, finely diced

⅓ cup onion, finely minced

2 cups cherry tomatoes (mixed colors if available), quartered

¼ cup fresh parsley or basil (or a combination), finely chopped

8 eggs

¼ cup potato starch flour or all-purpose flour

2 cups milk

1 teaspoon baking powder

Kosher salt and pepper to taste

1. Preheat oven to 425°F.

2. In a large oven-proof frying pan over medium heat, fry the bacon until crispy, stirring occasionally. Transfer the bacon to a bowl; drain off all but 1 teaspoon of the bacon fat from the pan. Use a pastry brush to brush the fat over the bottom and sides of the pan.

3. Toss the bacon with the onion, tomatoes, and parsley. Set aside.

4. Whisk together the eggs, flour, milk, and baking powder, then pour into the frying pan. Cook over medium-high heat for 2 minutes, then transfer the oven-proof pan to the second-to-top rack in the oven.

5. Cook for 15 minutes or until the *Æggekage* is puffed and golden. Remove from the oven and spread the bacon-tomato mixture in the middle "well"; sprinkle with salt and pepper. Serve immediately.

Æggekage with Potatoes, Onions, and *Gjetost*

Bake extra potatoes on steak night for breakfast the next day.

INGREDIENTS | SERVES 4–6

1 tablespoon canola or olive oil
1 tablespoon butter
3 baked potatoes, peeled and grated
1 onion, peeled and grated
1 green bell pepper, finely chopped
6 eggs
⅔ cup milk
1 teaspoon caraway seed
½ teaspoon salt
⅛ teaspoon pepper
½ cup *gjetost* cheese, grated

1. In a large oven-proof frying pan, melt the oil and butter over medium-high heat. Add the potatoes, onion, and bell pepper, and stir-fry about 10 minutes.

2. Whisk together the eggs, milk, caraway seed, salt, and pepper. Pour over potatoes in the frying pan and stir together. Reduce heat to low and cook for 5 minutes.

3. Sprinkle with the grated *gjetost* cheese and place in the oven on the top rack. Turn on the broiler and cook until the top of the *æggekage* is evenly browned, 5–7 minutes (keep an eye on it so it doesn't burn).

4. Remove and serve warm.

Norwegian Eggs Benedict

Substitute your favorite brand of English muffins if you like.

INGREDIENTS | SERVES 4

2 Sourdough Rye Muffins (see Chapter 5)
Butter, as needed
4 slices gravlax or lox
1 large avocado
4 poached eggs
Hollandaise Sauce (see sidebar recipe)
4 teaspoons cod roe or caviar

1. Slice, toast, and butter the rye muffins, then place the 4 halves on plates. Top each half with a slice of gravlax.

2. Thinly slice the avocado and arrange the pieces on top of the gravlax.

3. Place a poached egg on each muffin, then drizzle with Hollandaise sauce.

4. Top each serving with a teaspoon of cod roe and serve.

Hollondaise Sauce

Melt ¾ cup of butter in a saucepan until foamy; remove from heat. In the top of a double boiler over simmering water, whisk together 3 egg yolks, 2 tablespoons lemon juice, and a pinch of salt until the sauce thickens. Remove the top pan from the heat, and stir in ¼ cup of melted butter, a tablespoon at a time, whisking vigorously. Return the pan to the double boiler and beat in the rest of the butter in tablespoon increments until the sauce is creamy. Serve warm.

Crab Cakes Benedict

Crunchy crab cakes serve as the bread in this upscale version of eggs Benedict. The sauce is lighter than the traditional hollandaise—a lemony, eggless béarnaise with just a smidgeon of tarragon.

INGREDIENTS | SERVES 4

½ pound cooked dungeness crab meat

1½ cups dried rye bread crumbs (or panko bread crumbs)

¼ cup cream

1 egg, beaten

¼ cup green onions, finely minced

2 tablespoons celery, finely chopped

2 tablespoons lemon juice, divided use

2 tablespoons plus 2 teaspoons butter, divided use

1 tablespoon shallots, finely minced

1 tablespoon white wine vinegar

1 teaspoon dried tarragon

1 teaspoon lemon zest

¼ teaspoon salt

¼ teaspoon white pepper

½ cup crème fraîche or sour cream

1 tablespoon canola or olive oil

4 poached eggs

Perfect Poached Eggs

For perfect poached eggs, always use the freshest eggs you can find (within a day or two of purchase), and bring them to room temperature before poaching. Bring 2" of water and 1 tablespoon of vinegar in a frying pan to a strong simmer (just below the boiling point, around 180°F). Crack the eggs into individual ramekins or cups and gently drop them into the water. Poach for 4–5 minutes; remove with a slotted spoon.

1. Carefully pick through the crab meat to remove all cartilage and shells, then combine it with half of the bread crumbs, cream, egg, green onions, celery, and 1 tablespoon lemon juice. Form into 4 patties, then coat with the remaining bread crumbs. Place on a plate, cover with cling wrap, and chill for 1–2 hours before frying. Poach the eggs and make the sauce before frying.

2. For the sauce, melt 2 teaspoons butter in a medium saucepan, then sauté the shallots until soft, about 3 minutes. Stir in the vinegar, 1 tablespoon lemon juice, tarragon, lemon zest, salt, and pepper and bring to a boil; cook for 1 more minute. Strain the liquid, then return it to the saucepan. Stir in the sour cream and cook over low heat, stirring occasionally, until warmed through.

3. To fry the crab cakes, melt 2 tablespoons butter with 1 tablespoon oil in a skillet. Fry the patties, turning once, until golden and cooked through (about 4 minutes per side).

4. Transfer the crab cakes to plates, top with poached eggs, and drizzle with the tarragon sauce.

CHAPTER 10

Native Grains, Legumes, and Porridges

Spelt Berry Salad

Spelt berries, available at most organic food markets, are simply splendid when used in this side-dish salad. Far more nutritious than pasta, they have a sweet, nutty flavor and the perfect al dente crunch. For best results, make this salad a day ahead of time and place in the refrigerator.

INGREDIENTS | SERVES 6–8

1½ cups spelt berries

4½ cups water

1½ cups cherry tomatoes, halved

1 English cucumber, scrubbed and sliced

¼ cup red onion, chopped

½ cup celery, chopped

1 tablespoon lingonberry vinegar (or substitute white balsamic)

1 tablespoon canola oil or olive oil

1 teaspoon thyme

1 cup *Hushållsost* (farmer's cheese), cubed (or substitute mozzarella)

1. Cover the spelt berries with the water in a large pot and bring to a boil. Reduce heat to a steady simmer and cook, uncovered, for 1 hour or until the grain is tender and most of the water is absorbed. Rinse with cold water and drain well.

2. Toss the spelt with the vegetables. Whisk together the vinegar, oil, and thyme in a small bowl; stir into the salad.

3. Fold in the chopped cheese and place in the refrigerator for at least 1 hour before serving (overnight is better).

Hobbit Casserole

Spelt berries, rather than rice, work beautifully in this baked casserole, plump with the forest and cultivated mushrooms beloved by J. R. R. Tolkien's heroes.

INGREDIENTS | SERVES 4–6

1 ounce mixed dried mushrooms (chanterelles, morels, porcini)

Hot water, as needed to cover dried mushrooms

1 cup button mushrooms, quartered

1 medium onion, peeled and diced

2 cloves garlic, minced

¼ cup celery, diced

½ cup butter

1 teaspoon mixed dried herbs (thyme, oregano, rosemary)

1 cup spelt berries

2½ cups chicken broth

1. Cover the dried mushrooms with hot water and soak for 30 minutes. Drain, then pat dry with paper towels.

2. Preheat oven to 350°F. In a large frying pan over medium heat, sauté the button mushrooms, onion, garlic, and celery in the butter until the onion is opaque and the mushrooms begin to brown. Remove from heat and sprinkle with herbs.

3. Place the spelt berries in the bottom of an ungreased casserole dish. In a medium saucepan, heat the broth to boiling, then pour over the spelt berries. Stir in the sautéed vegetables and the mixed mushrooms.

4. Cover the casserole dish and bake in oven for 1 hour or until the broth is absorbed and the spelt berries are tender.

Barley "Risotto" with Chanterelles

By using the same cooking methods you would for Italian risotto, you can make a Nordic barley dish so creamy and decadent (yet inexpensive!) that you may never splurge on pricey Arborio rice again.

INGREDIENTS | SERVES 4–6

1 cup pearl barley

2 cups water

2 ounces dried chanterelle mushrooms

½ cup hot water

4½ cups chicken stock

3 tablespoons butter

1 tablespoon canola or olive oil

¼ cup red onion, finely chopped

1 cup white wine

5 cloves garlic, finely minced or pressed

¼ cup fresh parsley, finely chopped

1 cup grated *Våsterbotten* cheese (or substitute Parmesan)

¼ cup low-fat sour cream or crème fraîche

1. Immerse the pearl barley in 2 cups of water and allow to sit overnight.

2. Place dried chanterelles in the hot water and allow to soak for 30 minutes. Drain the mushrooms, reserving the water.

3. Pour the chicken stock in a small saucepan and warm over low heat.

4. Melt 2 tablespoons of the butter and the vegetable oil together in the bottom of a spacious pot. Sauté the onion at medium heat until opaque, about 10 minutes. Drain the barley and add it to the pot, stirring to cover it with the oil. Cook for 5 more minutes.

5. Pour in the white wine and reserved mushroom water and bring to a boil. Reduce heat to medium-low and allow to cook, uncovered, until the liquid has been reduced, about 10 minutes.

6. Pour ½ cup of the chicken stock into the barley and stir. Cook for 40 minutes or until barley is tender, adding more chicken broth in ½-cup increments as each addition simmers off.

7. In a separate pan, briefly sauté the mushrooms, garlic, and parsley in the remaining tablespoon of butter. When the barley is tender, fold it together with the mushroom mixture, grated cheese, and sour cream. Cook for an additional 5 minutes or until the cheese has melted and the barley is warmed through.

8. Serve with artisan bread and a fresh green salad.

Spelt "Risotto" with Asparagus and Shrimp

Celebrate spring's first tender asparagus with this creamy whole-grain "risotto."

INGREDIENTS | SERVES 4–6

5 cloves garlic

2 teaspoons olive oil

4½ cups vegetable stock

3 tablespoons butter

1 tablespoon canola or olive oil

¼ cup onion, finely chopped

1 cup asparagus spears, sliced in 1" pieces

1 cup spelt berries

1 pound uncooked shrimp, peeled

2 tablespoons fresh dill, finely chopped

1 cup grated *Västerbotten* cheese (or substitute Parmesan)

1. Preheat oven to 375°F. Place garlic cloves on a piece of aluminum foil, drizzle with 2 teaspoons olive oil, seal the foil into a packet, and roast in oven for 40 minutes. Cool and squeeze the roasted garlic cloves from the peels; finely chop.

2. Bring the vegetable stock to a steady simmer in a large pot.

3. Melt the butter and canola oil together in the bottom of a large pot, then sauté the onion and asparagus spears over medium-high heat until the onion is translucent, about 7 minutes.

4. Stir in the spelt berries and roasted garlic, then add enough of the simmering stock to cover. Reduce heat to medium and cook until the liquid is almost absorbed, then repeat the process for 40 minutes (adding more stock in ½-cup increments as each addition simmers off).

5. Once the spelt is tender, fold in the shrimp. Cook until the shrimp turns pink, about 5 minutes.

6. Stir in the chopped dill and grated cheese and serve.

Karelian Rice Pastries (*Karjalanpiirakat*)

One of Finland's most famous dishes, Karelian Rice Pastries can be served either as a snack or, when accompanied with a salad, as a light supper.

INGREDIENTS | SERVES 20

1 cup short-grained, glutinous rice (like pearl, sushi, or Calrose rice)

1 cup water

1 tablespoon butter

1½ teaspoons salt, divided use

4 cups milk

1½ cups rye flour (Bob's Red Mill works well)

1 cup all-purpose flour

1 cup warm water

½ cup milk plus ½ cup butter

2 hard-boiled eggs plus 2 tablespoons softened butter

1. For the rice porridge filling, rinse rice well and drain. In a medium saucepan, bring the water, 1 tablespoon butter, and ½ teaspoon of the salt to a rapid boil over high heat. Pour in the rice, stirring constantly to prevent sticking. Reduce heat to low, stirring rice until boiling is reduced to a simmer. Cover and simmer for 10–15 minutes until rice has absorbed most of the water.

2. Stir the milk into the rice. Bring the mixture to a boil once again, stirring constantly, then immediately reduce heat to low. Once boiling has reduced to a simmer, cover the pot and allow to cook, stirring occasionally, for 45 minutes. Remove pot from the heat and allow to cool to room temperature.

3. Preheat oven to 475°F. For the pastry crust, whisk together the flours and remaining 1 teaspoon salt in a large mixing bowl. Stir in the warm water to make a stiff dough.

4. Transfer the dough to a lightly floured counter, knead it a few times, then roll into a long "snake" 2" thick. Cut into 20 equal portions. Roll each portion into a thin circle 6" in diameter.

5. Spoon 3 tablespoons of the rice porridge in an oval shape in the center of each crust. Pull up the sides of the pastry just to the top edge of the filling and crimp (the rice should show in the middle). Place on a parchment paper–lined baking sheet.

6. Melt the remaining ½ cup milk and ½ cup butter together, then brush the tops and sides of each pastry well with half of this mixture. Bake for 10 minutes.

7. Remove from hot oven and brush the pastries with the remaining half of the milk-butter mixture. Transfer pastries immediately to a few zip-top bags and allow to cool for 1–2 hours (stacking them in the bags will help to soften the rye crust).

8. While the pastries cool, chop the hard-boiled eggs and fold into the 2 tablespoons softened butter. To serve, top each pastry with this egg butter. Karelian pastries can also be frozen, without the egg butter, for later enjoyment.

September Porridge

September is harvest season for apples and lingonberries, and nowhere are these two better combined than in this slightly sweet, slightly tart porridge from Finland.

INGREDIENTS | SERVES 4

2 cups water

2 cups apple, cranberry, or cranapple juice

2 cups lingonberries or cranberries

½ cup sugar

2 apples

2 cups instant rolled oats

½ teaspoon salt

½ teaspoon vanilla extract

1. Combine the water, juice, berries, and sugar in a nonreactive saucepan and bring to a low boil. Maintain the boil for 10–15 minutes until berries start to burst.

2. Meanwhile, peel, core, and grate the apples.

3. Add the instant oats to the saucepan and cook for 5 more minutes, until oats are creamy. Stir in grated apples, salt, and vanilla; remove from heat.

4. Taste for sweetness and, if preferred, add additional sugar. Serve warm with extra milk or cream on the side.

Danish Rye and Beer Porridge (*Øllebrød*)

Øllebrød, a traditional breakfast porridge enjoyed by Danes of all ages, is rich enough to also be served as a dessert, accompanied with whipped cream. If you dislike beer, it works well to use an equal amount of undiluted apple cider instead.

INGREDIENTS | SERVES 4

3 cups leftover seedless rye bread, cubed

3 cups water

1 cup low-alcohol beer or undiluted apple cider

1 cinnamon stick

Zest of 1 orange

½ cup brown sugar

1. Place the rye bread cubes in a medium-sized container with the water. Cover, and allow to soak overnight in the refrigerator.

2. Transfer the mixture to a large pot and add the beer, cinnamon stick, and orange zest. Bring to a boil, whisking steadily, then reduce heat to medium-low. Cover pot and cook for 10 minutes.

3. Remove the cinnamon stick from the porridge and transfer to a food processor; blend until velvety smooth. Return to the pot, stir in the sugar, and heat at medium-low until the sugar has dissolved and the porridge has warmed through.

Danish Oatmeal Porridge (*Havregrød*)

Oatmeal isn't just beloved by the Scots. Soften this oatmeal overnight for an easy and nourishing breakfast.

INGREDIENTS | SERVES 4

4 cups water

1 cinnamon stick

1 teaspoon salt

1 cup steel-cut oats

½ cup milk

2 teaspoons butter (optional)

1. Combine the water, cinnamon stick, and salt in a large pot and bring to a boil. Stir in the oats, then turn off the heat, cover the pot, and allow to sit undisturbed overnight.

2. In the morning, stir the milk into the oats and bring to a steady simmer. Cook uncovered for about 10 minutes or until the oats are cooked through.

3. Transfer to 4 bowls and top each with ½ teaspoon butter, if desired.

Bornholm Rye Porridge (*Rugmelsgrød*)

This is a rustic but oh-so-delicious rye porridge from Denmark's island of Bornholm.

INGREDIENTS | SERVES 4

4 cups water

1 teaspoon salt

2 cups coarse rye flour or rye flakes

Light syrup (in Swedish, *ljus sirap*) or Lyle's Golden Syrup, to taste

Whipping cream, to taste

1. Combine the water and salt in a medium saucepan and bring to a low boil.

2. Add the rye flour or rye flakes, stirring to incorporate.

3. Reduce heat to low; cook for an additional 15 minutes.

4. To serve, drizzle with light syrup and whipping cream to taste.

5. Alternatively, rye porridge is delectable when topped with a spoonful of Lingonberry Jam (see Chapter 7) or strawberry jam.

Jutland Buckwheat Porridge (*Tarregrød*)

Danes in Southern Jutland start their morning with a bowl of steaming buckwheat porridge, a foodway they adopted from Russia (tarregrød translates roughly as "Tatar grain," or grain from Russia).

INGREDIENTS | SERVES 4

4 cups whole milk
¾ cup buckwheat flour
1 teaspoon salt
4 teaspoons butter
4 teaspoons cinnamon-sugar

1. In a medium saucepan, bring milk to a steady simmer over medium heat.

2. Stir in the buckwheat flour; cook for 30 minutes, stirring occasionally.

3. Whisk the salt into the porridge. Transfer to 4 serving bowls. Top each bowl with a teaspoon of butter and a teaspoon of cinnamon-sugar.

Multigrain Buttermilk Porridge (*Kærnemælksvælling*)

Pearl barley, steel-cut oats, and cracked rye provide a rich contrast of texture in this hearty, vitamin-rich breakfast porridge.

INGREDIENTS | SERVES 4

¼ cup pearl barley
¼ cup steel-cut oats
¼ cup cracked rye kernels
¾ cup water
4 cups buttermilk
1 cinnamon stick
Zest of 1 small lemon
Sugar or brown sugar, to taste

1. In a medium saucepan, combine the grains in the water and bring to a boil. Reduce to a steady simmer, cover pot, and cook for 15 minutes.

2. Stir in the buttermilk, cinnamon stick, and lemon zest. Loosely cover pot and simmer for an additional 30 minutes, stirring occasionally.

3. Remove the cinnamon stick and transfer to bowls. Sweeten to individual taste with sugar or brown sugar.

Barley Porridge with Pears (*Byggrynsvaelling*)

Do you have a slow cooker? Then it's easy to wake up to a nourishing breakfast each morning—simply combine the elements of Byggrynsvaelling in your cooker the night before and let breakfast cook itself.

INGREDIENTS | SERVES 4

4 cups water

1 cup pearl barley

1 cinnamon stick

3 pears, peeled and coarsely chopped

1 teaspoon salt

Whipping cream (optional) to taste

Sugar to taste

1. Combine all of the ingredients except whipping cream and sugar in a 5-quart slow cooker.

2. Cover and cook on low heat for 8 hours.

3. In the morning, remove the cinnamon stick and transfer porridge to bowls. Drizzle with whipping cream and sweeten with sugar to taste.

Swedish Brown Beans (*Bruna Bönor*)

Swedish immigrants brought their native brown beans to the Midwest in the nineteenth century, and their descendants have been enjoying them ever since. Seek out Swedish brown beans in Scandinavian markets; their unique sweetness and tenderness far excel that of American bean varieties.

INGREDIENTS | SERVES 8

2 cups Swedish brown beans (or substitute navy beans)

5 cups water

½ cup brown sugar

3 tablespoons molasses (or Swedish dark syrup)

¼ cup apple cider vinegar

1 teaspoon salt

¼ cup water plus ¼ cup potato starch flour (or cornstarch)

1. Rinse the beans in a colander under flowing tap water, picking through them to remove any stones or discolored beans. In a large pot, cover the brown beans with 2 cups of water and allow to soak overnight.

2. Next day, add 3 more cups of water to the pot. Simmer on low heat for 2–3 hours or until tender.

3. Once beans are tender, stir in the brown sugar, molasses, apple cider vinegar, and salt. If beans are watery, whisk in potato starch/water mixture to thicken. Cover and simmer for 30 more minutes.

4. Serve warm as an accompaniment to pork or bacon.

Brown Bean Goulash

Swedish brown beans star in this vegetarian goulash, inspired by suggestions provided in a beautiful brochure distributed by the Association of Brown Bean Growers of Öland.

INGREDIENTS | SERVES 6

2 cups Swedish brown beans

4 cups salted water (2 teaspoons salt)

4 cups fresh cold water

1 large onion, chopped

1 cup mushrooms, halved or quartered

1 red bell pepper, chopped

3 cloves garlic, finely minced

2 teaspoons canola or olive oil

2 unpeeled potatoes, scrubbed and diced

1 (6-ounce) can tomato paste

1½ cups vegetable stock

½ cup red wine

¼ cup sweet or hot Hungarian paprika

½ teaspoon caraway seeds

½ teaspoon salt

¼ teaspoon pepper

Sour cream, to garnish

1. Rinse the beans in a colander under flowing tap water, picking through them to remove any stones or discolored beans. Soak the brown beans in the salted water for 14 hours. Rinse thoroughly, then place in a large pot with 4 cups fresh cold water. Bring to a low boil, reduce heat to a steady simmer, cover, and cook until the beans are tender (60–90 minutes).

2. In a large pot, sauté the onions, mushrooms, chopped pepper, and garlic in the oil until onions are opaque.

3. Add the beans, diced potatoes, tomato paste, vegetable stock, red wine, paprika, caraway seeds, salt, and pepper. Bring to a steady simmer, stirring to dissolve the tomato paste.

4. Cover and cook for 30–45 minutes until the potatoes are soft.

5. Serve garnished with dollops of sour cream, if desired.

Endangered Öland Brown Beans

Sweden's unique brown beans, grown on the island of Öland and sold since 1885, have become endangered as demand has decreased due to the import of cheaper non-native bean varieties. Farmers are increasingly devoting their fields to other, more financially lucrative crops (like, believe it or not, pumpkins!). Here's hoping international demand increases for one of Sweden's national culinary treasures.

Swedish Brown Bean Chili

While many Swedes emigrated to America in the 1800s, some returned to their homeland, taking with them American recipes for things like chili con carne. Here, native Nordic root vegetables are substituted for the meat to provide a Scandinavian flair to this healthy vegetarian entrée.

INGREDIENTS | SERVES 6

2 cups Swedish brown beans

4 cups salted water (2 teaspoons salt)

4 cups fresh cold water

½ cup celery root, chopped

2 carrots, peeled and chopped

1 parsnip, peeled and chopped

1 large onion, peeled and chopped

½ cup green bell pepper, chopped

3 cloves garlic, finely minced

2 (14½-ounce) cans diced tomatoes, undrained

1 (6-ounce) can tomato paste

1 cup vegetable stock

1 tablespoon chili powder

1 teaspoon ground cumin

½ cup *Hushållsost* cheese (or substitute Monterey jack), shredded

Sour cream, to garnish

1. Rinse the beans in a colander under flowing tap water, picking through them to remove any stones or discolored beans. Soak the brown beans in the salted water for 14 hours. Rinse thoroughly, then place in a large pot with 4 cups fresh cold water. Bring pot to a low boil, reduce heat to a steady simmer, cover, and cook until the beans are tender (60–90 minutes).

2. Combine the beans, chopped vegetables, undrained chopped tomatoes, tomato paste, vegetable stock, and the spices in a 5-quart slow cooker. Cover and cook for 8–10 hours on low or for 4–5 hours on high.

3. Transfer to bowls and garnish with shredded cheese and sour cream.

Savory Brown Bean Spread

*Instead of serving hummus with crackers or fresh vegetables,
try this savory alternative using Sweden's brown beans.*

INGREDIENTS | SERVES 6

1 cup Swedish brown beans

3 cups salted water (½ teaspoon salt)

3 cups fresh, cold water

2 cloves roasted garlic

2 tablespoons olive oil

3 tablespoons lemon juice

½ teaspoon salt

½ teaspoon oregano

1. Rinse the beans in a colander under flowing tap water, picking through them to remove any stones or discolored beans. Soak the brown beans in the salted water for 14 hours. Rinse thoroughly, then place in a pot with 3 cups fresh cold water. Bring pot to a low boil, reduce heat to a steady simmer, cover, and cook until the beans are tender (60–90 minutes). Rinse and drain.

2. Combine the beans and the rest of the ingredients in a food processor; pulse until smooth and creamy (if the spread is too thick, thin with water to taste).

3. Serve on rye crispbread or as a dip for fresh vegetables.

CHAPTER 11

Root and Cruciferous Vegetables

Hasselback Potatoes

Crunchy on the outside yet melt-in-your-mouth tender on the inside, these very special baked potatoes originated at the Restaurant Hasselbacken in Stockholm.

INGREDIENTS | SERVES 6

6 large baking potatoes

¼ cup melted butter

1½ teaspoons salt

¼ cup grated *Västerbotten* cheese (or substitute Parmesan)

¼ cup unseasoned bread crumbs

2 teaspoons finely chopped herbs (parsley, chives, dill, or oregano)

Potato Pastors

Potatoes were introduced to Norway around 1760 by parish pastors, who encouraged their flocks to embrace this vegetable that promised to end all hunger and famine. It seemed like a good idea at the time. The well-nourished population doubled—until 1847, when the potato blight hit and many lefse-starved Norwegians were forced to emigrate to America.

1. Preheat oven to 450°F. Peel the potatoes, removing all eyes and brown spots. Slice a thin ¼" layer from the bottom of each potato so it will sit flat.

2. Place a potato in a large serving spoon and cut downward into ¼" slices, leaving the bottom ¼" of the potato intact (you don't want to cut all the way through; the spoon will help prevent slicing all the way through the potato).

3. Place the sliced potato into a large bowl of ice water to prevent browning, and carefully flex the slices open, like an accordion. Repeat the process with the remaining potatoes.

4. Remove the potatoes from the water and dry well with a paper towel. Place in a greased casserole dish, sliced-side up; drizzle potatoes well with half of the melted butter, then season with the salt.

5. Bake in the oven for 30 minutes, basting occasionally with the butter that melts into the bottom of the pan.

6. Mix together the remaining butter, grated cheese, bread crumbs, and chopped herbs. Remove the potatoes from the oven and spoon the mixture over them, pushing some mixture between the layers; return to the oven and cook for an additional 20 minutes or until soft.

Jansson's Temptation (*Janssons Frestelse*)

Sweden's version of scalloped potatoes, Jansson's Temptation is said to have been christened for twentieth-century opera singer and gourmand Pelle Janzon.

INGREDIENTS | SERVES 6

5 large Idaho russet potatoes

2 large onions

25 Swedish spice-cured sprats

Salt and pepper, to season

1–2 cups whipping cream

2 tablespoons melted butter

1 cup rye bread crumbs

¼ cup fresh parsley, finely chopped

Swedish Anchovies

For best results, do not substitute tinned anchovies in this recipe; look for jars of spice-cured Swedish sprats (called "anchovies" in Sweden) in Scandinavian markets or online.

1. Preheat oven to 425°F. Scrub and peel the potatoes, then cut them into ¼" matchsticks. Place in a bowl of ice water for 10 minutes to leach out the excess starch.

2. Peel and slice the onions into thin strips. Butter a 9" × 13" casserole dish. Pat the potatoes dry with a paper towel. Place ⅓ of the potato matchsticks in the bottom of the dish, top with ½ of the onions, then layer ½ of the spiced sprats over the onions. Lightly season with salt and pepper. Repeat the layers, ending with the remaining third of the potatoes.

3. Pour enough of the cream over the casserole to fill the dish ¾ full. Stir together the butter, bread crumbs, and chopped parsley, then sprinkle on top of the casserole.

4. Bake on the center rack of the oven for 50 minutes.

Burning Love (*Brændende Kærlighed*)

For a healthier version of this Danish favorite, substitute turkey bacon for the bacon and use skim milk instead of whole.

INGREDIENTS | SERVES 6

6 baking potatoes
10 strips bacon
1 onion, peeled and thinly sliced
1 cup whole milk or half-and-half
2 tablespoons butter, room temperature

1. Peel the potatoes, place in a pot with enough water to cover by 2", and bring to a steady simmer. Cook until the potatoes break apart easily, about 25 minutes.

2. While the potatoes are cooking, dice the bacon finely and fry together with the sliced onion.

3. Drain the potatoes and mash together with the milk and butter until creamy.

4. Spoon the potatoes onto individual plates and make a small well in the center of each serving. Fill the well with the fried bacon and onions. Serve with a fresh salad.

Spring Potatoes with Horseradish and Dill

Samsø, a Danish island located off the Jutland Peninsula, is famous for its tender spring potatoes. For this recipe, try substituting thin-skinned white, red, or Yukon Gold potatoes.

INGREDIENTS | SERVES 4–6

2 pounds new potatoes
¼ cup melted butter
1 tablespoon kosher salt
2 tablespoons coarsely chopped dill
1 tablespoon freshly grated or prepared
  horseradish

The Versatile Potato

According to a Norwegian adage about any talented person: "Er litt som poteten; kan brukes til det meste." ("He is like a potato—good at everything.")

1. Preheat oven to 450°F. Scrub the potatoes well, place in a pot with enough water to cover by 1", and bring the pot to a low boil. Parboil for 7 minutes.

2. Drain and rinse the potatoes in cold water, then pierce each one with a fork in several places.

3. Whisk together the melted butter and salt; toss with the potatoes.

4. Place on a foil-lined baking sheet and roast in the oven for 30–40 minutes, until the potatoes are crispy on the outside (shake the pan at the 15-minute point to turn the potatoes.

5. Toss the warm potatoes with the chopped dill and horseradish and serve.

Sugar-Browned Potatoes

Anyone with a Danish grandmother knows how delicious brunede kartofler *are. Too rich for every day, they are a treat best reserved for Christmas and other special occasions.*

INGREDIENTS | SERVES 5–6

12–15 new or fingerling potatoes
2 tablespoons sugar
2 tablespoons butter

1. Place potatoes in a large saucepan and cover completely with water. Bring the potatoes to a boil, reduce heat to a steady simmer, and cook for 20 minutes or until tender. Drain, douse with cold water, and peel away the skins. Give the peeled potatoes another rinse, shaking the colander to remove excess water (the potatoes need to be a little damp in order for the sugar to best adhere).

2. Place the sugar in a large frying pan and allow to brown over low heat, watching to make sure it doesn't burn. When the sugar has begun to caramelize, stir in the butter and cook until the mixture begins to bubble.

3. Add the potatoes and stir to coat with the caramelized butter. Cook for 10 minutes or so until the potatoes have browned. Serve immediately.

Cauliflower with Dilled Shrimp Sauce

Steamed cauliflower serves as a healthy substitute for pasta in this savory main dish.

INGREDIENTS | SERVES 4–6

1 head cauliflower, rinsed and separated into florets

1 tablespoon olive oil plus 1 tablespoon butter

3 cloves garlic, finely minced

1 small red onion, peeled and finely chopped

1 pound precooked fancy bay shrimp, peeled

2 tablespoons butter

2 tablespoons flour

½ cup vegetable broth

⅔ cup low-fat milk

1 tablespoon fresh dill, finely minced

¼ cup toasted pine nuts

Spice It Up

Prefer a spicier dish? Add 1 teaspoon of your favorite curry powder to the garlic and onions as you sauté them.

1. Steam the cauliflower florets on the stove or in the microwave until fork-tender.

2. Melt the olive oil and 1 tablespoon of butter together in a spacious frying pan over medium heat, then add the garlic and onion and slowly sauté until the onion is opaque, stirring occasionally. Stir in the shrimp and remove from heat.

3. Melt the remaining 2 tablespoons of butter in a large pot over medium heat, then stir in the flour to make a roux. Pour the vegetable broth and then the milk into the roux in a steady stream, whisking constantly until the sauce thickens and begins to bubble. Add the shrimp mixture and the dill, reduce heat to medium-low, and cook until the shrimp are heated through, about 5 minutes.

4. Fold the shrimp sauce into the steamed cauliflower, garnish with pine nuts, and serve.

Rutabaga "Ham" with Brown Sugar Glaze (*Griljerad Kålrot*)

One of the trendiest recipes in today's Nordic cuisine is this festive rutabaga "ham," now often substituted for fat-laden baked hams on holiday tables.

INGREDIENTS | SERVES 4–6

1 large rutabaga (the biggest you can find) or 4 small rutabagas

Vegetable broth, as needed

1 onion, coarsely chopped

2 bay leaves

1 teaspoon whole allspice

1 teaspoon whole cloves

1 teaspoon white peppercorns

1 teaspoon salt

1 egg

¼ cup coarse Swedish mustard

1 cup bread crumbs, panko crumbs, or cracker crumbs

1 tablespoon chopped parsley

½ cup packed brown sugar

1 tablespoon flour

¼ teaspoon ginger

1½ tablespoons white wine or white balsamic vinegar

1½ tablespoons water

1. Peel the rutabaga, removing all green spots and rounding off the ends, if need be, so it approximates the shape of a small ham.

2. Place the rutabaga in a pot with enough vegetable broth to cover by 1". Add the chopped onion, bay leaves, allspice, cloves, peppercorns, and salt. Bring the pot to a steady simmer, cover, and cook until tender (1–2 hours, depending on the size of the rutabaga).

3. Preheat oven to 425°F. Drain the rutabaga, then pat well with a paper towel to dry.

4. Mix together the egg and mustard, then use a pastry brush to cover the entire surface of the rutabaga with the mixture.

5. Stir the bread crumbs and parsley together on a plate, then roll the rutabaga over in the crumbs so that they adhere to all surfaces.

6. Place the rutabaga in a greased casserole dish and roast in oven until golden brown, about 15 minutes.

7. For the glaze, combine the brown sugar, flour, ginger, wine or vinegar, and water in a small saucepan over low heat, stirring until the sugar has dissolved. Keep warm.

8. To serve, slice the rutabaga as you would a ham and drizzle with the brown sugar glaze.

Roasted Beets with Goat Cheese Butter

Crowned with a tangy Snøfrisk butter, these roasted beets can't be beat!

INGREDIENTS | SERVES 4–6

4 large beets
1 tablespoon olive oil
1 teaspoon anise seed
1 teaspoon lemon zest
4.4 ounces *Snøfrisk* cheese
½ stick of butter (2 ounces), softened

Beet Stains

To remove beet stains from your hands after slicing them, rub your hands with half of a cut lemon and coarse salt. Baking soda also works.

1. Scrub the beets well and cut off the ends, leaving 1" of stalk. Place in a pot and add enough water to cover by 1". Bring to a low boil, cover, and cook until fork-tender, about 30 minutes.

2. Rinse the beets under cold water, peel off the skins, and slice thinly.

3. Combine the olive oil, anise seed, and lemon zest, then toss together with the beet slices. Cream together the *Snøfrisk* and the butter.

4. Place the beet slices on a foil-lined roasting pan, drizzling any remaining marinade over them. Top each slice with a dollop of the *Snøfrisk*-butter blend; broil in oven for 2–3 minutes just until the butter begins to melt. Serve immediately.

Beetroot Pâté (*Punajuuripatee*)

You won't believe how good the combination of roasted beets, garlic, and blue cheese is in this colorful vegetable-based pâté.

INGREDIENTS | SERVES 8–10

5 beets

3 cloves garlic

2 onions, peeled and sliced

¼ cup olive oil

4 eggs

½ cup whipping cream

⅓ cup Danish blue cheese, crumbled

½ cup walnuts, chopped

½ teaspoon salt

½ teaspoon pepper

1. Preheat oven to 350°F. Scrub the beets well and place in a roasting pan with the garlic and onions. Cover, place in oven, and roast for 1 hour. Remove the pan from the oven and cool the beets enough so that you can handle them; lower oven temperature to 300°F.

2. Peel the beets and the garlic, then place in a food processor with the onion; process into a smooth purée. Add the olive oil, eggs, cream, blue cheese, walnuts, salt, and pepper; blend just until combined.

3. Transfer the mixture to a greased terrine or loaf pan, then place the pan in the center of a larger casserole dish. Add enough water to the casserole dish to fill half way.

4. Place the casserole dish (water bath) in the oven and cook for 1½ hours.

5. Remove from oven, then either offer the pâté warm or refrigerate and serve cool, accompanied with crackers or toast points.

Crispy Fried Leeks

Looking for a lighter alternative to french-fried onion rings?
Leeks, more delicate than onions, fry up into a tasty topping for hot dogs or casseroles.

INGREDIENTS | MAKES 1½ CUPS

2 leeks

3 cups canola oil

1 cup potato starch flour

1 teaspoon seasoned salt (like Lawry's)

¼ teaspoon pepper

Crispy Fried Onions

In Scandinavia, crispy fried onions are a popular topping for hot dogs. To make your own (which will be far lighter and crunchier than the kind that comes in a can), simply substitute 2 onions—sliced paper-thin with a mandolin or sharp knife—for the leeks in this recipe.

1. Cut off the green portion of the leek and discard, then slice the white part in half. Cut each half into 3" sections; then slice each section lengthwise into thin strips. Place the strips in a colander and rinse well under cold running water to remove any residual sand; shake the colander to remove excess water.

2. In a fryer or deep pot, heat the canola oil to 300°F.

3. Whisk together the potato starch flour, seasoned salt, and pepper, then lightly dredge the damp leeks in the flour to coat.

4. Use a slotted spoon to carefully transfer small batches of the floured leeks (about ¼ cup at a time) to the hot oil. Fry until golden, about 5 minutes, then remove them with the spoon to a plate lined with a paper towel to drain.

Root Vegetable Mash

Why settle for mashed potatoes when you can combine them with creamy, antioxidant-rich root vegetables like rutabagas and carrots?

INGREDIENTS | SERVES 8

3 pounds assorted root vegetables (potatoes, carrots, rutabagas, celery root)
1 teaspoon salt
2 large eggs
½ cup whipping cream
½ teaspoon ground nutmeg

1. Scrub the vegetables well. Peel and chop into a ½" dice.

2. Place cubed vegetables into a large saucepan and add enough water to cover by 1". Stir in the salt, and bring pot to a low boil. Reduce the heat to a steady simmer; cook the vegetables until tender, about 20 minutes.

3. Preheat oven to 425°F. Separate the eggs into yolks and whites; beat the whites until stiff peaks form.

4. Drain the vegetables well; return to the pot and stir in the egg yolks and whipping cream. Crush the vegetable mixture with a potato masher into a thick, smooth purée.

5. Gently fold the beaten egg whites into the vegetable mash; transfer to a buttered 1½ quart casserole dish and sprinkle with nutmeg.

6. Place in oven and cook for 30 minutes or until browned.

Kari's Cabbage Casserole (*Kållåda med Skinka*)

Add enough rich cheese, ham, and caraway seeds, and even something mundane like cabbage can be transformed into a dish for company!

INGREDIENTS | SERVES 6

4 cups water, lightly salted

3 cups shredded cabbage (either white or Napa)

1 tablespoon butter plus 1 tablespoon olive oil

1 large red onion, thinly sliced

½ green bell pepper, grated

2 cups chopped ham or leftover pork loin

5 eggs

1 cup grated *Hushållsost* (farmer's cheese), or substitute mozzarella

½ teaspoon salt

½ teaspoon freshly ground pepper

2 teaspoons caraway seeds

Hushållsost

Hushållsost (farmer's cheese) is a semi-soft, slightly tangy, cows' milk cheese produced and distributed by Scandic of Sweden. It's worth buying a large round, for it both freezes beautifully and, if wrapped well, lasts for months in the refrigerator.

1. Preheat oven to 400°F. In a large pot on the stovetop, bring lightly salted water to a boil. Add the shredded cabbage, reduce heat to a steady simmer, and cook, covered, for 10 minutes. Drain the cabbage and pat dry.

2. Melt 1 tablespoon butter plus 1 tablespoon olive oil in a large skillet. Add the onion and pepper and cook over medium-low heat, stirring occasionally, just until the onion begins to soften and brown.

3. Scatter the chopped ham in the bottom of a greased 9" × 13" casserole dish. Cover with the peppers and onions, then layer the cabbage on top.

4. Whisk together the eggs, grated cheese, salt, pepper, and caraway seeds; pour over the casserole.

5. Bake in oven for 40 minutes or until golden brown.

Creamed Kale (*Grønlangkål*)

Grønlangkål is a favorite holiday dish in Jutland, where it is always accompanied with Sugar-Browned Potatoes (Brunede Kartofler), see recipe in this chapter) and ham. In Vendsyssel, Denmark's northernmost district, grønlangkål is prepared slightly differently than in Jutland, and served with cinnamon-sugar.

INGREDIENTS | SERVES 6

1 pound kale
1½ teaspoons salt, divided use
3 tablespoons butter
3 tablespoons flour
2 cups half-and-half
1 tablespoon cinnamon-sugar

1. Clean the kale under running water, cutting away stalks and center veins.

2. Place the kale in a large pot with enough water to cover; sprinkle in ½ teaspoon of the salt. Bring pot to a steady simmer, cover, and cook until the kale is tender, about 20 minutes.

3. Drain the kale in a colander, pressing to release as much water as possible. Chop it finely.

4. Rinse and wipe the original pot clean, then melt the butter in it over medium heat. Whisk in the flour, then gradually incorporate the half-and-half in a steady stream. Cook, whisking constantly, until the sauce becomes thick and bubbly.

5. Fold the kale into the sauce, then stir in the remaining 1 teaspoon salt and the cinnamon-sugar. Heat until warmed through, about 5 minutes.

Danish Blue Kohlrabi

In Denmark, kohlrabi is called glaskål: *"glass cabbage." When lightly stewed with Danish blue cheese, it is a fantastic alternative to starchy side dishes like macaroni or potatoes.*

INGREDIENTS | SERVES 4

2 large kohlrabi

1 teaspoon salt, plus more to taste

5 tablespoons butter, divided use

1 small onion, finely diced

3 tablespoons flour

¼ cup half-and-half

2 tablespoons Danish blue cheese

Pepper to taste

Chopped chives or parsley for garnish

1. Use a sharp knife to remove the stalks and peel the skins from the kohlrabi; chop into an even ¼" dice. Place in a colander, sprinkle with 1 teaspoon salt, and allow to drain for 30 minutes. Rinse well, pressing out the excess water.

2. In a large frying pan over medium heat, melt 2 tablespoons of the butter. Add the chopped kohlrabi and onion, and fry until soft and golden brown, about 10 minutes. Transfer to a bowl or plate.

3. Melt the remaining butter in the pan and then stir in the flour to form a roux. Cook for 2–3 minutes, until bubbly, then stir in the half-and-half and the blue cheese. Add the kohlrabi and onion, and heat through until the liquid is absorbed, about 5 minutes.

4. Season to taste with salt and pepper, garnish with chives, and serve.

Carrot and Potato Bake

This is the perfect, golden harvest vegetable entrée to serve on a nippy autumn evening.

INGREDIENTS | SERVES 4

4 Yukon Gold potatoes

4 large carrots

1½ teaspoons dried thyme

3 cloves roasted garlic

1 teaspoon salt

¼ teaspoon pepper

1 cup grated *Hushållsost* (farmer's cheese) or substitute any semi-soft, mellow white cheese

1¼ cups half-and-half

Roasted Garlic

To roast garlic, simply cut the head off a jumbo garlic bulb, place it on aluminum foil, and drizzle with olive oil, sea salt, and pepper. Fold the aluminum foil over the bulb, sealing it into a packet, then place in an oven preheated to 375°F for 40 minutes.

1. Preheat oven to 350°F. Peel and thinly slice the potatoes and carrots, then place them in a pot with enough salted water to cover. Bring the water to a low boil; parboil the vegetables for 5 minutes. Drain and douse with cold water; pat dry with a paper towel.

2. Toss together the potatoes, carrots, thyme, roasted garlic, salt, pepper, and ½ cup of the shredded cheese; transfer to a greased 1½ quart casserole dish. Pour the half-and-half over the casserole, then sprinkle with the remaining cheese.

3. Bake on the center rack of the oven for 30 minutes or until golden.

Dilled Carrots

The innate sweetness of carrots is accentuated with just a bit of brown sugar and fresh dill.

INGREDIENTS | SERVES 4

1 cup water

1 tablespoon brown sugar

1 tablespoon butter, softened

1½ pounds baby carrots

1 teaspoon fresh dill, finely chopped

1 tablespoon lemon juice

1. In a medium saucepan, combine the water, brown sugar, butter, and carrots. Bring to a boil, reduce heat to a simmer, and cook until carrots are crisp-tender, about 8 minutes.

2. Use a slotted spoon to transfer the carrots to a bowl. Increase the heat under the pot to reduce the liquid to sauce consistency. Return the carrots to the pot and stir to coat.

3. Turn off the heat, transfer the glazed carrots to a serving bowl, and toss with the chopped dill and lemon juice.

CHAPTER 12

Cold Water Fish and Seafood

Poached Salmon with Green Sauce

Enhance the subtlety of lightly poached salmon with a fragrant and refreshing dill sauce.

INGREDIENTS | SERVES 6

5 cloves garlic, peeled

¼ rounded cup chopped walnuts

3 cups fresh dill, coarsely chopped

Zest of 1 large lemon

1 teaspoon salt

¾ cup canola oil

4 cups water

⅓ cup white wine vinegar

1 medium onion, chopped

½ teaspoon white peppercorns

½ teaspoon mustard seed

1 teaspoon dill seed

2 bay leaves

6 (6-ounce) salmon fillets

Salmon: The Wonder Fish

The health benefits of salmon—rich in protein, omega-3 fatty acids, and vitamin D—is justly praised. Excellent for lowering bad LDL cholesterol while raising good HDL cholesterol, salmon promotes heart health, stabilizes blood-sugar levels, helps prevent blood clots, improves memory, and is a natural antidepressant. It may also help to stave off Parkinson's disease and Alzheimer's disease. All this and salmon tastes good, too! Try to enjoy it at least twice a week as part of your Nordic diet.

1. For the green sauce, combine the garlic cloves and the walnuts in a food processor and pulse until finely chopped. Add the fresh dill, lemon zest, and salt; process into a thick paste. Add the oil in a steady stream, until the sauce has the consistency of a thick tomato sauce. Refrigerate for at least 30 minutes.

2. To poach the salmon, combine the water, white wine vinegar, onion, peppercorns, mustard seed, dill seed, and bay leaves in a large frying pan. Bring to a boil and simmer for 15 minutes.

3. Reduce the heat from a boil to a steady simmer, then slide the salmon fillets into the water. Cover and poach for 8–10 minutes, just until the salmon starts to flake.

4. Transfer the fillets briefly to a paper towel–lined plate and pat dry, then place them on warmed plates or a platter and drizzle the green sauce on top. Garnish with lemon wedges and serve.

Salmon Loaf with Marinated Cucumber Sauce

*To make marinated cucumbers, just follow the recipe for
Norwegian Cucumber Salad (Agurksalat) in Chapter 4.*

INGREDIENTS | SERVES 6

1 (14.75-ounce) can red salmon, undrained

2 eggs, beaten

⅔ cup cracker crumbs or bread crumbs

2 tablespoons onion, finely chopped

2 tablespoons celery, finely chopped

Zest and juice of 1 small lemon

½ teaspoon salt

¼ teaspoon white pepper

1 cup sour cream or crème fraîche

1 cup marinated cucumbers from
Norwegian Cucumber Salad (Agurksalat;
see Chapter 4), roughly chopped

2 teaspoons fresh dill, finely chopped

1. Preheat oven to 350°F. Gently fold together the salmon, eggs, cracker crumbs, onion, celery, lemon juice and zest, salt, and white pepper. Transfer the mixture to a greased loaf pan.

2. Bake on the center rack for 40 minutes or until browned.

3. As the salmon loaf bakes, stir together the sour cream, chopped marinated cucumbers, and dill. Refrigerate.

4. To serve, slice the warm salmon loaf and drizzle with the chilled cucumber sauce.

Fish Stock

Fish stock is a key element in intensifying the depth of flavor of many seafood casseroles, soups, and entrées. Use white-fleshed fish remnants rather than the oilier salmon to ensure a delicate stock.

INGREDIENTS | MAKES 8 CUPS

2 pounds white-fleshed fish heads,
bones, and roe (do not use the gills or
intestines)

8 cups cold water

1 cup dry white wine

1 onion, peeled and coarsely chopped

1 celery rib, coarsely chopped

6 fresh dill sprigs

10 white peppercorns

2 bay leaves

1. Stir together all of the ingredients in a large stockpot and bring to a boil. Reduce heat to a steady simmer and cook for 30 minutes, skimming off the froth as it rises to the surface.

2. Use a slotted spoon to remove the largest fish remnants and the vegetables from the pot; discard. Allow stock to cool.

3. Line a colander with two layers of cheesecloth and strain the stock into a large bowl to ensure that all fish bones and solids are removed.

4. Refrigerate homemade fish stock and use within 48 hours, or freeze for up to 3 months.

Seafood Au Gratin

Be sure to use homemade fish stock in this casserole fit for company, a dish that proves just how sophisticated "comfort food" can be.

INGREDIENTS | SERVES 6–8

2 pounds white fish fillets (sole, cod, halibut, or flounder)

1 teaspoon salt

¼ teaspoon white pepper

3 tablespoons fresh lemon juice

4 tablespoons butter, divided use

3 tablespoons flour

1 cup Fish Stock (see recipe in this chapter)

1 cup half-and-half

½ cup fresh dill, finely chopped

1 tablespoon lemon zest

3 cups mashed potatoes (homemade, not instant)

3 tablespoons grated Jarlsberg or *Västerbotten* cheese

1 cup cooked and peeled bay (tiny) shrimp

1. Preheat oven to 425°F. Make sure that all bones have been removed from the fish fillets, then season with salt and pepper. Place in a buttered 9" × 13" casserole dish, sprinkle with lemon juice, and dot with 1 tablespoon of the butter. Bake on center rack for 15 minutes.

2. Melt the remaining 3 tablespoons of butter in a medium saucepan at medium heat. When the butter turns frothy, stir in the flour to make a creamy roux. Once the flour is incorporated, whisk in the fish stock in a steady stream, followed by the half-and-half. Add the chopped dill and lemon zest; season with additional salt and pepper to taste. Simmer for 10 minutes or until warmed through, stirring occasionally.

3. Remove the casserole dish from the oven and increase heat to 475°F.

4. Pipe the mashed potatoes around the edges of the casserole dish, then pour the sauce over the center of the casserole. Sprinkle with grated cheese, then return to the oven and bake until browned, 10–15 minutes.

5. Garnish with the shrimp and additional fresh dill before serving.

Crispy Codfish Balls (*Torskeboller*)

There's no better way to use one of Scandinavia's primary exports—dried salt cod—than in these crunchy codfish balls. Your kids will eat them like tater tots!

INGREDIENTS | SERVES 4

1 pound dried salt cod
3 large potatoes
1 clove garlic, finely pressed
1 teaspoon dried dill
½ teaspoon lemon zest
2 egg whites
Canola oil for frying

Dill-Garlic Mayonnaise

To make a fast, no-fuss Dill-Garlic Mayonnaise, whisk together 1 cup of your favorite mayonnaise with 1–2 teaspoons of dried lemon-dill seasoning (to taste) and 1–2 cloves pressed garlic.

1. Rinse the salt cod well and cut into 2"-long pieces. Cover with cold water and soak for at least 24 hours and up to 3 days, replacing the water every 6 hours.

2. Peel the potatoes, roughly dice, and boil until tender. Drain, rinse with cold water, and then press through a potato ricer or use a masher to pound them into a smooth purée.

3. Pat the cod dry with paper towels, then shred it into tiny pieces with your fingers. Mix it into the potatoes, then stir in the remaining ingredients, except oil. Cover and chill in the refrigerator for 30 minutes.

4. Flour your hands and pat the batter into walnut-sized balls.

5. Add enough oil to a heavy pot or deep-fryer to fill to a depth of 3". Heat the oil until a drop of water sizzles when dropped in the pot. Carefully fry the codfish balls, 3–5 at a time, for 3 minutes or until golden brown. Remove from the oil and drain on paper towels.

6. Serve warm, with Dill-Garlic Mayonnaise (see sidebar recipe).

SAVU Smoked Salmon with Potatoes and Garlic

Trust it to the ingenious Finns to develop the easiest way in the world to smoke salmon!

SAVU Smoker Bags

Credit the Finns with inventing SAVU Smoker Bags (the Finnish word *savu* means "smoke"). Emeril Lagasse also distributes smoker bags under his Emerils brand; see *www.emerilstore.com*. Smoker bags are a miracle of Scandinavian simplicity: simply place the food you wish to smoke inside, seal, and either bake or grill it to smoky perfection.

1. Preheat oven to 475°F.

2. Slice the top off the garlic bulb to expose the cloves. Place the salmon, garlic, potatoes, and sugar cubes in the SAVU bag.

3. Seal the bag, place in the oven, and cook for 15 minutes. Reduce heat to 350°F. Carefully make a slit in the top of the bag to allow the salmon and potatoes to brown—*but take care that the escaping steam does not burn you.* Then cook for 15 more minutes or until the potatoes are tender.

4. Transfer the salmon to plates (removing the skin, if desired). Squeeze the roasted garlic from the cloves and toss with the potatoes. Serve alongside the smoked salmon, with warm rolls and a salad.

Smoked Trout with Summer Vegetables

During Walpurgis Night and Midsummer's Eve, Scandinavians often use their celebratory bonfires to roast freshly caught trout in the embers. You can achieve much the same effect at home (with a minimal fire hazard) by smoking trout and summer vegetables in a Finnish SAVU smoker bag.

INGREDIENTS | SERVES 6

2 pounds trout fillets, skin on
1 lemon, zested and thinly sliced
3 sugar cubes
1 SAVU Smoker Bag (Alder)
2 small zucchini, sliced
2 yellow squash, sliced
12 thin asparagus stalks, trimmed and cut into 3" pieces
1½ tablespoons canola or olive oil
1 teaspoon fresh thyme
½ teaspoon salt
¼ teaspoon pepper

1. Preheat oven to 475°F.

2. Place the trout fillets, lemon slices, and sugar cubes in the smoker bag.

3. Toss together the vegetables, lemon zest, oil, thyme, salt, and pepper. Place in the bag with the trout and seal.

4. Place the bag in the oven and cook for 15 minutes. Reduce heat to 350°F. Carefully make a slit in the top of the bag to allow the trout to brown slightly—*but take care that the escaping steam does not burn you.* Then cook for 5 more minutes.

5. Transfer the vegetables and the smoked trout to plates (removing the skin, if desired).

Grilled Trout with Minted Nettle Sauce

Delicate and earthy at the same time, grilled trout with minted nettle sauce is a perfect conclusion to a spring day spent fishing and foraging. The nettle-challenged chef can, of course, substitute baby spinach (safer but not quite so interesting and unique)!

INGREDIENTS | SERVES 4

⅓ cup butter, softened

2 tablespoons fresh parsley, finely chopped

3 tablespoons fresh mint, finely chopped

2 (1-pound) trout, gutted and cleaned

1 large lemon, thinly sliced

½ teaspoon salt

¼ teaspoon pepper

2½ cups water

2 cups packed nettle leaves (or baby spinach)

⅔ cup half-and-half

6 tablespoons butter, cubed

1. Beat together the softened butter, parsley, and 2 tablespoons of the mint, then spread inside the cavity of each fish. Place the lemon slices inside as well, then sprinkle the inside and outside of the fish with salt and pepper. Secure with toothpicks or kitchen string and place in the refrigerator for at least 30 minutes to allow the flavors to marry.

2. While the fish rest, bring water to a boil over high heat in a medium saucepan. Pull on rubber gloves and wash the nettles, removing all stems, and then drop them into the water and blanch for 5 minutes until tender (you can take off your gloves now!). Drain the cooked nettles well, removing as much water as possible, and chop them finely.

3. Pour the half-and-half into a saucepan and bring to a steady simmer over medium heat; cook until the cream has reduced to ¼ cup, stirring occasionally to prevent scorching. Reduce heat to low and whisk in the cubes of butter, one at a time.

4. Stir in the nettles and the remaining 1 tablespoon of the mint; thin to sauce consistency, if necessary, with additional half-and-half. Season to taste with salt and pepper, then keep sauce warm while you grill the fish.

5. Grease your grill grate well, then preheat on high. Reduce heat to medium, place the fish on the grill, and cook for 10 minutes, flipping once.

6. Debone and skin the grilled trout and transfer to warm plates. Serve, accompanied with the minted nettle sauce.

Boiled Crayfish (*Kräftor*) with Dill

Emulate the Swedes and serve August's beloved boiled crayfish with garlic mayonnaise, Västerbotten Pie (see Chapter 8), lager, ice-cold aquavit, and a strawberry cake.

INGREDIENTS | SERVES 6

4 quarts water (or enough to cover the crayfish in the pot)

½ cup salt

20 dill crowns

¼ cup sugar

1 bottle dark beer (optional)

8 pounds live large crayfish (15–20)

1. Bring the water, salt, dill crowns, sugar, and beer (if using) to a boil in a large stockpot.

2. Place the live crayfish in a basket sifter and lower into the boiling water. Cook for 10 minutes, then turn off the heat and allow the crayfish to cool in the water.

3. Use tongs to transfer the crayfish to a bowl; cover and refrigerate until well chilled.

4. To serve, transfer to a platter garnished with additional dill crowns.

Butter-Braised Halibut with Saffron

Lightly braising fish in butter is a simple way to produce a gourmet-class dish without a lot of effort. Any firm-fleshed fish (salmon, tilapia, cod) can be substituted. Cook this over low to medium-low heat (don't let it boil) to prevent the butter liquid from separating.

INGREDIENTS | SERVES 6

1 clove garlic, finely minced

1 shallot, finely minced

½ cup Fish Stock (see recipe in this chapter)

1 tablespoon kosher salt (or 1½ teaspoons regular salt)

1 pound homemade or European-style unsalted butter (Kerrygold or Plugra brands), melted

1 pinch saffron threads (about ⅛ teaspoon), crumbled

2 pounds halibut steaks or cheeks

1. In a heavy-bottomed frying pan just large enough to hold the fish, combine the garlic, shallots, fish stock, and salt and bring to a simmer over medium-low heat.

2. Gradually whisk the melted butter into the liquid, stirring steadily. Heat to 130°F, then stir in the crumbled saffron.

3. Place the fish in the pan and poach for 15–20 minutes or until cooked through (spoon the liquid over the top of the fish a few times as it poaches).

4. Transfer to plates and spoon some of the poaching butter over the fish, if desired. Accompany with rice and steamed vegetables.

Salt Baked Salmon

When fully encased in salt, this dramatic baked salmon retains an unparalleled juiciness while absorbing just enough flavor from the fennel and spices. Serve it with flair at the table, using a hammer to crack open the hardened salt.

INGREDIENTS | SERVES 16–20

1 whole salmon (7–9 pounds), scaled, gutted, and with gills removed

1 egg white per pound of salt (8–10)

1½ pounds of kosher or sea salt per pound of salmon (8–10 pounds)

½ tablespoon mixed (black, red, white) peppercorns

2 teaspoons whole cloves

15 whole star anise

1 large fennel bulb

1. Preheat oven to 425°F. Line a large roasting pan or baking sheet large enough to hold the salmon with heavy aluminum foil.

2. Whip the egg whites to firm peaks, then fold together with the salt to form a stiff paste, the consistency of wet sand, that holds together when squeezed.

3. Place ⅓ of the salt-egg paste in a ½"-thick layer over the bottom of the foil-lined pan. Sprinkle half of the spices evenly over the salt paste.

4. Cut the fennel bulb in half and coarsely chop the fennel tops; core and thinly slice the bulb. Stuff the sliced bulb and fennel tops into the center of the salmon.

5. Place the salmon on the salt paste, then sprinkle the remaining spices on top. Use your hands to pack the rest of the paste over the top and around the sides of the fish, completely encasing it in the salt mixture.

6. Bake in the oven for 10 minutes per pound, until an instant-read thermometer stuck into the center of the fish registers 125°F (check it at 40 minutes). Remove from oven and allow to sit for 15 minutes before serving.

7. To serve, dramatically crack the salt crust open with a hammer. Peel the salt and the skin away from the fish, taking care to remove as much salt as possible. Slice the top half of the fish in serving size portions and transfer to plates; discard the fennel and the fish skeleton. Then slice the bottom half, lifting the individual pieces of salmon carefully away from the skin.

Baked Salmon with Caviar Cream in Puff Pastry

No, puff pastry isn't Nordic (although it's available in Scandinavian shops). Salmon caviar is, though, and it makes the perfect filling to top salmon encased in puff pastry.

INGREDIENTS | SERVES 6

1 whole skinless salmon fillet (1–1½ pounds), all pinbones removed

12 ounces cream cheese, softened

½ cup sour cream

Zest and juice of 1 small lemon

3½ ounces (100 grams) black salmon caviar (Royal Sweden brand works well)

2 tablespoons chives, finely minced

2 8" × 11" sheets puff pastry

5 cups fresh spinach leaves

1 egg, beaten

Norwegian Food for Thought

Det er håp i hengende snore: "There is hope as long as your fishing line is in the water" (Norwegian proverb).

1. Preheat oven to 450°F. Trim the edges of the salmon so that all sides are even.

2. Using a whisk (or whisk attachment of an electric beater), beat together the cream cheese, sour cream, and lemon juice. Drain and rinse the caviar, then gently fold it and the chives into the whipped cream cheese with a spatula.

3. Grease a large baking sheet. Roll the 2 puff pastry sheets into rectangles that are 1" wider than the salmon fillet. Transfer 1 pastry sheet to the baking sheet.

4. Place the salmon fillet on top of the puff pastry sheet and drizzle with the lemon zest. Cover with two or three layers of spinach leaves.

5. Spoon the caviar cream evenly across the top of the fillet, then cover with the second sheet of puff pastry. Seal and trim the edges and brush the top and sides of the pastry with the beaten egg. Cut 3 or 4 slits in the top crust.

6. Bake for 20 minutes or until puffed and golden. Cool slightly, then slice and serve.

Nordic Fish Pizza

The most-consumed food in Scandinavia isn't meatballs or gravlax—it's pizza! Still, there's no reason that pizza can't be part of a healthy Nordic diet, particularly when an herbed spelt crust supports smoked salmon, red onions, and tomatoes.

INGREDIENTS | SERVES 6

⅔ cup finger-warm water (105°F–110°F)

1½ teaspoons sugar

1½ teaspoons quick-rising yeast

1½ tablespoons plus ¾ cup canola oil, divided use

1 teaspoon salt

1 teaspoon dill or fennel seeds

2 cups light spelt flour

3 cups fresh dill, coarsely chopped

3 cloves garlic

1 red onion, thinly sliced and separated into rings

¼ pound smoked salmon, diced small

2 Meyer lemons, thinly sliced

⅔ cup dill Havarti cheese, shredded

1. In a medium bowl, stir together water, sugar, and yeast. Allow to sit for 15 minutes until the yeast bubbles, then mix together with 1½ tablespoons canola oil, salt, and dill or fennel seeds. Stir in flour.

2. Place into an oiled bowl, turning to cover with the oil. Cover with a tea towel and allow to rise in a warm place until doubled, about 1 hour. Punch down and roll into a crust.

3. While pizza dough is rising, preheat a pizza stone in your oven at 475°F for 30 minutes.

4. Reduce heat to 400°F. Lightly dust a pizza peel with cornmeal, place the pizza crust on it, and slide the pizza into the oven to prebake for 10 minutes.

5. Place ¾ cup canola oil, 3 cups chopped dill, and garlic in a food processor and pulse into a smooth sauce.

6. Remove the prebaked pizza crust from the oven; spread the dill sauce evenly across the top. Arrange the red onion rings, smoked salmon, and lemon slices over the sauce, then sprinkle with the grated cheese.

7. Return the pizza to the oven and cook until the cheese has melted, about 10 minutes.

Norwegian Fish Pudding (*Fiskepudding*)

A true classic, Norwegian Fish Pudding is not only wonderful in its own right, but it can also be used as the base for fish cakes and fish balls. Slice it and serve it as is with Shrimp Sauce (see recipe in this chapter), or lightly fry the slices for a crispier entrée.

INGREDIENTS | SERVES 6

1½ pounds white fish (haddock, cod, or halibut), skinned and deboned

2 teaspoons salt

½ cup crushed ice

1½ tablespoons potato starch flour (or substitute cornstarch)

3 egg whites

1½ cups cream, well chilled

⅛ teaspoon ground nutmeg

1 tablespoon butter, softened

2 tablespoons dried rye bread crumbs

A kettle full of boiling water

Shrimp Sauce to taste (see recipe in this chapter)

1. Chop the fish into 2" chunks, place in the bowl of a food processor (equipped with its blade), cover, and refrigerate for 30 minutes. Place a mixing bowl (of a stand mixer, if you have one) in the freezer to chill, as well.

2. Place the chilled bowl with the fish on the processor and sprinkle in the salt. Pulse for a few seconds, then add the crushed ice and the potato starch flour. Pulse again to combine.

3. Place the egg whites in the chilled mixing bowl and use the whip attachment (or a balloon whisk) to beat them to soft peaks. Fold the fish paste into the beaten eggs whites. With the mixer on low, gradually pour the cream in a steady stream into the bowl until the mixture has turned into a thick, smooth purée. Increase the speed to high and whip for 2–3 minutes, until light and fluffy.

4. Preheat oven to 350°F. Use the softened butter to grease a 1½-quart loaf pan, then dust the bottom and sides with the dried bread crumbs. Spoon the fish batter into the pan, cover it tightly with aluminum foil, then place the pan in the center of a larger casserole dish. Add enough boiling water to the casserole to fill it ¾ of the way up.

5. Place the casserole dish in the oven on the middle rack and bake for 60–70 minutes, making sure that the water bath simmers but does not reach a boil. The pudding is done when a bamboo skewer inserted in the middle comes out clean and dry.

6. To serve, pour off any juices that may have collected on the top of the pudding. Invert the pan onto a warmed platter, cut into slices, and accompany with Shrimp Sauce.

Shrimp Sauce

Enjoy this shrimp sauce as a topping for Norwegian Fiskepudding, on pasta, or over buttered wild rice.

INGREDIENTS | MAKES 2 CUPS

1½ sticks butter (¾ cup), divided use

¼ cup flour

2 cups half-and-half

1 teaspoon salt

½ teaspoon white pepper

½ cup dry white wine

4 shallots, finely chopped

16 ounces uncooked shrimp, peeled and deveined

⅓ cup fresh dill, finely chopped

1. Melt ¼ cup of the butter in a saucepan over medium heat until frothy. Whisk in the flour and cook for 2–3 minutes, until the roux begins to bubble. Stir in the half-and-half, salt, and white pepper; cook, stirring constantly, until the mixture thickens, 5–7 minutes. Whisk in the wine and reduce heat to low.

2. In a frying pan over medium heat, melt the remaining butter. Stir in the shallots, and sauté just until they soften and begin to brown; add the shrimp and cook 5 more minutes, stirring occasionally, until the shrimp turn pink.

3. Fold the sautéed shrimp and shallots into the sauce, mix in the dill, and season with additional salt and pepper to taste.

Fish Dumplings (*Fiskefarse*) with Curry Sauce

Norwegian Fiskefarse *begin with the same components as* Fiskepudding, *but after the fish is processed into a smooth batter, it is formed into small dumplings that are quickly poached before serving with a savory sauce.*

INGREDIENTS | SERVES 6

1½ pounds white fish (haddock, cod, or halibut), skinned and deboned

2½ teaspoons salt, divided use

½ cup crushed ice

1½ tablespoons potato starch flour (or substitute cornstarch)

3 egg whites

1½ cups cream, well chilled

¼ cup butter

¼ cup flour

2 cups milk

¼ teaspoon white pepper

1½ teaspoons curry powder

Other Sauce Suggestions

Not a curry fan? Norwegian *fiskefarse* are also quite good when served with dill sauce, Shrimp Sauce (see recipe in this chapter), or lobster sauce (these canned varieties are all packaged and distributed by Sweden's Abba Seafood company).

1. Chop the fish into 2" chunks, place in the bowl of a food processor (equipped with its blade), cover, and refrigerate for 30 minutes. Place a mixing bowl (of a stand mixer, if you have one) in the freezer to chill as well.

2. Place the chilled bowl with the fish on the processor and sprinkle in 2 teaspoons of the salt. Pulse for a few seconds, then add the crushed ice and the potato starch flour. Pulse again to combine.

3. Place the egg whites in the chilled mixing bowl and use the whip attachment (or a balloon whisk) to beat them to soft peaks. Fold the fish paste into the beaten egg whites. Then, with the mixer on low, gradually pour the cream in a steady stream into the bowl until the mixture has turned into a thick, smooth purée. Increase the mixer speed to high and whip for 2–3 minutes, until light and fluffy.

4. Cover the bowl with plastic wrap and refrigerate for 30 minutes.

5. While the fish chills, make a curry sauce by melting the butter in a saucepan until frothy. Stir in the flour to make a roux, then gradually whisk in the milk. After the sauce thickens, stir in remaining ½ teaspoon salt, the white pepper, and curry powder; reduce heat to low and keep warm.

6. To make the dumplings, flour your hands and roll 1 tablespoon of the fish at a time into 1"-long balls. Fill a pot with salted water to the depth of 4", bring to a low boil, then gently lower the dumplings into the water. Poach for 2–3 minutes or until firm. Remove, drain, and serve warm with the curry sauce.

CHAPTER 13

Lamb Dishes

Swedish Frost-Bump Lamb (*Tjälknöl*) with Cardamom-Currant Sauce

While tjälknöl ("frost bump") is most often prepared in Sweden from frozen wild game roasts, it's perhaps even better when made with lamb.

INGREDIENTS | SERVES 8–10

1 (6-pound) boneless leg of lamb, frozen

6 cups water

6 tablespoons salt

3 cloves garlic, pressed

1 tablespoon coriander seeds

1 teaspoon fennel seeds

2 bay leaves

Cardamom-Currant Sauce (see sidebar recipe)

Cardamom-Currant Sauce

Combine ⅓ cup red wine or port, 1 cup red currant jelly, 1 tablespoon grated orange zest, ½ tablespoon grated lemon zest, ½ cup orange juice, 1 tablespoon brown sugar, and 1 teaspoon ground cardamom in a saucepan. Bring to a simmer over medium heat; reduce heat to low and cook for 15 minutes, stirring occasionally. Remove from the heat and allow to cool and thicken.

1. Preheat oven to 170°F.

2. Place the frozen lamb on a rack in a roasting pan, then place it on the lowest rack of the oven.

3. Cook the lamb until a thermometer inserted in the thickest part of the roast registers 150°F (check it at 8 hours, then every half hour thereafter until it reaches 150°F). Remove from the oven.

4. To make the brine, combine the water, salt, garlic, coriander seeds, fennel seeds, and bay leaves in a large pot and bring to a boil. Stir until all of the salt has dissolved, then remove from heat and allow to cool completely.

5. Place the roasted lamb into the brine (the brine needs to cover the lamb completely), then refrigerate for 5 hours.

6. To serve, remove the lamb from the brine, pat dry, and slice thinly. Accompany the dish with the Cardamom-Currant Sauce.

Roasted Lamb Stuffed with Mushroom Pilaf

This recipe features tender roasted lamb, enriched with a blend of forest mushrooms and barley.

INGREDIENTS | SERVES 8

3 ounces dried chanterelle, morel, and porcini mushrooms

2 tablespoons canola or olive oil, divided use

1 cup button mushrooms, finely chopped

½ red onion, finely chopped

1 celery stalk, finely chopped

1 tablespoon garlic, finely chopped

1 cup cooked barley

¼ cup fresh thyme leaves, divided use

1 boned and butterflied leg of lamb, fell removed

1 teaspoon salt

½ teaspoon pepper

1. Place the dried mushrooms in enough hot water to cover and let them sit for 30 minutes to reconstitute. Drain, pat dry, then coarsely chop.

2. Preheat oven to 400°F. Heat a frying pan over a medium burner, pour in 1 tablespoon of the oil, then sauté the button mushrooms, onion, celery, and garlic until they soften. Remove from heat and stir in the reconstituted wild mushrooms, barley, and 2 tablespoons of the thyme.

3. Place the lamb, skin side down, on a counter and pound with a meat mallet to an even ½" thickness. Spread the stuffing over the meat, leaving a ½" border around the edges. Roll tightly, jellyroll fashion, then tie the bundle with kitchen string.

4. Rub the outside of the lamb with the remaining tablespoon of oil, then sprinkle with the remaining thyme, salt, and pepper. Place on a rack, seam-side down, over a roasting pan.

5. Roast the lamb in the middle of the oven for 30 minutes, then reduce heat to 360°F and roast for an additional hour. Remove from the oven, tent with foil for 15 minutes, then slice and serve.

Juniper Smoked Leg of Lamb

Brining lamb then smoking it over juniper branches gives it a special flavor reminiscent of the smoked lamb from Iceland and Finland. Although juniper berries are safe for adults, you should not consume them if you are pregnant, have cancer or kidney disease, or are younger than 12.

INGREDIENTS | SERVES 8–10

2 tablespoons juniper berries, divided use

2 tablespoons peppercorns

3 bay leaves, crumbled

½ cup plus 1 teaspoon salt, divided use

½ cup sugar

2 quarts water

1 leg of lamb, boned and butterflied, fell removed

3 cups alder chips

A few juniper branches

5 cloves garlic, chopped

1 tablespoon lemon zest

3 tablespoons lemon juice

½ teaspoon pepper

½ cup canola or olive oil

Hangikjöt

The preparation and enjoyment of *hangikjöt*—lamb, mutton, or even horse-meat that has been brined, cold-smoked, then hung to dry for several weeks—is a time-honored tradition in Iceland. Unfortunately, it is a difficult dish to replicate in an American home kitchen, requiring a lengthy bout of cold-smoking in a smoke-house environment (traditionally, the meat was smoked over dried sheep dung). For a great description of how to prepare *hangikjöt*, go online and visit one of the best Icelandic recipe sites on the web: Jo's Icelandic Recipes (*www.isholf.is/gullis/jo*).

1. Place 1 tablespoon of the juniper berries, peppercorns, crumbled bay leaves, ½ cup salt, and sugar in a food processor and pulse until the berries and peppercorns are ground. Combine with 2 quarts water into a brine in a dish large enough to hold the lamb. Place the lamb in the brine, making sure it is fully covered; if not, add more water. Cover and refrigerate for 24 hours.

2. Soak the alder chips in enough water to cover for 1 hour. Place the juniper branches in a bucket of water.

3. Combine the remaining tablespoon of juniper berries, garlic, lemon zest, lemon juice, 1 teaspoon salt, and pepper in a food processor, then pulse into a paste. Pour the oil into the paste in a steady stream, pulsing steadily to combine.

4. Remove the lamb from the brine, then place the brine in the water pan of your smoker. Prick the lamb all over deeply with a sharp knife, then rub the paste into the skin.

5. Spread 1 cup of the soaked alder chips over the coals or heating element of the smoker; place the water pan with the brine into position. Grease the top rack, place the lamb on top, and close the smoker. Smoke for 2–3 hours, turning the lamb and adding more chips every hour, until a thermometer inserted into the thickest portion registers 135°F.

6. When the thermometer registers 135°F, shake the juniper branches to remove excess water, then place them directly on top of the heating element. Cover the smoker and continue to smoke until the lamb reaches an internal temperature of 145°F (for medium rare). Remove from the smoker, allow to sit for 15 minutes, then carve.

Cabbage Rolls with Ground Lamb (*Kåldolmar med Lammfärs*)

Lightly blanched cabbage leaves provide a healthy "wrap" for ground lamb and onions in this Swedish classic.

INGREDIENTS | SERVES 4

8 large cabbage leaves
1 pound ground lamb
½ cup fresh bread crumbs
¼ cup onion, finely minced
1 cup whipping cream, divided use
1 egg
2 tablespoons fresh parsley, minced
2 teaspoons fresh thyme, minced
1 teaspoon salt
¼ teaspoon pepper
1 cup rice (your choice), cooked
3 tablespoons butter
2 tablespoons Swedish light syrup or
  light corn syrup
⅔ cup white wine

1. Preheat oven to 400°F. Place the cabbage leaves in a large frying pan with enough water to cover by ½"; bring to a boil and maintain boil for 1 minute. Drain the leaves through a colander and rinse with cold water; pat the pan dry with a towel.

2. Combine the lamb, bread crumbs, onion, ½ cup of the whipping cream, egg, parsley, thyme, salt, and pepper in a food processor; pulse until combined into a smooth paste. Fold this mixture together with the prepared rice.

3. Place ⅛ of the mixture near the short (stem) end of a cabbage leaf and roll up, like an enchilada, tucking in the ends as you go. Repeat for the remaining cabbage rolls.

4. Melt the butter in the frying pan over medium heat, then stir in the syrup. Place the rolls in the pan, seam-side down, and fry until golden, turning once. Transfer the rolls, seam-side down, to a 9" × 13" casserole dish. Increase the heat under the pan to high and pour in the wine to deglaze, scraping up the browned bits. Whisk well, then pour this mixture over the cabbage rolls in the baking dish. Place in oven and bake for 1 hour or until tender and cooked through.

5. Remove the cabbage rolls from the casserole and drain the pan juices into the frying pan. Boil over high heat until reduced to a glaze-like consistency, then stir in the remaining ½ cup whipping cream. Season this sauce with salt and pepper to taste, then drizzle over the cabbage rolls.

Juniper-Braised Lamb Shanks

Proof-positive of the unparalleled tenderness that results from slow-cooking lamb, these lamb shanks almost melt off the bone. Accompany them with egg noodles or garlic mashed potatoes to soak up the rich sauce.

INGREDIENTS | SERVES 6

6 lamb shanks
Salt and pepper to season lamb
¼ cup canola oil
1 onion, peeled and finely diced
1 celery rib, finely diced
1 large carrot, finely diced
1 tablespoon flour
3 cloves garlic, minced
½ cup good red wine
1 cup chicken broth
1 tablespoon white wine vinegar
1 cup water
2 teaspoons juniper berries (or substitute 6 sprigs fresh thyme)
5 anchovies, chopped

Juniper Berries

Sharply pungent juniper berries are a favorite seasoning in Scandinavia, used to add a resinous note to game dishes, to flavor schnapps and pickled herring, or as a key ingredient in marinades. Juniper berries can be used both fresh and dried; simply remove them from dishes (as you would a bay leaf) after cooking. Warning: because they have diuretic properties and can cause abdominal cramping, juniper berries should not be used in food to be served to children under 12, persons with kidney disease or cancer, or women who are pregnant/nursing.

1. Preheat oven to 325°F.

2. Season the lamb shanks with salt and pepper. Heat the oil in a large frying pan over medium-high heat, add the lamb shanks, and sear on all sides (about 2 minutes per side). Transfer the shanks to a roasting pan large enough to hold them in a single layer.

3. Pour off all but 3 tablespoons of the fat from the pan, then add the onion, celery, and carrot. Cook over medium-high until the vegetables are soft and begin to brown, about 7 minutes. Stir the flour and garlic into the vegetables and cook for 1 minute more.

4. Pour the wine over the vegetables and bring to a boil. Add the chicken broth, vinegar, water, juniper berries, and anchovies. Bring to a boil once more, then remove from heat.

5. Pour the sauce over the lamb shanks. Use heavy-duty aluminum foil to cover the roasting pan, sealing tightly around the edges. Roast for 1 hour, then remove the foil and turn the shanks over. Replace the foil and cook for 1 additional hour until tender. Transfer the shanks to a serving bowl and tent with foil to keep warm.

6. Pour the liquids from the roasting pan into a saucepan and boil over high heat until reduced by half, about 10 minutes, skimming off fat as it rises to the top. Season to taste with additional salt and pepper, pour over the lamb shanks, and serve.

Rustic Lamb Pie with *Snøfrisk* Cheese

Use your favorite double pie crust for this elegantly simple ground lamb pie, or—if you have time—make the Spelt Pie Crust from Chapter 9.

INGREDIENTS | SERVES 6

2 Spelt Pie Crusts (see Chapter 9, or substitute your favorite double crust)

1 pound ground lamb

1 cup fresh mushrooms, sliced

½ cup red onion, chopped

2 cloves garlic, finely chopped

½ teaspoon pepper

¼ teaspoon dried thyme

1 can condensed cream of potato soup

1 (4.4-ounce) package *Snøfrisk* fresh spreadable cheese, room temperature

½ cup sour cream

1 egg, beaten

1. Preheat oven to 375°F. Line the bottom of a 9" pie pan with the first crust.

2. In a large skillet over medium-high heat, brown the ground lamb, mushrooms, onion, and garlic together until the meat has cooked through, stirring to prevent sticking, about 10 minutes. Drain off any accumulated fat.

3. Add the pepper, thyme, potato soup, and *Snøfrisk*, stirring until the cheese has melted. Fold in the sour cream, then transfer the mixture to the pie crust.

4. Top with the second crust; seal and flute the edges, and cut a few vents in the top. Brush well with the beaten egg.

5. Bake for 45–50 minutes or until the crust is golden brown. Remove from oven, allow to sit for 10 minutes, then slice and serve.

Lamb Kabobs with Salt-Grilled Potatoes

You'll love these grilled Icelandic lamb kabobs, accompanied with salt-grilled potatoes and tarragon-infused Béarnaise sauce.

INGREDIENTS | SERVES 10

½ cup olive oil

¼ cup white wine vinegar

4 cloves garlic, pressed

1 tablespoon dried tarragon

1 teaspoon salt

1 teaspoon pepper

1 boneless leg of lamb

2 pounds baby potatoes

Kosher salt, as needed

Béarnaise sauce (homemade or made from a Knorr packet)

Easy Eggless Béarnaise Sauce

Sauté 1 tablespoon minced shallots in 2 teaspoons butter until soft, about 3 minutes. Stir in 1 tablespoon white wine vinegar, 1 tablespoon lemon juice, 1 teaspoon dried tarragon, and 1 teaspoon lemon zest and bring to a boil; cook for 1 more minute. Strain the liquid, then return it to the saucepan; stir in ½ cup sour cream and cook over low heat, stirring occasionally, until warmed through. Season to taste with salt and pepper.

1. Whisk together the oil, vinegar, garlic, tarragon, salt, and pepper into a marinade. Chop the lamb into 2" cubes, then cover with the marinade. Refrigerate for 1 hour.

2. Cover the bottom of 2 (8" or 9") aluminum foil pans with kosher salt. Distribute the potatoes in a single layer in the pans, then add enough salt to cover. Place on the top rack of a grill set at medium heat, close the lid, and bake for 45 minutes or until fork-tender. Remove from the grill, then increase the heat to high.

3. Thread the marinated lamb onto skewers. Place them on the grill, reduce heat to medium-high, and grill until done, turning to brown all sides evenly, about 10 minutes

4. To serve, brush the salt off the potatoes, then place them in a serving dish. Accompany the lamb and potatoes with Béarnaise Sauce and a salad.

Lamb Loaf with Savory Mushroom Sauce

Ground lamb, typically less fatty than hamburger, also creates a denser, more flavorful loaf. Keep the loaf simple, then sauce it up with a savory mushroom-blue cheese gravy.

INGREDIENTS | SERVES 8

¾ cup milk

1 egg, beaten

½ cup rye crispbread, finely crumbled

¼ cup onion, finely chopped

1 tablespoon fresh parsley, finely chopped

1 teaspoon dried sage, divided use

1 teaspoon salt

⅛ teaspoon pepper

2 pounds ground lamb

3 ounces mixed dried mushrooms (chanterelle, moral, porcini)

1 cup boiling water

1 tablespoon canola or olive oil

1 tablespoon butter

1 cup button mushrooms, quartered

½ ounce Danish blue cheese, crumbled

2 teaspoons Lingonberry Jam (see Chapter 7, or substitute red currant jelly)

½ cup half-and-half

Salt and pepper to taste

1. Preheat oven to 350°F.

2. In a large bowl, combine the milk, egg, crispbread crumbs, onion, parsley, ½ teaspoon of the sage, salt, and pepper, then use your hands to mix the ground lamb into the mixture. Form into a loaf and place in a greased 9" × 5" loaf pan.

3. Bake for 1 hour or until internal temperature of lamb meatloaf registers 160°F.

4. As the meatloaf cooks, make your sauce: Place the dried mushrooms in the boiling water and allow to reconstitute for 15 minutes. Drain, reserving ½ cup of the mushroom liquid.

5. Melt the oil and butter together in a saucepan, then add the button mushrooms and sauté over medium-high heat until the mushrooms begin to weep, about 3 minutes. Reduce heat to medium, then stir in the reconstituted mushrooms, the reserved mushroom liquid, the remaining ½ teaspoon dried sage, blue cheese, Lingonberry Jam, and half-and-half. Warm through, then season with salt and pepper to taste.

6. To serve, slice the lamb loaf and drizzle with the sauce.

Caraway-Encrusted Rack of Lamb with Chilled Dill Sauce

One thing that should never be overlooked—like seasoning—by those who seek to boost flavors is the sensory explosion that occurs when you pair warm-from-the-oven roasted meat with an ice-cold sauce. It's like jumping into a chilly, pristine forest lake immediately after a Finnish sauna.

INGREDIENTS | SERVES 6

1 shallot, peeled and finely minced

1 large garlic clove, peeled and finely minced

1 teaspoon kosher salt

½ teaspoon white pepper

1 tablespoon lemon juice

¼ cup fresh dill, finely chopped

8 ounces *skyr* or plain low-fat Greek yogurt

2 trimmed racks of lamb (1½ pounds each)

1 teaspoon dried dill

Salt and black pepper to season

1 tablespoon vegetable oil

1 tablespoon butter

1 tablespoon caraway seeds

2 tablespoons fresh rye breadcrumbs

3 tablespoons Swedish or Dijon mustard

To Sear or Not to Sear

It's true that it is unnecessary to sear domestic meat (lean beef and pork) before roasting (at least with the intent of "sealing" in the juices, which is an old wives' tale). However, searing does promote the Maillard reaction: the caramelization that makes the outside crust of meat so delicious. With a fatty meat like lamb—especially if it's encrusted with a breading on the outside—go ahead and sear to your heart's content (so long as it's only for a minute or two on each side).

1. For the sauce, combine the shallot, garlic, kosher salt, white pepper, lemon juice, and dill, then fold it together with the *skyr* or yogurt. Cover and refrigerate for at least 3 hours.

2. Preheat oven to 400°F.

3. Sprinkle both sides of the lamb racks with the dried dill and a pinch of salt and black pepper. Heat vegetable oil in a frying pan over a medium-high burner, then sear the lamb racks on both sides, about 2 minutes per side. Remove from the heat; place the racks, bone-side down, in a roasting pan.

4. Return the pan to the burner and add the butter. Once it's frothy, stir in the caraway seeds and bread crumbs, and stir-fry until the crumbs have browned, about 3 minutes. Season the crumbs with a generous pinch of salt and pepper; remove from heat.

5. Spread the top and sides of the lamb racks with the mustard, then press the breading mixture evenly over the racks. Bake in the oven for 20 minutes or until a thermometer registers 130°F (for medium-rare). Remove from oven, tent with foil, and allow to sit for 10 minutes.

6. To serve, cut the lamb racks into two-rib slices and plate, accompanied with the chilled dill sauce.

Smoked Lamb Chops with a Lingonberry Sauce Reduction

Reverse-searing these lamb chops after oven-smoking gives them a crispy edge not possible by smoking alone and also adds a richer flavor to the lingonberry sauce reduction. Serve with the smoked potatoes and a simple shelled pea salad as a luscious late-spring supper.

INGREDIENTS | SERVES 4

2 tablespoons canola oil

4 tablespoons lingonberry vinegar, divided use (or substitute cranberry vinegar)

1 teaspoon white pepper

1 teaspoon salt

8 (1½"-thick) lamb chops

12 new potatoes, halved

1 SAVU Smoker Bag (Alder)

2 tablespoons butter

½ cup white wine

2 shallots, minced

½ cup lamb broth (or substitute vegetable broth)

¼ cup Lingonberry Jam (see Chapter 7)

½ teaspoon ground cardamom

1. Whisk the 2 tablespoons canola oil, 3 tablespoons lingonberry vinegar, white pepper, and salt into a marinade. Place the lamb chops in a pan just large enough to hold them in a single layer; pour the marinade over them, cover, and refrigerate for 2 hours.

2. Preheat oven to 475°F. Place the lamb chops and potatoes in the smoker bag, seal the bag tightly, and cook for 15 minutes. Reduce heat to 350°F and cook for 20 more minutes.

3. Melt the butter over medium-high heat in a large frying pan, then transfer the smoked lamb chops immediately from the bag to the pan. Sear for 1 minute on each side; transfer to a plate and tent with foil.

4. Pour the wine into the pan to deglaze the bottom, scraping up any browned bits, then toss in the shallots, stirring constantly until the wine has reduced almost completely. Whisk in the broth and maintain a fast simmer until the liquid has reduced by half.

5. Add the Lingonberry Jam, remaining tablespoon of lingonberry vinegar, and cardamom. Stir until the mixture thickens into a smooth reduction, about 5 minutes.

6. Transfer the lamb chops and potatoes to individual plates and drizzle with the lingonberry sauce reduction.

Swedish Lamb Fricassee (*Svensk Lammefrikassé*)

Farm-fresh vegetables combined with grass-fed lamb in a creamy sauce; this dish is a salute to the superiority of simple ingredients when they're harvested and cooked in season.

INGREDIENTS | SERVES 4

3 tablespoons canola or olive oil

2 pounds lamb, cut in 1" chunks

2 cups lamb broth (or water)

Salt and pepper to season

2 whole leeks, washed and chopped

3 large carrots, peeled and chopped into matchsticks

1 turnip, peeled and chopped

1 stalk celery, diced

2 tablespoons potato starch flour (or cornstarch) plus 2 tablespoons water

½ cup fresh dill, minced

½ cup shelled peas

Slow Cooker Lamb Broth

To make lamb broth, place 4 pounds of lamb bones in a slow cooker. Add enough water to cover by 2", 2 tablespoons cider vinegar, 1 chopped carrot, 1 chopped onion, and 1 chopped celery stalk. Cook on low for at least 12 and up to 24 hours, skimming off the froth occasionally. Use immediately or freeze until needed.

1. Heat the oil in the bottom of a large frying pan over medium heat. Add the lamb and sauté on all sides until it's browned. Pour the lamb broth (or water) over the lamb, add a pinch of salt and pepper, turn the heat to medium-low, and cover. Cook for 1 hour or until the lamb is tender and cooked through (check it occasionally and skim off any froth that rises to the top).

2. Add the leeks, carrots, turnip, and celery to the pan, increase heat to medium, and simmer, uncovered, until the vegetables are crisp-tender, about 15–20 minutes.

3. Once the vegetables are cooked, transfer them and the lamb to a deep serving bowl. Whisk the potato starch flour and the 2 tablespoons water together, then stir this into the remaining pan liquid to thicken. Stir in the chopped dill and the fresh peas, then immediately fold the sauce into the lamb and vegetables in the serving dish.

4. Serve in bowls, with warm homemade bread or flatbread.

Lamb Pâté

Enjoy this tender pâté as is, as an appetizer on toasted bread points, or use it to accent Company Lamb in Puff Pastry (see recipe in this chapter).

INGREDIENTS | SERVES 6–8

4 slices thick-cut smoked bacon, finely chopped

1 pound lamb liver

2 shallots, peeled and finely diced

½ cup mushrooms, finely diced

1 clove garlic, peeled and finely diced

1 tablespoon fresh thyme, chopped

½ teaspoon cayenne pepper

2 tablespoons brandy

1. Fry the bacon in a skillet over medium-high heat until crispy.

2. Add the lamb liver, shallots, mushrooms, garlic, thyme, and cayenne; stir-fry until the liver is cooked through but still moist and slightly pink inside. Transfer the contents of the pan to a food processor, then deglaze the pan with the brandy. Scrape up the browned pits and then pour into the processor.

3. Pulse the mixture until it is as coarse or as fine as you like it (if it's too thick, thin it with olive oil or melted butter).

4. Use a spatula to spread the pâté in a narrow mold or in individual ramekins. Allow to cool to room temperature, then transfer to the refrigerator and chill for at least 30 minutes before serving.

Company Lamb in Puff Pastry

Wow your guests with lamb, pâté, and a duxelle of mushrooms tucked into puff pastry.

INGREDIENTS | SERVES 4

1 pound fresh mushrooms

1 tablespoon shallots, finely diced

½ cup white wine

2 teaspoons fresh rosemary, finely minced

4 (4-ounce) boneless lamb steaks

Salt and pepper to taste

1 tablespoon butter

1 tablespoon canola or olive oil

1 sheet puff pastry, thawed

⅓ cup Lamb Pâté (see recipe in this chapter)

2 eggs, beaten with 1 tablespoon water into an egg wash

1. Place the mushrooms and shallots in a food processor and pulse until finely ground. Heat a nonstick frying pan over medium-high; transfer the mushrooms to the pan and cook, stirring often, until the mushrooms have released most of their water. When they are dry, pour in the wine to deglaze the pan. Stir in the rosemary and simmer until the liquid has all been absorbed. Remove from heat and cool.

2. Season the lamb steaks on both sides with salt and pepper. Heat the butter and oil together in a frying pan over medium-high heat, add the lamb, and sear on each side, about 2 minutes per side. Transfer to a plate and allow to cool.

3. On a floured counter, cut the sheet of pastry into quarters, then roll out each quarter until it's large enough to completely encase a steak (about 4½"). Take half of the cooled mushroom mixture and distribute it evenly between the centers of the pastry sheets.

4. Use half of the pâté to "frost" one side of the cooled steaks, then place them, pâté-side down, on the mushrooms. "Frost" the tops with the remaining pâté, then divide the remaining mushrooms on top, pressing down slightly with the back of a spoon.

5. Use a pastry brush to coat all of the exposed edges of the pastry well with the egg wash, then fold up the edges to encase the lamb. Seal the edges, then place them seam-side down on a baking sheet. Chill in the refrigerator for 30 minutes.

6. Preheat oven to 400°F. Brush the tops and sides of the pastry bundles with the remaining egg wash and prick the tops in a few places with a fork to vent. Place in the oven and cook until golden brown, about 25 minutes.

Chocolate Waffles (Chapter 7)

Våsterbotten Cheese Crisps with Fresh Pears (Chapter 2)

Gingersnap Meatballs (Chapter 2)

Chilled Cucumber Soup (Chapter 3)

Lamb Kabobs with Salt-Grilled Potatoes (Chapter 13)

Chocolate Sticky Cake/*Kladdkaka* (Chapter 18)

Hasselback Potatoes (Chapter 11)

Carrot and Potato Bake (Chapter 11)

Karelian Hot Pot/*Karjalanpaisti* (Chapter 3)

Flying Jacob/*Flygende Jacob* (Chapter 14)

Danish Oatmeal Porridge/*Havregrød* (Chapter 10)

Venison Steaks with Juniper Berry Sauce (Chapter 15)

Icelandic Scones/*Skonsur* (Chapter 5)

Swedish Hash/*Pytt i Panna* (Chapter 14)

Jarlsberg Omelette (Chapter 9)

Danish *Tykmælk* (Chapter 8)

Finnish Strawberry Snow/*Mansikkalumi* (Chapter 16)

Macaroni Casserole with *Nøkkelost* Cheese (Chapter 8)

Danish *Æggekage* ("Egg Cake") with Bacon and Tomatoes (Chapter 9)

Danish Apple Soup/*Aeblesuppe* (Chapter 16)

Finnish Cinnamon Pastries/*Korvapuusti* (Chapter 17)

New Potato Salad (Chapter 4)

Finnish Oven-Baked Pancake/*Pannakakku* (Chapter 7)

Smoked Trout with Summer Vegetables (Chapter 12)

CHAPTER 14

Domestic Pork, Beef, and Poultry

Fruit-Stuffed Pork Tenderloin

This recipe features juicy pork tenderloin stuffed to the seams with prunes, apples, and dried cranberries.

INGREDIENTS | SERVES 6–8

8½ cups water, divided use
8 tablespoons kosher salt
8 tablespoons brown sugar
1 tablespoon whole cloves
2 cinnamon sticks, crumbled
1 (4-pound) pork tenderloin, boned
8 pitted prunes
¼ cup dried cranberries
1 large apple, peeled and chopped
½ teaspoon ground ginger
¼ teaspoon ground allspice
½ teaspoon salt
¼ teaspoon white pepper
2 cups white wine
1 tablespoon cornstarch plus 1 tablespoon water, whisked into a slurry
4 tablespoons red currant jam or Lingonberry Jam (see Chapter 7)

1. To make your brine, bring 8 cups of the water, kosher salt, brown sugar, cloves, and crumbled cinnamon sticks to a boil. Reduce heat to a steady simmer and cook for 15 minutes. Remove from heat and cool completely.

2. Using a sharp knife, slit the tenderloin open length-wise and parallel to the counter, so that it looks like an envelope (don't cut all of the way through the loin). Submerge the tenderloin completely in the brine, cover, and refrigerate for at least 12 hours.

3. Remove the tenderloin from the brine and pat dry. Place the prunes and the dried cranberries in a bowl with enough hot water to cover; allow to plump for 20 minutes.

4. Drain the prunes and cranberries, then coarsely chop the prunes. Toss together with the cranberries and chopped apple, then spoon the mixture evenly into the slit of the pork loin. Tie the loin with kitchen string to secure the stuffing inside, then sprinkle the loin on all sides with the ground ginger, allspice, salt, and white pepper.

5. Preheat oven to 325°F. Place the stuffed pork loin on a rack in the middle of a roasting pan, then pour the white wine and ½ cup of water in the bottom of the pan. Place in the oven and cook for 45 minutes, or until a meat thermometer registers 145°F, basting with the pan juices every 20 minutes.

Fruit-Stuffed Pork Tenderloin (continued)

To Sear or Not to Sear Redux: The Maillard Reaction

One of the greatest misconceptions of the past century has been that searing meat before cooking it "seals" in the juices. In fact, an initial searing actually reduces the moisture content of meat ("scarring" it and making it weep moisture much like a burn does). In order to both retain moisture and achieve the Maillard reaction responsible for browning and intensifying the flavor of a roast, replace the initial sear with a short broil in the oven at the end of the cooking cycle.

6. Remove the pan from the oven; increase the heat to 500°F. Transfer the pork to a cutting board, strain the pan juices into a heat-resistant measuring cup, then place the tenderloin back in the pan. Return it to the top rack of the oven and broil the pork loin, 1–2 minutes per side, flipping once (watch it carefully to prevent over-browning). Remove the pork loin from the oven, return it to the cutting board, and tent it over with aluminum foil for 10 minutes.

7. For your sauce, skim away the fat from the pan juices, then transfer the liquid to a saucepan. Heat the pan on the stove, bringing it to a steady simmer and cooking until the liquid is reduced to 1½ cups; slowly whisk in the slurry to thicken the sauce. Stir in the jam.

8. To serve, remove the string from the stuffed pork loin and cut into 1" slices. Place on a platter, presenting the gravy on the side.

Roast Pork with Crackling

Although far too rich to consume every day, roast pork with crackling is a beloved holiday treat in Iceland and Denmark, where the juicy outer layer of fat is served alongside the meat. Enjoy with gusto and delight (then swear off fast-food burgers for a month).

INGREDIENTS | SERVES 8–10

1 gallon water

1 cup table salt

½ cup maple syrup, molasses, or Swedish dark syrup

1 tablespoon whole cloves

1 (5-pound) pork shoulder with a thick layer of fat

1 tablespoon kosher salt

1 teaspoon fennel seeds

1 teaspoon whole mustard seeds

3 bay leaves, crumbled

3 cups boiling water

Brining Pork

Although today's pork is far leaner (and healthier) than it was in our grandparents' day, the downside of this is that the meat is also much less juicy. Compensate for this by always brining pork loins and pork chops at least 12 hours before cooking. You can be creative with your brine—start with 8 cups water or apple juice, 8 tablespoons kosher salt, and 8 tablespoons sugar, then add additional herbs and/or spices to your taste.

1. Combine 1 gallon water, table salt, maple syrup, and whole cloves into a brine. Submerge the pork completely, cover, and refrigerate for at least 12 hours but no longer than 24. Remove the pork from the brine, rinse, and pat dry with paper towels.

2. Preheat oven to 450°F. Use a sharp knife to score the outside layer of fat into a cross-hatch pattern.

3. Mix together the kosher salt, fennel seeds, mustard seeds, and crumbled bay leaves, then rub the mixture all over the pork, including down into the seams of the cross-hatched fat.

4. Place the roast on a rack over a deep roasting pan and bake in the center of the oven until the crackling is crisp and golden, about 30 minutes. Reduce the heat to 350°F and pour boiling water into the bottom of the roasting pan (*be careful that the steam does not burn you!*). Cook for an additional hour until a thermometer inserted in the center of the roast registers 160°F.

5. When the roast is fully cooked, remove the crackling, slice into thin pieces, and serve alongside the sliced pork.

Mock Hare (*Forloren Hare*)

You've got to love the Danes' name for meatloaf: "Mock Hare." This makes a beautiful company dish—slice the "hare" thin, offer a generous tossed salad alongside, and serve with new potatoes and crusty bread to soak up the rich gravy.

INGREDIENTS | SERVES 8

½ pound minced veal

½ pound minced pork

½ cup dried bread crumbs

1 medium onion, peeled and finely minced

¼ cup fresh parsley, finely chopped

1 egg

½ cup half-and-half, divided use

¼ cup seltzer water

10–12 slices bacon

1 cup milk

1 cup beef bouillon

1 tablespoon flour

1 tablespoon water

1 tablespoon red currant jelly

1 teaspoon gravy browning (Kitchen Bouquet or other)

Salt and pepper to taste

1. Preheat oven to 435°F. Combine the veal, pork, bread crumbs, onion, parsley, egg, ¼ cup of the half-and-half, and seltzer water in a food processor; pulse until finely chopped. Form into a loaf, ½" shorter than your bacon strips.

2. Overlap 4 slices of bacon side-by-side in the bottom of a deep casserole dish, then place the meatloaf on top. Encase the top and sides completely, from one end of the loaf to the other, with slightly overlapping strips of bacon.

3. Place in the oven and cook for 15 minutes to brown the bacon. Reduce heat to 325°F; whisk together the milk and beef bouillon, then pour them into the pan around the meatloaf. Cook for an additional 30 minutes.

4. To make a sauce for the meatloaf, transfer the cooked loaf to a cutting board. Skim the fat from the pan liquid then transfer the liquid to a saucepan, along with the remaining ¼ cup of half-and-half. In a separate bowl, make a slurry of the flour and water. Bring the sauce to a steady simmer, then stir in the slurry to thicken. Whisk in the red currant jelly and gravy browning; season to taste with salt and pepper.

5. Slice the meatloaf into 8 thin slices and serve with potatoes, the sauce, and a large salad.

Swedish Castle Fry (*Slotsstek*)

This is a basic recipe for Swedish "Royal Pot Roast" (historically called "Castle Fry" since the days when large roasts of meat were enjoyed primarily by the rich), adapted for the slow cooker.

INGREDIENTS | SERVES 4

1 (4-pound) boneless chuck roast

½ teaspoon salt

¼ teaspoon pepper

1 red onion, peeled and cut into thin wedges

1 celery stalk, coarsely chopped

2 cups beef bouillon

5 Abba Seafood brand anchovy-style sprat fillets (or substitute regular anchovies)

4 teaspoons anchovy paste

5 peppercorns

5 whole allspice

2 bay leaves

1 tablespoon white vinegar

2 tablespoons Swedish dark syrup (or substitute molasses)

1 tablespoon flour

1 tablespoon water

4 tablespoons red currant or Lingonberry Jam (see Chapter 7)

1. Season the roast all over with the salt and pepper.

2. Place the red onion and celery in the bottom of your slow cooker, then transfer the roast to the cooker.

3. In a large bowl, whisk together the bouillon, sprats, anchovy paste, peppercorns, allspice, bay leaves, vinegar, and dark syrup; pour over the roast. Cover the slow cooker and cook on low for 8–10 hours or on high for 4–5 hours.

4. After the roast has cooked, transfer it to a cutting board, allow to cool slightly, then slice. Strain the solids from the liquid that remains in the slow cooker. Pour the strained juices into a saucepan and heat to a simmer. Whisk the flour and water together into a slurry, and stir into the juices to thicken. Stir in the red currant or Lingonberry Jam; serve as an accompaniment to the roast.

Danish *Millionbøf*

The expressive name of this simple yet tasty Danish meat sauce refers to the millions of pieces that the ground beef crumbles into when fried. Serve it over mashed potatoes for a hearty winter dinner.

INGREDIENTS | SERVES 4

1 tablespoon butter
1 tablespoon canola oil
1 pound lean hamburger
1 large onion, finely chopped
1 tablespoon flour
2⅓ cups beef bouillon
2 teaspoons gravy browning (Kitchen Bouquet or other)
Salt and pepper to taste
Mashed potatoes

1. Melt the butter and oil together over medium heat in a large frying pan. Stir in the hamburger and chopped onion, and fry until the hamburger is browned.

2. Sprinkle the flour over the hamburger, give it a stir, then pour in the bouillon. Increase heat until the mixture bubbles, then reduce to a low simmer. Cover and cook until most of the liquid has been absorbed, about 20 minutes. Stir in the Kitchen Bouquet to darken; season to taste with salt and pepper.

3. Serve the hamburger mixture over mashed potatoes.

Swedish Hash (*Pytt i Panna*)

Pytt i panna (also pyttipanna) is the consummate "leftover" recipe. Simply use whatever meat you have left over from the previous evening meal (steak, ham, lamb) to flavor this tasty "next day" hash.

INGREDIENTS | SERVES 6

6 slices bacon
4 baking potatoes, peeled and diced
3 tablespoons butter
1 medium onion, peeled and diced
1 teaspoon white pepper
½ teaspoon salt
1 pinch of ground allspice
1–2 cups leftover meat, diced small
6 eggs

1. Chop the bacon into ¼" pieces and fry in a large frying pan until golden. Drain off the bacon fat, then add the diced potatoes and butter to the pan. Cook over medium-high heat, stirring constantly, until the potatoes are golden.

2. Add the onion to the pan and stir-fry until cooked through, about 5 minutes.

3. Sprinkle the mixture with the white pepper, salt, and allspice, then stir in the leftover cubed meat. Cook for an additional 5 minutes, stirring constantly to prevent sticking.

4. In a separate pan, fry the 6 eggs sunny-side up.

5. Transfer the hash to plates and top each portion with a fried egg. Accompany with pickled beets and gherkin pickles.

Biff à la Lindström

*Here's a homemade version of Sweden's own piquant hamburgers,
developed by chef Henrik Lindström at the Hotell Witt in Kalmar in 1862.*

INGREDIENTS | SERVES 4

1 pound ground beef

⅔ cup onion, finely chopped

5 eggs, divided use

¼ cup seltzer water

¾ cup pickled beets, chopped into a ¼" dice

2 tablespoons pickled beet juice

1 tablespoon capers

1 teaspoon salt

¼ teaspoon pepper

3 tablespoons butter

1 tablespoon canola or olive oil

1. Gently fold all of the ingredients together except for the butter, oil, and 4 of the eggs. The mixture will be soft and sticky.

2. Flour your hands, then with a light touch form the mixture into 4 large patties.

3. Heat 2 tablespoons of the butter and the oil in a frying pan over medium heat; fry the patties to your desired doneness. Transfer to plates.

4. Melt the remaining tablespoon of butter in the pan and fry the remaining eggs, sunny-side up.

5. Place a fried egg on each of the burgers and serve.

Flying Jacob (*Flygende Jacob*)

*Tradition has it that this popular "comfort" dish was created by a Swedish Air Freight worker,
Ove Jacobsson. Use a store-bought rotisserie chicken to simplify the preparation.*

INGREDIENTS | SERVES 4–6

1 fully cooked rotisserie chicken

3 cups cooked rice

4 bananas

2 cups light cream

⅔ cup chili sauce or spicy ketchup

8 ounces bacon, fried and crumbled

¾ cup peanuts, chopped

1. Preheat oven to 395°F. Pull the meat off the rotisserie chicken, discarding the skin and bones. Coarsely shred the chicken.

2. Spread the cooked rice in the bottom of a casserole dish and then cover with the shredded chicken. Slice the bananas and place them in a single layer over the chicken.

3. Whip the cream to soft peaks, then fold the chili sauce into it. Use a spatula to spread it over the bananas, then sprinkle the crumbled bacon and chopped peanuts over the top.

4. Place the casserole in the oven and cook for 20 minutes, until the sauce browns.

5. Remove from the oven and serve.

Salmon-Stuffed Chicken Breasts with Dill Sauce

Shh! Don't tell your guests, but making this sophisticated entrée is incredibly easy . . . so much so that you may well find yourself preparing it as an everyday go-to supper.

INGREDIENTS | SERVES 4

⅔ cup sour cream

2 tablespoons milk

½ teaspoon prepared horseradish (optional)

1 tablespoon plus 1 teaspoon fresh dill, finely minced

4 boneless chicken breasts

1 cup hot-smoked salmon, flaked

2 tablespoons minced red onion

1 (8-ounce) package cream cheese

1 clove garlic, finely minced

Seasoned bread crumbs, as needed

How to Butterfly a Chicken Breast

To butterfly a chicken breast, lay it on a cutting board with the smooth side down. Cut away the small inner tender filet and reserve for later use. Turn the breast over, then carefully cut through the width of the breast, lengthwise, stopping ¼" before you reach the other edge. Open the breast so it looks like a butterfly, then place it between layers of wax paper or plastic wrap and pound it thin.

1. Whisk together the sour cream, milk, horseradish, and 1 tablespoon of the minced dill into a smooth sauce. Cover and refrigerate while the chicken cooks.

2. Preheat oven to 375°F. Use a sharp knife to butterfly each chicken breast. Open the breasts up, place them between two sheets of waxed paper (or in a plastic bag), and pound them thin (¼" thick).

3. Fold together the remaining teaspoon dill, smoked salmon, minced onion, cream cheese, and garlic. Divide the mixture evenly between the chicken breasts; wrap and roll each breast and secure with toothpicks or kitchen string. Roll the breasts in the seasoned bread crumbs and place in a lightly greased 9" × 13" casserole dish.

4. Bake in the oven for 30–40 minutes or until the juices run clear.

5. To serve, slice each chicken breast into cross-sections; place on plates and drizzle with the chilled dill sauce.

Boneless Birds (*Benløse Fugler*)

A miracle of Norwegian frugality, this old-fashioned recipe for Boneless Birds transforms cheap cuts of meat into an economical yet tasty meal.

INGREDIENTS | SERVES 8

2 pounds beef round, veal cutlets, or lamb flank steak

8 raw bacon slices

½ cup onion, chopped

1 teaspoon dried thyme

2 cloves garlic, finely minced

¼ cup flour lightly seasoned with salt and pepper

2 tablespoons canola oil

2 tablespoons butter

4 cups beef bouillon

1 tablespoon flour plus ¼ cup ice water, combined in a slurry

Salt and pepper to taste

Mashed potatoes to taste

Birds of a Feather (or Not)

There are variations on "boneless birds" throughout Europe. The French call the dish called oiseau sans tête, "headless birds," and typically prepare it with veal; on the island of Mallorca, it is called the "chaplain's doves." The Italians enjoy uccelletti scappati, "little escaped birds," utilizing skirt steak and replacing the bacon with—of course—prosciutto.

1. Cut the meat into 8 equal (¼-pound) pieces and pound paper-thin with a meat mallet or rolling pin.

2. Cut the bacon strips in half, then place two of the halves side-by-side on each piece of meat. In a bowl toss together the chopped onion, thyme, and garlic, then place 1 tablespoon of the mixture on the end of each "bird." Roll the meat tightly, starting at the end with the onion stuffing; secure with kitchen string or toothpicks. Dredge the meat rolls in the seasoned flour.

3. Over medium heat, melt the canola oil and butter together in the bottom of a stockpot large enough to hold the "birds" in a single layer. Brown the rolls on all sides, then pour the beef bouillon over them.

4. Reduce the heat to low, cover, and simmer for 2 hours, or until tender.

5. Transfer the birds to a plate and keep warm. Skim away any fat that has accumulated at the top of the broth, bring the liquid to a simmer over medium-high heat, and add the flour-water slurry. Cook, stirring constantly, until the juice thickens into a brown sauce. Season to taste with salt and pepper.

6. Slice each "bird" into 2–3 pieces and arrange the slices on plates or on a platter. Serve with mashed potatoes and the brown sauce.

Chicken Fricassee

Originally developed as a way to make tough old stewing hens palatable, chicken fricassee is even better when made with young, organic chickens. Use fresh, not frozen, birds for the best depth of flavor.

INGREDIENTS | SERVES 5–6

1 (½-ounce) package dried porcini or morel mushrooms

Warm water, as needed

½ cup flour

½ teaspoon salt

¼ teaspoon pepper

¼ teaspoon fennel seed

1 chicken, cut into 8 pieces

3 tablespoons butter

2 tablespoons canola oil

½ cup button mushrooms, sliced

½ cup onion, peeled and chopped

½ cup carrots, peeled and chopped

½ cup chopped fennel bulb

2 cups white wine

1 bay leaf

¼ cup half-and-half

1. Place the dried mushrooms in enough warm water to cover and allow to plump for 30 minutes. Drain.

2. Reserve 1 tablespoon of the flour. In a bowl, combine the remaining flour, salt, pepper, and fennel seed, then toss each piece of chicken in the mixture to coat.

3. In the bottom of a frying pan large enough to hold the chicken pieces in a single layer, melt the butter and canola oil together over medium-high heat. Add the chicken pieces and brown well on both sides, about 8 minutes.

4. Remove the chicken from the pan to a plate. Place the mushrooms and vegetables in the pan and sauté until crisp-tender, about 7 minutes. Return the chicken to the pan, along with the white wine and bay leaf. Bring to a boil, then reduce heat to medium-low. Cover and simmer for 35 minutes or until the juices run clear.

5. Transfer the chicken and vegetables to a plate and tent with aluminum foil to keep warm.

6. Whisk the reserved 1 tablespoon of flour into the half-and-half to form a slurry, then stir this into the pan juices to thicken them into a sauce.

7. Transfer the chicken and vegetables to pasta bowls, cover with the sauce, and serve.

SAVU Smoked Chicken and Winter Vegetable Medley

*Succulent oven-smoked chicken and winter vegetables will brighten your day,
with no need to venture outside in the cold and dark of winter.*

INGREDIENTS | SERVES 4–6

4 cups lemon-lime soda

¼ cup canola oil

½ teaspoon salt

1 teaspoon garlic powder

4 boneless chicken breasts, skinned

1 SAVU Smoker Bag (Alder)

1 large beet, greens removed

3 carrots, peeled and coarsely chopped

3 potatoes, coarsely chopped

3 rosemary springs

1 small lemon, sliced

1. Whisk together the lemon-lime soda, canola oil, salt, and garlic powder in a large bowl. Submerge the chicken breasts in this brine, cover, and refrigerate for at least 2 hours.

2. Preheat oven to 425°F. Drain the chicken from the brine and place it in the smoker bag along with the remaining ingredients.

3. Seal the smoker bag, place it in the oven, and cook for 30 minutes.

4. Reduce heat to 175°F. Carefully cut a slit in the top of the bag, then peel back the sides slightly to allow the chicken to brown—*take care not to burn yourself on the escaping steam.* Cook for 15 more minutes or until the chicken and vegetables are cooked through.

5. To serve, peel and coarsely chop the beet, then toss it together with the smoked potatoes and carrots. Thinly slice the chicken breasts and transfer them to plates; accompany with the smoked vegetable medley.

Swedish Chicken

Since the 1970s, versions of this recipe have been swapped around on handwritten recipe cards in so many American communities that it's almost impossible to trace the original source. It's certainly delicious enough to be Swedish!

INGREDIENTS | SERVES 8

8 strips bacon

1 (3-ounce) jar dried beef

4 whole boneless chicken breasts, skin removed

8 ounces sour cream

1 can cream of mushroom soup

1 8-ounce can mushroom pieces, drained

2 teaspoons chopped chives for garnish

1. Preheat oven to 300°F. Partially fry bacon so that it is browned on both sides but still pliable. Drain on paper towels.

2. Arrange the dried beef in overlapping layers on the bottom of a 9" × 13" casserole dish.

3. Cut each chicken breast in half, cross-wise, into 2 equal portions. Fold the 8 half-breasts into bundles, tucking the edges under, then bend a strip of the bacon around each one and secure with a toothpick. Place the bundles in the dish over the dried beef.

4. Fold together the sour cream, soup, and drained mushroom pieces. Spread over the top of the chicken bundles.

5. Bake in the oven, uncovered, for 2 hours.

6. Serve warm, garnished with chopped chives, accompanied with rice or noodles.

Kari's Chicken Danablu

Denmark's richly marbled Danablu cheese, also called Danish blue cheese, is substituted for Swiss cheese in this Nordic-themed version of chicken cordon bleu.

INGREDIENTS | SERVES 4

4 chicken breast halves, pounded paper-thin

Salt and pepper to taste

6 slices bacon

2 shallots, peeled and finely minced

6 ounces Danablu cheese, crumbled

⅔ cup fine, dried rye bread crumbs

¼ teaspoon caraway seeds

1 egg

1 cup milk

1 tablespoon butter

1 tablespoon flour

Danablu Cheese

Danablu cheese, frequently recognized as "overall world champion" in Wisconsin's World Championship Cheese Contest, was developed by Danish dairyman Marius Boel in the 1920s.

1. Preheat oven to 350°F. Season both sides of the pounded chicken breasts with salt and pepper.

2. Fry the bacon until crisp, drain on paper towels, then crumble. Distribute the bacon and the shallots evenly over the tops of the chicken. Sprinkle half of the crumbled blue cheese over the bacon and shallots, reserving the rest for the cheese sauce.

3. Roll each breast tightly over the filling, jellyroll fashion, and secure with toothpicks or kitchen string. Combine the bread crumbs and the caraway seed in a pie plate; whisk together the egg and ¼ cup of the milk in a mixing bowl. Dip each rolled chicken breast in the egg wash to cover, then roll in the bread crumbs. Arrange side-by-side in a greased 9" × 13" casserole dish, place in the oven, and cook for 30 minutes.

4. As the chicken cooks, melt the butter in a saucepan over medium heat and stir in the flour. When the roux begins to bubble, stir in the remaining milk. Once the sauce begins to thicken, add the remaining blue cheese, stirring until it melts. Reduce heat to low and keep warm, stirring occasionally.

5. Transfer the cooked chicken to plates, drizzle with the blue cheese sauce, and serve.

CHAPTER 15

Wild Game and Fowl

Venison Steaks with Juniper Berry Sauce

You'll feel like a 20-minute gourmet master as you prepare perfectly roasted venison steaks, enhancing them with a piney juniper berry sauce. You can substitute gin for the juniper berries if preparing this for people who shouldn't ingest the berries (children under 12 or people who are pregnant or have cancer or kidney disease).

INGREDIENTS | SERVES 6

2 tablespoons canola or olive oil

1 tablespoon butter

6 boneless venison haunch steaks or fillets

Sea salt and pepper to taste

1½ cups good red wine

8 juniper berries, crushed (or substitute 4 teaspoons gin)

2 shallots, peeled and finely minced

1½ cups beef or game stock

Venison *En Papillote* ("In Parchment" in French)

Cooks have used buttered paper to wrap venison during the roasting process since the 1700s; the buttered parchment truly helps to keep this very lean meat juicy. Simply wrap your steaks or roasts in a piece of buttered parchment paper before placing them in the oven (or take a page out of Chef Gordon Ramsay's book and use the foil wraps from stick butter for smaller cuts).

1. Preheat oven to 400°F. Melt the oil and butter together in a frying pan over medium-high heat. Season the venison steaks on both sides with salt and pepper, then sear in the pan on both sides just until browned. Wrap each steak in a piece of buttered parchment paper, place in a baking dish large enough to hold the steaks in a single layer, and roast in the oven for 8 minutes. Remove and allow the steaks to rest for 10 minutes before unwrapping.

2. As the venison roasts, prepare your sauce: deglaze the pan with the red wine, then add the crushed juniper berries and shallots, scraping up the browned bits. When the liquid has reduced by half, add the stock. Reduce heat to medium and simmer until the sauce is again reduced by half; strain out the solids and transfer the juniper sauce to a serving boat.

3. Plate the venison and serve the sauce on the side.

Venison *Gjetost* Burgers

*Cheeseburgers just don't get any better than this recipe,
featuring ground meat and mushroom patties topped with melted Norwegian gjetost.*

INGREDIENTS | SERVES 8

6 slices bacon

1 teaspoon minced garlic

¼ cup green onions, finely chopped

2 pounds ground venison

⅔ cup mushrooms, finely chopped

3 tablespoons sour cream or *skyr* (or substitute low-fat Greek yogurt)

1 tablespoon fresh parsley, finely chopped

8 slices Ski Queen brand *gjetost* cheese

1. Fry the bacon until crispy; transfer to paper towels to drain. Pour off all but 2 tablespoons of the grease from the pan.

2. Add the garlic and green onions to the pan and cook until softened, about 3 minutes.

3. Use your hands to mix together the venison, bacon, sautéed onions and garlic, mushrooms, sour cream, and parsley. Form 8 patties; refrigerate for 30 minutes.

4. Fry the patties on a grill or griddle, flipping a few times, until they've reached the desired doneness. In the last minute of cooking, place the *gjetost* slices on top to melt.

5. Serve as is, on buns or crispbread, or folded into flatbread.

Wild Game Hot Pot

Finland's classic Karelian Hot Pot takes a walk on the wild side in this flavorful dish.

INGREDIENTS | SERVES 6–8

2 onions, peeled and thinly sliced

3 pounds mixed wild game stew scraps (venison, boar, hare, moose, elk)

1 teaspoon salt

2 teaspoons peppercorns

8 whole allspice berries

4 juniper berries, crushed (optional)

2–3 cups water

1. Place half of the sliced onions in the bottom of a slow cooker and cover with half of the meat.

2. Sprinkle the layer with half of the salt, peppercorns, allspice, and juniper berries.

3. Repeat the layers, then pour in just enough water to barely cover the meat.

4. Cover the slow cooker, set on low, and cook for 8–10 hours.

5. Serve accompanied with mashed potatoes and lingonberries.

Norwegian Hunter Stew with Elk or Venison

*This is a hearty game stew, perfect to make in celebration of
the first snowflakes of late autumn or early winter.*

INGREDIENTS | SERVES 6

½ cup flour

½ teaspoon salt

¼ teaspoon pepper

2 pounds moose, elk, or venison meat,
cut in 1" cubes

1 tablespoon butter

2 tablespoons canola or olive oil

1 large onion, peeled and chopped

3 cups beef or game broth

4 large potatoes, peeled and chopped

3 carrots, peeled and chopped

½ rutabaga, peeled and chopped

2 stalks celery, chopped

⅔ cup fresh wild mushrooms (or
substitute button mushrooms),
coarsely sliced

⅓ cup sour cream

1 tablespoon fresh thyme, chopped

1. Season the flour with the salt and pepper, then toss with the meat to coat. In the bottom of a large pot, melt the butter and oil over medium-high heat; add the meat and brown evenly on all sides. Add the onion and cook until it softens, about 8 minutes.

2. Pour the stock over the meat, reduce heat to medium-low, cover, and cook until the meat is tender, skimming off foam as it arises (check the meat for doneness at 1 hour).

3. Add the vegetables and mushrooms, and continue to simmer for 20–30 minutes until the vegetables are tender.

4. Fold the sour cream into the stew to thicken, and stir in the fresh thyme; cook for 5 more minutes, until the stew is heated through.

An Elk by Any Other Name . . .

Is a moose (Alces alces). At least in Scandinavia and in Great Britain, where they refer to moose as "elk." Confusing, right? This means that whenever you translate an original recipe, you should keep in mind that it's Bullwinkle they're talking about when they use the word älg (in Swedish) or elg (Norwegian and Danish). The animal that Americans refer to as an elk, or wapiti (Cervus canadensis), is actually a large variety of deer, native only to the Americas and East Asia. Feel free to substitute venison or American elk meat for any of the moose recipes here—the taste won't be quite the same, but they'll work for those without a supply of moose meat.

Venison Heart with Fruited Barley Stuffing

In Norway, a land of avid hunters, it isn't uncommon to find recipes for stuffed reindeer (caribou) heart. Venison works equally well.

INGREDIENTS | SERVES 2

1 venison, caribou, or moose heart

2 shallots, chopped

2 tablespoons butter

1 cup barley, cooked

¾ cup mixed dried fruit (prunes, apricots, apples, cranberries)

¼ cup slivered almonds, toasted

1 teaspoon dried sage, crumbled

1 bay leaf

Water to cover in pot

1 egg, beaten

1 cup seasoned bread crumbs

Have a Heart

If hunters had perfect eyesight and wild game were always heart-shot, there wouldn't be much cause for cooking the heart. Yet hunters sometimes make efficient and lethal head, neck, or lung shots—and it's criminal to waste one of the most flavorful parts of the animal. Be sure to remove the tough outer membrane and the arteries of the heart, rinsing it well to remove any blood, before using. For a simple treatment, simply slice the heart thin and pan-sear it very lightly and quickly (it will dry out if you overcook it) in butter over high heat. Gently boiling a heart also results in delicious fare; if boiled, leave the outer membrane intact until after cooking to ensure moist, tender meat.

1. Rinse the heart well under cold running water. Use a sharp knife to remove the veins, valves, fat, and membranes. Venison fat is not tasty.

2. Sauté the shallots in the butter in a frying pan over medium heat, about 3 minutes. Remove from heat and combine with the barley, dried fruit, almonds, and sage.

3. Slice open the side of the heart and stuff with the fruited barley mixture. Use kitchen string or skewers to tightly close the opening over the stuffing (it's best if you sew the sides together with string).

4. Place the heart in a large pot with the bay leaf and add enough water to cover by 2". Bring the pot to a boil, maintaining the boil for 5 minutes. Reduce heat to medium-low, cover, and simmer for 1½ hours.

5. Preheat oven to 350°F. Remove the heart from the pot, pat dry with paper towels, then brush all over with the beaten egg. Roll in bread crumbs to cover, then place in a pan and roast in the oven for 30 minutes. Remove from oven and rest for 10 minutes before serving.

Frost-Bump Elk (*Tjälknöl*)

Tjälknöl was "accidentally" developed by Swede Ragnhild Nilsson after she asked her husband to defrost a wild game roast in the oven. He forgot the roast, and it slowly cooked overnight. Hoping to save the roast, Nilsson soaked it in a marinade for a few hours, producing a dish so good that it captured the 1982 price for "Best Regional Dish."

INGREDIENTS | SERVES 8–10

1 (6-pound) boneless elk or moose roast, frozen

6 cups water

6 tablespoons salt

2 tablespoons sugar

3 cloves garlic, pressed

2 tablespoons juniper berries, crushed (or substitute fresh rosemary)

2 bay leaves

1. Preheat oven to 170°F.

2. Place the frozen roast on a rack in a roasting pan, then put it on the lowest rack of the oven.

3. Cook the roast until a thermometer inserted in the thickest part of the roast registers 150°F (check it at 8 hours, then every half hour thereafter until it reaches 150°F). Remove from the oven.

4. To make the brine, in a large pot combine the water, salt, sugar, garlic, juniper berries (or rosemary), and bay leaves and bring to a boil. Stir until all of the salt has dissolved, then remove from heat and allow to cool completely.

5. Place the roast into the brine (the brine needs to cover it completely), then refrigerate for 5 hours.

6. To serve, remove the roast from the brine, pat dry, and slice thinly.

Drunken Moose with Cinnamon Apples

In Sweden in the autumn, it's apparently not unheard of to run across "tipsy" moose, drunk on fermenting apples.

INGREDIENTS | SERVES 6–8

- 1 cup pearl onions, peeled
- 2 cloves garlic, minced
- 3 carrots, peeled and cut into matchsticks
- 1 (4-pound) moose roast (or substitute elk or venison)
- ¼ teaspoon pepper
- ½ teaspoon salt
- ¼ cup hard cider
- 1 cup apple cider or apple juice
- 2 tablespoons Swedish light syrup or golden syrup
- 1 teaspoon ground allspice
- ½ teaspoon ground ginger
- ¼ teaspoon ground cloves
- 2 tablespoons potato starch flour or cornstarch plus 2 tablespoons water
- 2 tablespoons butter
- Four apples, peeled and chopped into a ½" dice
- 1 tablespoon brown sugar
- ½ teaspoon cinnamon

How to Tree a Moose

In September 2011, folks in Särö, Sweden (south of Gothenberg), had to rescue a moose, "drunk" after eating fermented apples, that got herself tangled in the middle of an apple tree as she reached for her fruit fix.

1. Place the onions, garlic, and carrots in the bottom of a 5- or 6-quart slow cooker.

2. Season the roast on all sides with the pepper and salt, then place it on top of the vegetables.

3. Whisk together the hard cider, apple cider, light syrup, allspice, ginger, and cloves, then pour over the roast. Cover and cook on low for 10 hours.

4. Transfer the roast to a plate and tent with foil to keep warm.

5. Strain the cooking liquid, discard the solids, and skim off any fat. Return it to the slow cooker, whisk in the combined potato starch flour and water slurry, and increase heat to high. Cover and cook, stirring occasionally, until the sauce has thickened.

6. As the sauce cooks, melt the butter in a frying pan over medium-high heat. Add the apples, brown sugar, and cinnamon, and sauté for 15 minutes or until crisp-tender.

7. Stir the apples into the sauce. Slice and plate the roast, then drizzle with the sauce.

Roasted Wild Boar with *Gjetost*-Lager Sauce

Tough wild boar shoulders melt to toothsome tenderness when slow-cooked in a low-heat oven. Be sure to brine the pork overnight before preparing; this will really help to eliminate any gaminess. Accompany with potatoes and buttered kohlrabi or Brussels sprouts.

INGREDIENTS | SERVES 8–10

8 cups water

1 cup kosher salt

1 cup brown sugar

¼ cup crushed juniper berries (or substitute fresh rosemary)

3 bay leaves, crumbled

1 (4-pound) boneless wild boar shoulder

12 ounces chopped bacon or pancetta

2 large onions, peeled and chopped

1 cup celery, chopped

4½ cups Danish lager

2 tablespoons butter

2 tablespoons flour

1 teaspoon Swedish or Dijon mustard

1½ cups shredded *gjetost* (Ski Queen brand)

¾ cup sour cream

1. In a pot, combine the 8 cups water, kosher salt, brown sugar, juniper berries, and crumbled bay leaves, and heat to boiling over high heat, stirring to dissolve the sugar. Once the sugar has fully dissolved, remove mixture from heat and cool completely. Immerse the boar shoulder completely in the marinade, cover, and refrigerate for 12 hours.

2. Preheat oven to 325°F. Remove the boar from the brine and pat dry.

3. In the bottom of an oven-proof pot or Dutch oven, fry the chopped bacon together with the onion and celery until the bacon is brown and crispy. Remove from the burner. Place the boar in the pot with the bacon and vegetables, then pour 4 cups of the lager over the shoulder. Cover and place in the oven; cook for 1½ hours or until tender, turning once halfway through the cooking cycle. Remove the boar, transfer it to a cutting board, and allow it to rest while you prepare the sauce.

4. For the sauce, melt the butter in a saucepan over medium-low heat, adding the flour once the butter begins to froth. Whisk to form a roux. Once this roux begins to bubble but before it browns, whisk in the mustard and the remaining ½ cup lager. Gradually add the shredded *gjetost*, stirring until the cheese melts. Fold in the sour cream and cook for 3–5 more minutes until the sauce is warmed through.

5. To serve, slice the meat and drizzle with the sauce.

Lingonberry-Glazed Smoked Boar Tenderloin

Accompany this smoked wild boar tenderloin with Swedish Brown Beans (Bruna Bönor; see Chapter 10) and baked apples.

INGREDIENTS | SERVES 4–6

1 teaspoon ground thyme

3 star anise

1 teaspoon ground ginger

1 tablespoon sugar

3 tablespoons salt

1 teaspoon pepper

4 cups water

2 (1-pound) wild boar tenderloins

1 cup hickory chips

⅔ cup Lingonberry Jam (see Chapter 7)

¼ cup orange juice

1. Combine the thyme, star anise, ginger, sugar, salt, pepper, and water in a large saucepan and bring to a boil, stirring until the sugar and salt have dissolved. Cool to room temperature, then pour the marinade over the tenderloins. Cover and refrigerate for 12 hours.

2. Soak the hickory chips in enough water to cover for at least 1 hour.

3. In a small saucepan over medium-low heat, stir together the Lingonberry Jam and orange juice to make a glaze.

4. Drain the chips and place them in your smoker over the heating element; pour the marinade into the smoke pan. Grease the top rack of the smoker, then place the tenderloins on them; baste with the lingonberry glaze. Cook for 5 minutes, then turn over, baste again, and cook until a digital thermometer inserted in the meat registers 150°F, about 5 minutes.

5. Slice, drizzle with the remaining glaze, and serve.

Swedish-Style Duck Meatballs in Cloudberry Sauce

These are savory wild duck meatballs in a traditional Swedish sauce slightly sweetened with cloudberries. Thanks to Hank Shaw, author of Hunt, Gather, Cook: Finding the Forgotten Feast *(Rodale Books: 2011), for sharing his expertise during the development of these duck recipes.*

INGREDIENTS | SERVES 6–8

2½ pounds duck meat, chilled

1 pound pork fat (fatback or fatty bacon slices), chilled

4 slices stale bread, crusts removed

⅔ cup milk

2 teaspoons salt

1 teaspoon ground nutmeg

1 teaspoon ground cardamom

1 teaspoon pepper

2 eggs

Canola oil for frying

1 tablespoon butter

2 tablespoons flour

3 shallots, peeled and finely minced

2 cloves garlic, peeled and finely minced

1½ cups duck or chicken broth

½ cup sour cream

¼ cup cloudberry jam (or substitute Lingonberry Jam; see Chapter 7)

"Must-Have" Wild Game Cooking Resources

There are two indispensible cookbooks that articulate the magic of cooking local game: Andreas Viestad's *Kitchen of Light: The New Scandinavian Cooking* (Artisan: 2003), and Hank Shaw's, *Hunt, Gather, Cook*. Viestad, the Norwegian host of the public television series *The New Scandinavian Cooking*, has been a driving force in promoting the benefits of a diet based on cold-climate foods. American Hank Shaw is one of the most exciting writers defining the "back to local" wild food movement in America. Check out his award-winning website, "Hunter Angler Gardener Cook" (*http://honest-food.net*). twice nominated for a James Beard Foundation Award.

1. Chop the duck meat and the pork fat into ½" pieces and either run them through a meat grinder or pulse them in a food processor until minced. Cover and place in the refrigerator for 20 minutes.

2. Tear the stale bread into small pieces and cover with the milk; allow to sit until the bread absorbs all of the milk, about 15 minutes. Use a fork to mash the bread and milk into a paste.

3. Place the ground duck and pork in a large bowl; sprinkle with the salt, nutmeg, cardamom, and pepper. Add the eggs and bread mixture, then use your hands to lightly combine the ingredients into a mass.

4. Form meatballs between your palms, using a tablespoon of the mixture to form each 1½" meatball. Place on a plate, then chill for at least 30 minutes or up to 1 hour.

5. Fill a heavy frying pan with ¼" of oil (enough to half submerge the meatballs). Heat over medium-high until a drop of water sizzles on the surface; reduce the heat to medium, add the meatballs, and cook for 6 minutes, turning once, until golden brown. Remove and drain on paper towels.

6. For the sauce, remove all but 1 tablespoon of the grease from the frying pan. Stir in the butter over medium-high heat until it froths; add the shallots and garlic and sauté until they begin to soften, about 5 minutes. Stir the flour into the pan. Pour in the broth; simmer until the liquid thickens to sauce consistency. Reduce heat to medium-low; fold in the sour cream, meatballs, and cloudberry jam. Cook until the meatballs are warmed through, about 10 minutes.

7. Serve with new potatoes and additional cloudberry jam.

Roast Mallard with Orange-Elderflower Glaze

Rich and succulent, roast mallard is a delight for anyone who prefers dark meat. Look for orange-elderflower marmalade (Sylt Fläder & Apelsin) at IKEA. If you need to substitute domesticated or very fatty wild ducks for this recipe, follow the cooking instructions in the sidebar, as these require different cooking times and temperatures.

INGREDIENTS | SERVES 4

2 lean mallards

¼ cup orange-elderflower marmalade

¼ cup elderflower-orange cordial

1 tablespoon white wine vinegar

1 large orange, quartered

Softened butter, as needed

Sea salt and pepper to taste

City Ducks

Slow, lazy domesticated ducks required slow, lazy roasting. Preheat oven to 350°F. Prepare and glaze your duck, place it in the oven, and roast for 1 hour, basting every 20 minutes. At the 1-hour point, glaze the duck well again, increase heat to 450°F, and roast for 10 more minutes. Remove from oven, glaze one final time, tent with foil, and allow to sit for 15–30 minutes (the ideal internal temperature for duck is between 135°F and 140°F).

1. Preheat oven to 450°F for 30 minutes, allowing ducks to rest at room temperature while the oven heats.

2. As the oven heats, make your glaze: In a saucepan combine ¼ cup of the marmalade, the cordial, and white wine vinegar. Bring to a low boil over medium-high heat; reduce heat to low, and cook until thick and syrupy, about 7 minutes.

3. Use a sharp knife to prick the skin (not the meat) of the fatty portions of the duck. Rub each duck all over with the orange quarters, then stick 2 orange quarters inside each duck. Generously spread the softened butter over the duck, then season generously with salt and pepper. Coat the duck all over with the glaze.

4. Place the ducks on the rack of a roasting pan, place in the oven, and roast until the internal temperature reaches 135°F, about 20–25 minutes. Remove from oven, transfer to a cutting board, coat once again with any remaining glaze, tent with foil, and allow to rest for 10 minutes before serving.

Cardamom-Honey Roasted Rabbit

Virtually cholesterol-free, rabbit is one of the healthiest of white meats. Here it is slow-roasted in a light glaze of cardamom and honey. Serve with roasted carrots and a radish salad for a whimsical conversation starter.

INGREDIENTS | SERVES 4

4 tablespoons honey
2 tablespoons white wine or sherry
1 teaspoon freshly ground cardamom
½ teaspoon pepper
1 rabbit, cut into pieces
1 package baby carrots (about 2 cups)
1 lemon, thinly sliced

1. Preheat oven to 350°F. In a small saucepan warm the honey over medium-low heat for 3 minutes, then stir in the wine, cardamom, and pepper. Remove from heat and place in a bowl with the rabbit, tossing to coat all sides. Allow to sit at room temperature for 30 minutes.

2. Place the carrots and lemon slices in the bottom of a lightly greased roasting pan. Place the rabbit pieces on top, then brush well with the marinade once more.

3. Roast the rabbit in the oven for 1½ hours or until a digital thermometer registers 160°F.

4. Remove from the oven, transfer the rabbit to plates, and serve with the roasted carrots and a radish salad.

Norwegian Rabbit in Cabbage (*Kanin i Kål*)

This recipe is adapted from the Norwegian classic, fårikål ("sheep in cabbage"). Serve with homemade flatbread and boiled potatoes.

INGREDIENTS | SERVES 4

1 rabbit, cut into pieces
12 peppercorns
2 teaspoons caraway
2 tablespoons all-purpose flour
2 teaspoons salt
1 Savoy cabbage, sliced into thick wedges
1 leek, cleaned and cut into matchsticks
2 cups boiling water

1. Place half of the rabbit pieces in the bottom of a 5-quart slow cooker or large pot. Sprinkle with 3 of the peppercorns, ½ teaspoon of the caraway, ½ tablespoon of the flour, and ½ teaspoon of the salt.

2. Place half of the cabbage and leeks on top of the rabbit pieces, and repeat the seasoning.

3. Repeat the two layers, seasoning each and ending with the cabbage/leek layer.

4. Pour the boiling water over the layers. If using a slow cooker, cover and cook on low for 10 hours. If using a pot, bring the contents to a boil, reduce the heat to low, cover, and simmer for 2 hours or until the meat falls off the bone.

CHAPTER 16

Scandinavian Berry and Fruit Dishes

Blueberry Soup

Although lovely when served cold, blueberry soup is appreciated even more when offered warm as an après-ski pick-me-up.

INGREDIENTS | SERVES 4

4 cups water

¼ cup sugar

4 cups wild (or regular) blueberries, fresh or frozen

3 tablespoons potato starch flour or cornstarch

3 tablespoons ice water

Vasaloppet

Warm blueberry soup is a staple concession at Vasaloppet, the world's longest and oldest ski marathon held in Sweden on the first Sunday in March.

1. In a large saucepan, bring water and sugar to a boil, stirring to dissolve sugar. Add blueberries, reduce heat to a simmer, and cook until berries begin to pop, about 10 minutes.

2. Whisk together the potato starch flour and ice water; stir into the blueberries to thicken to soup consistency (if soup becomes too thick, just add additional water in tablespoon increments to dilute).

3. Serve soup warm, garnished with a dollop of whipped cream, or refrigerate for 1 hour and serve cold.

Sweet Soup (*Søtsuppe*)

The perfect winter warmer, Sweet Soup can be made from any combination of dried fruit you have on hand.

INGREDIENTS | SERVES 6

1 tablespoon pearl tapioca

5½ cups water

½ cup dried apples, finely chopped

½ cup raisins

½ cup pitted prunes, finely chopped

½ cup dried cherries, apricots, or peaches

1 small lemon, thickly sliced

1 cinnamon stick

1 cup apple or cranberry juice

1. In a small bowl, place tapioca with ½ cup of the water and soak overnight.

2. In a large pot, bring the remaining 5 cups water to a boil. Add tapioca mixture, dried fruit, raisins, prunes, lemon slices, and cinnamon stick. Reduce heat to a steady simmer and cook for 30 minutes, stirring occasionally.

3. Stir in fruit juice and cook for 5 more minutes. Remove lemon slices and cinnamon stick and serve.

4. Sweet Soup is lovely served either warm or cold.

Rhubarb Soup (*Rabarbersoppa*)

Celebrate the first fresh rhubarb of the season with this refreshing dessert soup.

INGREDIENTS | SERVES 4

1½ pounds rhubarb, as red as you can find

3 cups water

1½ cups sugar

2 teaspoons lemon zest

1 tablespoon potato starch flour or cornstarch

1 tablespoon ice water

1. Clean and, if tough, peel the rhubarb, then cut stalks into 1" dice.

2. Combine water, sugar, and lemon zest together in a nonreactive pan. Bring to a boil and add rhubarb; reduce heat to a simmer and cook until rhubarb is soft, about 15 minutes. Turn off heat.

3. Purée the mixture using an immersion blender or carefully blend in batches in a food processor. Bring soup back to a steady simmer.

4. Whisk together the potato starch flour and ice water, then stir into the soup to thicken. Cook for an additional 5 minutes.

5. Serve soup warm with ice cream, or chill and serve cold as a refreshing summer starter or dessert.

Danish Apple Soup (*Aeblesuppe*)

Danish apple soup (in Norwegian, eplesuppe) can be served either warm or cold, depending on the season.

INGREDIENTS | SERVES 4

1 cup sugar
4 cups water
Juice and zest of 1 lemon
1 cinnamon stick
½ teaspoon freshly ground cardamom
¼ teaspoon ground cloves
4 red apples
1½ tablespoons potato starch flour
1½ tablespoons ice water

1. Over low heat, stir the sugar in a frying pan until it turns amber. Remove from heat and whisk in the water in a steady stream; return to the burner again and stir in the lemon zest, lemon juice, cinnamon, cardamom, and cloves. Increase heat to medium and simmer for 10 minutes, stirring a few times to thoroughly dissolve the caramelized sugar.

2. Core, pare, and peel the apples, then slice them directly into the pot. Cook until fork-tender, about 15 minutes.

3. Use a slotted spoon to remove about ¼ cup of the apples and the cinnamon stick from the pot; set aside. Use an immersion blender to purée the remaining soup.

4. Whisk together the potato starch flour and the 1½ tablespoons ice water, then stir into the soup to thicken. Simmer for 3–4 more minutes, stirring constantly. Remove from heat.

5. Return the reserved apples to the soup and serve warm, or refrigerate for at least an hour if serving cold.

Stablemaster's Fool (*Tallimestarin Kiisseli*)

No joke—the juice from tangy berries like gooseberries or currants lends zest to this old-fashioned pudding.

INGREDIENTS | SERVES 6

2 cups gooseberries, currants, lingonberries, or cranberries

4 cups water

1 cup sugar

¼ cup potato starch flour

¼ cup warm water

2 tablespoons butter

1½ cups rye bread crumbs

2 tablespoons cocoa powder

¼ cup cinnamon sugar

1 cup whipping cream, whipped to stiff peaks

Stablemasters, Rye, and Cocoa

It's interesting that older Finnish and Swedish cookbooks often attribute two different recipes—this "fool" (a pudding with puréed fruit and whipping cream) and a version of Skansk apple cake—to an anonymous "stablemaster." What unites the two recipes is that they both incorporate rye breadcrumbs and cocoa.

1. Place the berries in a nonreactive saucepan with 4 cups of water and bring to a boil. Reduce heat to a steady simmer and cook until the berries have popped. Strain the mixture to remove the berry pulp, returning the juice to the pan. Return to a simmer and stir in the sugar.

2. Whisk together the potato starch flour and the ¼ cup warm water, then pour in a slow stream into the simmering juice, stirring constantly. Bring the mixture to a boil; once it thickens, remove immediately from the heat and cool.

3. Melt the butter in a frying pan until it begins to foam. Stir in the rye bread crumbs, cocoa powder, and cinnamon sugar, then fry over medium heat until the crumbs are crisp and caramelized.

4. To serve, transfer the dessert to individual bowls and sprinkle with the caramelized bread crumbs, offering the whipped cream on the side.

Plum Soup

Use red or deep purple plums to give this late-summer soup a rich color.

INGREDIENTS | SERVES 4

2 pounds red or English plums

5 cups water

1 cup sugar

1 cinnamon stick or 3 star anise

2 tablespoons potato starch flour or cornstarch

2 tablespoons water

⅔ cup whipping cream, sweetened with 1 tablespoon sugar

1. Wash, halve, stone, and peel the plums. Stir together the 5 cups water, sugar, and cinnamon stick in a saucepan; bring to a boil. Add the plums, return to a low boil, and cook until the plums have softened, about 15 minutes. Use a potato masher to further break apart the plums.

2. Whisk together the potato starch flour and 2 tablespoons water, then pour in a steady stream into the soup, stirring constantly. Cook at a low boil for 5 more minutes until the soup starts to thicken.

3. Remove from heat, cool on a back burner, and serve at room temperature with the sweetened whipping cream.

Rose Hip Soup (*Nypesuppe*)

Rose hips, rich in vitamin C, are a much-valued base for soups and jams throughout northern Europe. You can find the dried rose hips in many organic or ethnic food stores.

INGREDIENTS | SERVES 8

2 cups dried rose hips

5 cups water

3 tablespoons honey

2 tablespoons lemon juice or cider vinegar

2 tablespoons potato starch flour or cornstarch

2 tablespoons warm water

⅔ cup whipping cream, sweetened with 1 tablespoon vanilla sugar

¼ cup almond slivers, toasted

1. Place the rose hips, water, honey, and lemon juice in a nonreactive saucepan and bring to a boil. Reduce heat to a simmer and cook until soft, about 20 minutes.

2. When the rose hips are soft, use a food processor to purée the mixture, then strain through a fine-meshed colander to separate out the juice. Return juice to the pan and simmer.

3. Whisk together the potato starch flour and 2 tablespoons warm water, then pour into the rose-hip juice. Bring the soup to a boil, stirring constantly; once the soup has thickened, remove from heat and cool.

4. Whip the sweetened cream to soft peaks. Sprinkle with toasted almonds.

Finnish Strawberry Snow (*Mansikkalumi*)

For an alternative presentation, freeze strawberry snow in molds and serve in place of ice cream on a warm summer evening.

INGREDIENTS | SERVES 6

2 cups fresh strawberries or 2 (10-ounce) packages frozen strawberries, defrosted and drained.

½ cup sugar

8 teaspoons meringue powder

½ cup warm water

¾ cup heavy cream, whipped to stiff peaks

Additional sliced strawberries for garnish

1. Combine the strawberries and sugar in a bowl and pound with a potato masher into a smooth purée (or use a food processor to purée the berries).

2. Using an electric mixer, stir together the meringue powder and warm water, then whip to stiff peaks.

3. With a spatula, gently fold first the strawberry purée and then the whipped cream into the whipped meringue.

4. Transfer to bowls, garnish with sliced strawberries, and serve.

Blueberry Cream (*Blåbärsgrädde*)

You can use either fresh or frozen blueberries or huckleberries for this easy dessert. Serve it as is, or use it to replace the whipped cream filling in many Nordic cakes or semlor (sweet Lenten buns).

INGREDIENTS | SERVES 4

¼ cup sugar

2 cups blueberries

1½ cups whipping cream

½ cup sour cream or crème fraîche

1. Stir the sugar into the blueberries, then crush them with a potato masher or in a food processor.

2. Whip the cream to stiff peaks, then fold in the sour cream.

3. Gently fold the blueberries into the cream.

4. Eat immediately or refrigerate until serving.

Danish Red Berry Pudding with Cream (*Rødgrød med Fløde*)

Considered to be the Danes' national dessert—as well as a source of amusement when non-Danish speakers attempt to pronounce its name—Rødgrød med Fløde is vibrant with red fruits like currants, raspberries, and strawberries.

INGREDIENTS | SERVES 6

2 pounds bright red berries (red currants, raspberries, strawberries, or combination)

4 cups water

1 cup sugar

¼ cup potato starch flour or cornstarch

¼ cup ice water

1 cup heavy cream, sweetened with 1 tablespoon vanilla sugar

Blanched almond slivers and additional berries to garnish

1. Thoroughly clean and hull the berries, discarding any bad ones. Combine with 4 cups water in a large nonreactive pot; cook over medium heat for 15 minutes until the berries soften.

2. Remove berry mixture from heat and cool slightly, then press the mixture through a sieve or colander lined with cheesecloth. Discard the seeds and remaining pulp.

3. Return the berry juice to the burner and whisk in sugar; bring the juice to a low boil, then lower heat to a steady simmer. Dissolve the potato starch flour in ¼ cup ice water, then pour in a steady stream into the juice, stirring constantly until the mixture reaches the consistency of a heavy syrup.

4. Remove from heat, cool to room temperature, then pour into either a single bowl or individual glass serving bowls.

5. Serve immediately or chill in refrigerator for up to 2 days; garnish with sweetened cream, blanched almonds, and additional berries.

Savory Pear Soup

Not all Scandinavian fruit soups are sweet; pears and apples are often used in partnership with vegetables like potatoes in fantastic lunch or dinner soup entrées.

INGREDIENTS | SERVES 4

4 large pears
1 medium onion
2 potatoes
2 tablespoons canola or olive oil
2 garlic cloves, minced
1 tablespoon freshly grated ginger root
1 tablespoon granulated chicken bouillon
5 cups water
½ teaspoon salt
¼ teaspoon white pepper

1. Peel, pare, and finely chop the pears, onion, and potatoes.

2. In a large soup pot, heat the oil and then add the chopped pears, onion, potatoes, garlic, and ginger root. Fry over medium heat until the vegetables begin to soften, about 8 minutes, then sprinkle with the chicken bouillon.

3. Add the water, stir, and reduce heat to a low, steady simmer. Cover and allow to cook for 25–30 minutes.

4. Purée the soup with an immersion blender or hand mixer; if it is too thick for your taste, dilute with more water. Season with salt and white pepper.

5. Serve warm, accompanied by a salad and good rye bread.

Cloudberry Cream Parfait

Arctic cloudberry jam, gently folded into rich whipped cream, is layered with almond rusk crumbs in this light dessert.

INGREDIENTS | SERVES 6

2½ tablespoons butter
2 cups almond rusk crumbs, or substitute biscotti
¼ cup sugar
1 vanilla bean (or substitute ½ teaspoon vanilla extract)
2 cups whipping cream
1 cup cloudberry jam

1. Melt butter in a frying pan on medium heat. Stir in the almond rusk crumbs and sugar; fry the mixture, stirring constantly, until the crumbs are toasted. Remove from heat and cool.

2. Slice the vanilla bean in half and scrape the seeds into the cream. Whip the cream until stiff peaks form, then lightly fold cloudberry jam into the whipped cream.

3. Reserve 1½ tablespoons of the toasted crumbs for garnish. Alternate 3 layers of the rusk crumbs and cloudberry cream in individual parfait glasses, ending with the cloudberry cream. Sprinkle with reserved crumbs to garnish.

4. Chill in the freezer until glasses are frosty and cream has set slightly (about 15 minutes), then serve.

Cloudberry Mousse

Tastes vary, so sample this cloudberry mousse as you prepare it and add additional sugar if you find it too tart. Just don't sample it so much that there's none left for dessert!

INGREDIENTS | SERVES 4

⅔ cup cloudberry jam

2 tablespoons cloudberry (or other berry) liqueur

¼ cup sugar

1 tablespoon unflavored gelatin powder

¼ cup cold water

¼ cup boiling water

1 cup whipping cream

3 egg whites

1. Stir together the cloudberry jam and berry liqueur.

2. Whisk together the sugar and gelatin powder, then sprinkle into ¼ cup of cold water. Allow to sit for 15 minutes, then combine with ¼ cup boiling water, stirring until dissolved. Pour the mixture into the cloudberry jam and mix well. Allow to cool.

3. Whip the cream until stiff peaks form, then gently fold together with the berry mixture.

4. Beat the egg whites to solid peaks; fold into the berry cream.

5. Refrigerate for 3 hours before serving.

Magic Lingonberry Porridge (*Klappgröt*)

The time it takes to whip this magic dessert porridge (Klappgröt in Swedish, Vispipuuro in Finnish) into airy perfection can be reduced if you first chill the bowl of your electric mixer.

INGREDIENTS | SERVES 4

2½ cups water

1 cup sugar

2 cups lingonberries, or substitute cranberries or Lingonberry Jam (see Chapter 7)

1 cup semolina

1. Combine the water, sugar, and lingonberries in a nonreactive saucepan and bring to a low boil. Maintain boil for 15 minutes.

2. Strain the mixture through a fine-meshed colander into a large measuring cup, then return the juice to the pan. Bring back to a simmer over medium-high heat and then whisk in the semolina. Cook, stirring occasionally, for 8 minutes. Remove from heat and cool to room temperature.

3. Transfer the porridge to a chilled electric mixer bowl. Using the whisk attachment, beat on high until the porridge is light and foamy, at least 10 (up to 30) minutes.

4. Serve with cold milk or cream and additional fresh berries.

Lingonberry Applesauce

If you're careful not to cook the lingonberries too long, they'll look like the tapioca in Thai bubble tea—a fun alternative to regular old applesauce.

INGREDIENTS | MAKES 4 CUPS

½ cup water

2 tablespoons lemon juice

½ teaspoon ground cardamom

8 large apples (about 4 pounds)

¼ cup sugar

1 cup lingonberries

Can I Use Cranberries?

Certainly. But because cranberries are larger and denser than lingonberries, you might need to microwave the cranberries in the final cooking stage for a minute or two longer—until they've lost most of their crunch but still retain their shape.

1. In a microwave-safe bowl mix together the water, lemon juice, and cardamom

2. Peel, core, and slice the apples directly into the bowl.

3. Cover and microwave at high for 5 minutes.

4. Stir in the sugar and microwave at high for 5 more minutes.

5. Use a potato masher or an immersion blender to process the applesauce into a very smooth purée. Gently fold the lingonberries into the warm sauce; microwave for 1 more minute (you don't want to cook the mixture so long that the lingonberries burst).

6. Either can the applesauce in hot jars or refrigerate and use within 2 weeks.

Apple "Porcupines" (Æble Pindsvin)

Children will gobble up these prickly little fellows, baked apples topped with creamy meringue and almonds.

INGREDIENTS | SERVES 6

3 baking apples

2½ cups water

¼ cup sugar

2 tablespoons lemon juice

2 egg whites

½ cup Superfine sugar

½ teaspoon cinnamon

¼ teaspoon allspice

½ cup almond slices

12 currants

1. Peel the apples and cut in half, from the top down. Remove the cores.

2. Combine the water, ¼ cup sugar, and lemon juice in a frying pan just big enough to hold the apples in a single layer; bring to a boil, then reduce heat to a simmer.

3. Place the apples cut-side down in the simmering water. Cover pan and cook just until the apples begin to soften, turning once (you want the apples to be tender enough to pierce with a fork, but not so soft that they fall apart).

4. Preheat oven to 325°F. For the meringue, use a hand mixer or the whisk attachment of a stand mixer to vigorously beat the egg whites (alternatively, you can use meringue powder instead of the egg whites, following the directions on the can). After peaks have begun to form, slowly add the Superfine sugar until it is all absorbed into the meringue.

5. Place the apples cut-side down on a baking sheet and sprinkle with cinnamon and allspice. Frost each apple with meringue, then insert almond slices into the meringue to make it look like a porcupine. Place two currants at the end of each apple to serve as eyes.

6. Place in oven and bake for 25 minutes until the meringue is golden.

CHAPTER 17

Fika Favorites: Coffee Breads, Quickbreads, and Coffeecakes

Swedish Cinnamon Rolls (*Kanelbullar*)

Swedish cinnamon rolls are a classic complement to fika coffee breaks.
Unlike U.S. cinnamon buns, the Swedish version contains less sugar and are unglazed.
Add golden raisins to the filling for an extra-special touch.

INGREDIENTS | SERVES 24

1 cup milk

¼ cup softened butter

⅓ cup white sugar

1 egg, beaten

1 teaspoon salt

2 teaspoons freshly ground cardamom

1 package active dry yeast (2¼ teaspoons)

4–4½ cups all-purpose or bread flour

⅓ cup melted butter

½ cup brown sugar

3 tablespoons cinnamon

¼ cup chopped walnuts or pecans (optional)

1½ cups golden raisins, plumped in warm water then drained (optional)

1 egg plus 1 tablespoon water, beaten into an egg wash

3 tablespoons pearl sugar or sparkling sugar

Swedish *Fika*

In Sweden, it's common to take two or three coffee breaks a day; not 10-minute affairs where you gossip around the water cooler, but real, refreshing breaks where you leave your work premises long enough to meet with friends to fika at a local hot-spot, relaxing together with a cup of coffee and a snack. Makes you want to emigrate to Sweden, doesn't it?

1. In a small saucepan, heat milk to a light boil, turning off heat when the milk reaches the scalding point. Transfer scalded milk to a mixing bowl. Stir in the ¼ cup softened butter, white sugar, egg, salt, and cardamom. Let mixture cool until finger-warm (still quite warm, but just cool enough to touch). Stir in the yeast and let the mixture sit for 10 minutes.

2. Add flour into mixture ½ cup at a time until dough is firm and pulls away from the side of your mixing bowl. (*Tip*: If using a stand mixer, exchange the mixing paddle for the dough hook after you've added the first 2 cups of flour. Use the dough hook to mix and knead the dough as you add the remaining 2–2½ cups of flour.)

3. Cover the dough in the mixing bowl with a clean towel and let rise in a warm place until doubled, about 1 hour. Punch down the dough, then remove from bowl. On a floured counter, knead dough lightly until smooth and shiny.

4. Roll each half of the dough into an 8" × 14" rectangle, pressing down slightly on the rolling pin to remove any air bubbles. Brush each rectangle with the ⅓ cup melted butter.

5. Mix together the brown sugar and cinnamon, then sprinkle evenly over the rectangles. Sprinkle the nuts and raisins, if using, in an even layer on top.

6. Tightly roll each rectangle, jellyroll fashion, to form a 12"-long snake. Use a sharp knife to cut each roll into 12 (1") slices. Put each roll in a cupcake wrapper and place on a baking sheet. Cover with a tea towel and allow to double in size, about 45 minutes.

7. Preheat oven to 425°F. Brush the cinnamon rolls with egg wash and sprinkle with pearl sugar. Place on the middle rack of the oven and bake for 7 minutes or until done.

Kari's "Icelandic" *Snúður*

In Iceland, cinnamon rolls are called snúður ("turns") and are frosted with chocolate or glazes, like American donuts. This is a special tribute version of these decadent buns, using a date filling and a brown-sugar penuche frosting.

INGREDIENTS | SERVES 24

¾ cup butter, chilled

5–6½ cups all-purpose flour, divided use

3 level tablespoons plus 1 cup packed brown sugar, divided use

1 teaspoon cinnamon

1¼ cups milk, divided use

1 cup butter, divided use

¼ cup sugar

1 teaspoon salt

1 egg, beaten

1 package active dry yeast

⅓ cup melted butter

1½ cups dates

¾ cup chopped walnuts or pecans

2 cups (or less) powdered sugar

1. Preheat oven to 350°F. Using a pastry blender, cut together the chilled butter, 1½ cups flour, 3 tablespoons brown sugar, and cinnamon until it looks like coarse crumbs. Spread on a rimmed baking sheet, place in the oven, and bake for 15 minutes until golden. Remove from the oven, cool, then crumble. Turn off the oven.

2. Heat 1 cup milk just to the scalding point. Turn off the heat, stir in ½ cup of the butter, the sugar, and salt. Allow to cook until finger-warm; stir in the beaten egg and the yeast, then transfer to a mixing bowl.

3. Add remaining 4–5 cups flour into mixture ½ cup at a time until dough is firm and pulls away from the side of your bowl. (*Tip*: If using a stand mixer, swap the mixing paddle for the dough hook after the first 2 cups of flour. Use the hook as you add the remaining 2–3 cups of flour.)

4. Cover the dough in mixing bowl with a clean towel and let it rise in a warm place until doubled, about 1 hour. Punch down the dough, then remove from bowl. On a floured counter, knead dough lightly until smooth and shiny.

5. Roll each half of the dough into an 8" × 14" rectangle. Brush each rectangle with the ⅓ cup melted butter. Sprinkle the crumb mixture, chopped dates, and nuts evenly over the rectangles, then roll up tightly, jellyroll fashion. Seal the seams, then cut each length into 12 (1") slices. Place on a greased cookie sheet and allow to rise in a warm place until doubled, about 45 minutes.

6. Preheat oven to 375°F. Bake the rolls for 15–20 minutes until golden. Cool on a rack.

7. For the penuche frosting, melt ½ cup butter in a saucepan, then stir in 1 cup packed brown sugar. Bring to a boil, reduce heat to medium-low (a bubbling simmer), and continue to cook for 2 minutes, stirring constantly. Add remaining ¼ cup milk and return to a boil, continuing to stir. Cool to lukewarm, then beat in enough of the powdered sugar to bring the mixture to a spreadable consistency. Use immediately to frost the buns.

Finnish Cinnamon Pastries (*Korvapuusti*)

Don't be alarmed if a Finn offers to give you a slapped ear.
That's the Finnish name for these interestingly shaped cardamom buns: "slapped ears."

INGREDIENTS | SERVES 14

1 cup finger-warm milk

½ cup melted butter, cooled to room temperature, divided use

1 package active dry yeast (2¼ teaspoons)

½ cup sugar

1 teaspoon salt

1 tablespoon freshly ground cardamom

2 eggs

4–5 cups all-purpose flour

¾ cup packed brown sugar

2 tablespoons cinnamon

Pearl sugar or sparkling sugar to taste

1. In a large mixing bowl, combine the milk, ¼ cup of the melted butter, yeast, and sugar. Stir in the salt, cardamom, and 1 of the eggs, then gradually incorporate flour until the dough pulls away from the side of the bowl. (*Tip:* If using a stand mixer, exchange the mixing paddle for the dough hook after you've added the first 2 cups of flour. Use the dough hook to mix and knead the dough as you add the remaining 2–3 cups of flour.) Place the kneaded dough in a greased bowl, turning once to coat with the shortening. Cover with a towel and allow to rise 1 hour or until doubled.

2. Punch down the dough, then divide into two equal halves. Roll each half into an 8" × 14" rectangle; brush each half with the remaining ¼ cup of melted butter, then sprinkle with the brown sugar and cinnamon.

3. Starting from the long side, tightly roll each rectangle into a tube, jellyroll fashion. Use a sharp knife to cut each roll diagonally into 7 triangular rolls (starting at one end of the roll, slant your knife to the right to make the first diagonal cut, then slant it to the left to make the second, producing a triangular slice).

4. Place each slice point up on a greased baking sheet, then use a spoon to press down each tip to form ear-shaped rolls. Cover with a clean towel and allow to rise another hour until doubled.

5. Preheat oven to 400°F. Beat the remaining egg, then use this to brush the top and sides of each roll. Sprinkle with pearl sugar. Bake on center rack for 10–15 minutes or until golden brown.

Braided Cardamom Bread

Braided cardamom bread has been known to convert those unfamiliar with cardamom to a professed love of Scandinavia's most ubiquitous spice.

INGREDIENTS | MAKES 2 LOAVES

1 package active dry yeast (2¼ teaspoons)

¼ cup warm water

1 cup milk, scalded then cooled until finger-warm

¼ cup softened butter

⅓ cup white sugar

1 teaspoon salt

1 egg, beaten

1½ teaspoons freshly ground cardamom

4–4½ cups all-purpose or bread flour

Milk for basting loaves

Pearl or sparkling sugar to taste

Scandinavian Baking Lessons

What's the best way to learn how to bake the Nordic way? Join a local Scandinavian-American cultural organization. Most require only that you have a desire to promote Nordic culture in your community. You're certain to find members who are happy to cook by your side and share recipes handed down to them by their grandparents. A few great organizations to check out are Daughters of Norway, Sons of Norway, Danish Sisterhood of America, Vasa Order of America (Swedish-American), Icelandic National League of North America, and Finlandia Foundation National.

1. Stir the yeast into the warm water and allow it to proof for 15 minutes, until it becomes foamy (if it doesn't start to bubble, buy new yeast and try again).

2. Combine the milk, butter, sugar, salt, beaten egg, and carda-mom in the bowl of a stand mixer. Stir in the yeast mixture and 2 cups of the flour. Equip the mixer with its paddle blade, turn to low, and gradually increase the speed to medium as the flour incorporates into the liquid. Beat until smooth.

3. Replace the mixer paddle with the dough hook, and add enough of the remaining 2½ cups of flour to make a slightly stiff dough that pulls away from the side of the mixer. Increase the speed to medium-high to high and knead dough until it is smooth and glossy.

4. Turn the dough out onto a lightly floured counter and knead 2–3 times.

5. Place the dough in a greased bowl and roll it over once, bringing the greased side up. Cover with a tea towel and place in a warm spot to rise until doubled, about 1 hour. Punch the dough down.

6. Divide the dough into 2 equal halves, and then divide these halves into 3–4 equal portions. Roll each portion into a 15"-long snake. Lay 3–4 of these ropes parallel to one another and braid them together loosely, tucking the ends under and pinching to seal. Repeat with the remaining set of "snakes." Place on greased cookie sheet, cover with the tea towel, and allow to rise until doubled.

7. Preheat oven to 350°F. Brush the braids with milk, sprinkle with the pearl or sparkling sugar, and bake for 15–20 minutes, until golden.

Lemon Cardamom Wreath

Once you've mastered making the basic cardamom dough used for baked goods like cinnamon rolls and cardamom bread, you're ready to try your hand at even fancier yeasted breads like this cardamom wreath, filled with candied lemon and chopped pecans.

INGREDIENTS | MAKES 2 TEA WREATHS

1 package active dry yeast (2¼ teaspoons)

¼ cup warm water

1 cup milk

¼ cup softened butter

½ cup white sugar

2 eggs, beaten

1 teaspoon salt

1½ teaspoons freshly ground cardamom

4–5 cups all-purpose or bread flour

6 tablespoons lemon curd

4 ounces candied lemon peel

4 ounces candied citron

1 cup chopped pecans

1 cup powdered sugar

1½ tablespoons milk

1 tablespoon lemon juice

Grated lemon zest and sparkling sugar for garnish

1. Stir the yeast into the warm water and allow it to proof for 15 minutes, until it becomes foamy.

2. In a saucepan bring the milk to just scalding, then pour into the bowl of a stand mixer. Stir in the butter, sugar, eggs, salt, and ground cardamom. Let mixture cool until finger-warm. Stir in the yeast mixture and let sit for 10 minutes.

3. Add flour into mixture ½ cup at a time until dough is firm and pulls away from the side of your mixing bowl. Knead until smooth and glossy. (*Tip*: If using a stand mixer, exchange the mixing paddle for the dough hook after you've added the first 2 cups of flour. Use the dough hook to mix and knead the dough as you add the remaining 2–3 cups of flour.)

4. Place the dough in a greased bowl and roll it over once, bringing the greased side up. Cover with a tea towel and place in a warm spot to rise until doubled, about 1 hour. Punch down the dough, then remove from bowl. On a floured counter, knead dough lightly until smooth and shiny.

5. After dough has risen, punch down and divide in half. Use a rolling pin to form each half into an 8" × 14" rectangle. Spread 3 tablespoons of lemon curd on each half; divide the candied lemon peel, citron, and pecans evenly, and sprinkle over top of the lemon curd.

Lemon Cardamom Wreath continued

6. Starting at the wide side, tightly roll each rectangle, jellyroll fashion, into a cylinder. Pinch together seams, then shape roll into a circle, pinching together the two ends. Place rings on lightly greased baking sheets, seam down. With scissors or a sharp knife, cut down two-thirds through each ring at 1" intervals. Gently pull and twist each section outward so that it lays on its side but is still connected to the wreath. Cover with a clean towel and allow to rise for an additional hour until doubled.

7. Preheat oven to 350°F. Bake the wreaths on middle rack of oven for 15–20 minutes until lightly browned. Whisk together the powdered sugar, milk, and lemon juice to make a light glaze; spread on the warm wreathes and sprinkle with grated lemon zest and sparkling sugar.

Swedish *Semlor* Buns

Swedish semlor *buns are a treat traditionally served on Shrove Tuesday in Sweden. Making them was a way to use up eggs before the austerities of the Lenten season. Today you'll find* semlor *buns available from January through Easter.*

INGREDIENTS | SERVES 16

1 package active dry yeast (2¼ teaspoons)

¼ cup warm water

¾ cup milk, scalded then cooled until finger-warm

¼ cup softened butter

½ cup white sugar

2 eggs, beaten

1 teaspoon salt

½ teaspoon ground cardamom

4 cups all-purpose or bread flour

1 egg mixed with 1 tablespoon water into an egg wash

½ cup milk (or less)

8 ounces almond paste, grated

½ cup whipping cream

2 tablespoons powdered sugar

1. Stir the yeast into the warm water and allow to proof until it bubbles, about 15 minutes.

2. In a large mixing bowl combine the warmed milk, butter, sugar, eggs, salt, and ground cardamom. Stir into the yeast mixture.

3. Add flour into mixture ½ cup at a time until dough is firm and pulls away from the side of your mixing bowl. Knead until smooth and shiny. (*Tip*: If using a stand mixer, exchange the mixing paddle for the dough hook after you've added the first 2 cups of flour. Use the dough hook to mix and knead the dough as you add the remaining 2 cups of flour.)

4. Place the dough in a greased bowl and roll it over once, bringing the greased side up. Cover with a tea towel and place in a warm spot to rise until doubled, about 1 hour. Punch down the dough, then remove from bowl. On a floured counter, knead dough lightly until smooth and shiny.

5. After dough has risen, punch down and divide in half, then divide each half into 8 equal portions. Shape the portions into spherical buns, then place them on a greased baking sheet. Cover loosely with a towel and allow to rise for 1 hour.

6. Preheat oven to 400°F. Brush the tops and sides of the buns with the egg wash, then place in the preheated oven and cook for 12 minutes or until golden. Remove from the oven and cool on racks.

Swedish *Semlor* Buns continued

7. After the buns have cooled, slice the top almost off the bun, ⅓ of the way from the top, so that it forms an attached "lid." Spoon out the interior of the buns, break into crumbs, and place into a small bowl. Add just enough of the ½ cup milk to moisten the bread, then mix in the grated almond paste. Continue to whisk the crumbs and paste together, adding enough milk so the mixture has almost the consistency of pudding. Spoon the almond mixture back into the buns.

8. Combine whipping cream with powdered sugar and whip to stiff peaks. Pipe into the buns, on top of the almond paste filling, place the lid of each bun down, then sprinkle with additional powdered sugar.

Saffron Bread (*Saffransbröd*)

The same basic dough used for Sweden's Saint Lucia Buns is used here for this fragrant yeasted saffron bread.

INGREDIENTS | MAKES 1 LOAF

1 cup milk

½ cup softened butter, divided use

¾ cup sugar, divided use

1 teaspoon salt

½ teaspoon ground saffron or ¼ teaspoon saffron threads (dried in 250°F oven for 20 minutes, then crumbled)

1 package yeast (2¼ teaspoons)

1 egg, beaten

4–5 cups all-purpose flour

⅔ cup raisins, dried currants, or cherries (or combination), plumped in warm water

1 egg plus 1 tablespoon water, whisked into an egg wash

Pearl sugar or sparkling sugar to taste

1. Heat the milk to the scalding point, then turn off the heat. Stir in ¼ cup of the butter, ½ cup of the sugar, salt, and ground saffron. Pour mixture into mixing bowl and allow to cool until finger-warm. Stir in yeast and let sit for 10 minutes.

2. Stir the beaten egg into liquid, then add the flour into mixture ½ cup at a time until dough is firm and pulls away from the side of your mixing bowl. Knead the dough until it is smooth and glossy. (*Tip*: If using a stand mixer, replace the mixing paddle with the dough hook after you've added the first 2 cups of flour. Use the dough hook to mix and knead the dough as you add the remaining 2–3 cups of flour.)

3. Cover the dough in the mixing bowl with a clean towel and let rise until doubled, about 1 hour. Punch down the dough, then remove from bowl.

4. On a floured counter, roll dough into an 8" × 14" rectangle. Brush this with the remaining butter, then sprinkle with remaining ¼ cup sugar and the plumped dried fruit. Roll jellyroll fashion into a tube, then pinch along the seam and ends to close.

5. With scissors or a sharp knife, cut loaves into ½"-long partial slices. (Take care not to cut through the rolls completely; only snip about ⅔ of the way down.) Gently separate the slices, pulling the first one to the right, the second to the left, then repeating for the length of the loaf. Cover with a clean towel and allow to rise about 1 hour.

6. Preheat oven to 375°F. Brush the risen loaf with egg wash, sprinkle with pearl sugar, and bake for 30 minutes or until done.

Rhubarb Muffins

Sweet yet tangy, these rhubarb muffins are the perfect vehicle for homemade butter and a dollop of strawberry jam.

INGREDIENTS | SERVES 12

¾ cup sugar

¼ cup butter

1 egg

½ cup plain *skyr* (Siggi's) or strained nonfat Greek yogurt

¼ cup milk

1 cup spelt flour

1 cup all-purpose flour

1 teaspoon baking powder

¼ teaspoon salt

1 teaspoon vanilla sugar (or substitute 1 teaspoon vanilla extract)

¼ cup candied ginger, minced

2 cups rhubarb, chopped

1. Preheat oven to 375°F. Grease or place cupcake wrappers in a 12-cup muffin tin.

2. Cream together the sugar and butter, then stir in the egg until incorporated. Lightly stir in the *skyr* and the milk. In a separate large mixing bowl, whisk together the flours, baking powder, salt, and vanilla sugar, then mix into the batter just until all of the dry ingredients have been incorporated.

3. Fold the candied ginger and rhubarb into the batter.

4. Spoon the batter into the prepared muffin tins and bake for 20–25 minutes.

Ten-Minute Chocolate Coffeecake

When you don't have time to bake a yeasted coffee bread, this egg-free yet rich chocolate coffeecake is ready in 10 minutes, thanks to modern microwave technology.

INGREDIENTS | SERVES 4–6

1½ cups all-purpose flour

1 cup sugar

3 tablespoons unsweetened cocoa

3 teaspoons instant coffee

1 teaspoon baking powder

½ teaspoon baking soda

¼ teaspoon salt

1 cup cold water

⅓ cup canola oil

1 tablespoon white vinegar

1 teaspoon cardamom extract (or substitute vanilla)

Powdered sugar to taste

1. In a mixing bowl, whisk together the flour, sugar, cocoa, instant coffee, baking powder, baking soda, and salt.

2. Stir in the water, canola oil, vinegar, and cardamom extract.

3. Pour into a microwave-safe baking dish and microwave on high for 6–8 minutes (turning the dish every 2 minutes if your microwave isn't equipped with a turntable). Test the cake for doneness with a toothpick inserted in the middle of the cake (it should come out clean).

4. Sprinkle the warm cake with powdered sugar and serve.

Danish Leaf Cake (*Bladenkage*)

Also called grønkage ("green cake") or, by mothers with young sons, "poison cake," this bright green almond cake with its chocolate ganache topping is a favorite among Danish children. Try baking it as a Halloween treat for your favorite munchkins.

INGREDIENTS | SERVES 12

1 cup butter or margarine

1 cup sugar

2 eggs

2 cups all-purpose flour

1 teaspoon baking powder

⅔ cup milk

1 tablespoon almond extract

2 teaspoons green food coloring

12 ounces semisweet chocolate

⅔ cup heavy cream

Chocolate Ganache (almond flavoring) to frost (see sidebar recipe)

Chocolate Ganache

To make Chocolate Ganache, finely chop 12 ounces of good semisweet chocolate. Bring ⅔ cup heavy cream just to the scalding (boiling) point over medium-high heat, then remove from the burner and whisk in the chocolate and 1 teaspoon of flavored extract (vanilla, almond, or cardamom). Whisk vigorously until the ganache is smooth and creamy. Cool slightly, then use to frost cakes or cookies. The ganache will thicken more the longer it sits, so keep an eye on it and use it at your desired thickness—thinner for a glaze, thicker for a frosting.

1. Preheat oven to 395°F.

2. Cream together the butter and sugar until fluffy, then add the eggs one at a time.

3. In a separate bowl, whisk the flour and baking powder together, then stir into the batter.

4. Combine the milk, almond extract, and food coloring, and then mix this liquid into the cake batter.

5. Pour into a greased 9" square cake pan and bake for 30 minutes, or until a toothpick inserted in the center of the cake comes out clean. Remove from oven and cool completely before glazing with Chocolate Ganache.

Mor Monsen's Coffeecake

Golden Norwegian "Mother Monsen's Cake" freezes beautifully, so it's nice to keep one in the freezer in anticipation of unexpected guests or just as a treat to pull out on a lazy weekend morning.

INGREDIENTS | SERVES 10

1¼ cups butter, softened

1¼ cups sugar

6 eggs, separated

1½ cups flour

1 teaspoon baking powder

Zest of 1 lemon

½ cup currants, plumped in warm water, then drained

½ cup sliced almonds

¼ cup pearl or sparkling sugar

1. Preheat oven to 350°F. Cream together the butter and sugar, then add the egg yolks one at a time. Mix in the flour, baking powder, and lemon zest.

2. Whisk the egg whites into firm peaks, then fold them gently into the batter.

3. Spoon the batter into a greased and floured 9" × 13" pan. Scatter the currants, almonds, and pearl sugar over the top; then press them down slightly with a spoon so they are partly submerged into the batter.

4. Bake in the oven for 25–30 minutes or until a toothpick inserted in the center comes out clean. Cool cake in the pan, then turn it out and cut into diamond shapes.

Banana Spelt Bread

Sugar-free, this moist banana bread is made using 3 of the healthy ingredients native to the Nordic terroir: spelt flour, skyr (Icelandic yogurt), and walnuts. Make it the night before serving to allow the flavors time to meld.

INGREDIENTS | MAKES 1 LOAF

3 tablespoons canola oil

½ cup unsweetened applesauce

2 eggs

3 ripe bananas, mashed

½ cup chopped walnuts, toasted

1 teaspoon cardamom, freshly ground

1 (6-ounce) container vanilla Siggi's *skyr* (or nonfat Greek yogurt, strained)

2 cups spelt flour (or substitute all-purpose)

1 teaspoon baking soda

½ teaspoon baking powder

½ teaspoon salt

1. Preheat oven to 350°F. Mix together the canola oil and applesauce, then beat in the eggs one at a time. Stir in the mashed bananas, walnuts, and cardamom. Fold in the *skyr* (or strained yogurt).

2. In another bowl, whisk together the flour, baking soda, baking powder, and salt; mix into the batter just until combined.

3. Pour the batter into a greased 9" × 5" loaf pan. Bake on the center rack of the oven for 1 hour, or until a toothpick inserted in the center returns clean.

4. Allow the bread to rest in the pan for 15 minutes, then turn it out to cool on a rack.

Danish *Kringler*

Making Danish Kringler is a labor you'll love—the pastry, layered with butter, is rolled three times over on itself in a process that is best spread over 2–3 days (to allow the pastry layers to chill properly). The result is worth the time: a flaky, tender, almondy pretzel that will melt in your mouth.

INGREDIENTS | MAKES 2 KRINGLER

1 package active dry yeast (2¼ teaspoons)

¼ cup finger-warm water

½ cup finger-warm milk

3 tablespoons sugar

½ teaspoon salt

1 egg

2 cups all-purpose flour

¾ cup butter, chilled

¼ cup butter, softened

2 cups powdered sugar

2 tablespoons milk

1 (3-ounce) package almond paste

1 cup golden raisins, plumped in hot water

Sparkling sugar to taste

Slivered almonds to taste

1. Dissolve the yeast in the warm water in a mixing bowl. Once it begins to bubble, after about 15 minutes, mix in the finger-warm milk, sugar, salt, and egg. Stir in the flour just until incorporated (do *not* overwork the dough). Wrap in cling wrap and chill in the refrigerator overnight.

2. Remove the chilled butter from the refrigerator and grate it; divide into two equal parts. Roll out the dough on a floured counter into an 8" × 12" rectangle. Spread ½ of the butter over ⅔ of the rectangle (the far left-hand ⅔). Fold the remaining right-hand, unbuttered ⅓ over the middle ⅓ of the rectangle, then fold the left-hand (buttered) ⅓ over on top of the middle to form a tight 8" × 4" rectangle. Chill for 10 minutes.

3. Roll the chilled dough out again into an 8" × 12" rectangle. Repeat the same process with the remaining butter.

4. Now roll the dough out to an 8" × 16" rectangle. Lift the right-hand end of the rectangle and fold it into the exact middle of the dough; lift the left-hand end and fold it too into the exact middle (you'll now have an 8" × 8" square). Fold the left-hand side entirely over the right-hand side (producing an 8" × 4" rectangle). Chill for 30 minutes.

5. Roll the dough one last time into an 8" × 12" rectangle. Fold the right-hand ⅓ over the middle ⅓, then the left-hand ⅓ over the middle. Divide down the middle into two 2" × 8" halves.

6. Roll each half into a 6" × 20" rectangle.

Danish *Kringler* continued

So Many *Kringler*, So Little Time

There are a multitude of varieties of kringler in Denmark: saltkringler (savory pretzels), kommenskringler (small unsweetened yeasted pretzels sprinkled with caraway), and sukkerkringler (sweetened pretzels topped with sugar). The distinctive kringle pretzel shape has been used as a signboard denoting bakeries since the Middle Ages.

7. Cream together the ¼ cup softened butter, the powdered sugar, milk, and almond paste, then fold in the raisins. Spread this filling down the center ⅓ of each rectangle. Fold the bottom edge up over the filling, then the top edge down over to make a roll; pinch the seams and ends together well.

8. Place the first roll on a lightly greased baking sheet, folding its two ends up, around, and down into the middle of the roll to form a pretzel shape (without the twist). Repeat with the second roll. Cover with a clean tea towel and allow to rise in a warm place for 1 hour.

9. Preheat oven to 375°F. Brush the tops of the pastries with a little milk, then sprinkle with sparkling sugar and slivered almonds. Bake in the oven for 25 minutes, until golden brown.

Danish Coconut Dream Cake (*Drømmekage*)

Coconut lovers will have very happy dreams in anticipation of waking up to this Danish coffeecake.

INGREDIENTS | SERVES 12

3 eggs

1 cup sugar

2 cups flour

3 teaspoons baking powder

1 teaspoon vanilla sugar

12 tablespoons butter

1½ cups milk

1⅓ cups coconut flakes

1¼ cups brown sugar

Alletiders Kokebog ("Alletiders Cookbook")

If you love to browse Danish recipe collections, check out the web-based, interactive cookbook Alletiders Kokebog (*www.dk-kogebogen.dk*). Not only does it have a fabulous collection of user-contributed coffeecake (and other) recipes, but it also has an inspired (and inspiring) "empty your refrigerator" search feature where you can type in the ingredients you have on hand and it will generate recipes using them. Brilliant!

1. Preheat oven to 400°F.

2. In a large double boiler, whisk together the eggs and sugar over boiling water until the mixture has thickened enough to coat a spoon. Remove from heat.

3. Whisk together the flour, baking powder, and vanilla sugar, then use a spatula to lightly fold the flour into the custard.

4. Melt 4 tablespoons of the butter and 1 cup of the milk together on the stove or in the microwave (1 minute on high), then stir this into the batter. Pour the batter into a greased and floured rectangular (9" × 13") cake pan.

5. Bake on the middle rack of the oven for 20 minutes or until a toothpick inserted in the middle returns clean.

6. As the cake bakes, in a saucepan combine the remaining 8 tablespoons (½ cup) butter, coconut flakes, brown sugar, and remaining ½ cup milk. Heat over medium-low until the sugar has melted and the mixture is warmed through, stirring constantly.

7. Remove the cake from the oven and increase the heat to 450°F.

8. Spread the coconut topping over the warm cake and return to the oven. Bake for 5 more minutes to allow the topping to caramelize. Remove from the oven and serve either warm or cold.

Lingonberry Swirl Quickbread

Either Lingonberry Jam (see Chapter 7) or stirred lingonberries can be used for this Nordic quickbread.

INGREDIENTS | MAKES 1 LOAF

¼ cup butter, softened

1 cup sugar

1 egg

2 cups all-purpose flour

1 teaspoon baking powder

½ teaspoon baking soda

½ teaspoon salt

1 cup buttermilk

1½ cups Lingonberry Jam (see Chapter 7)

2 tablespoons slivered almonds

1. Preheat oven to 350°F.

2. In a large mixing bowl, cream together the butter and sugar. Stir in the egg.

3. In a separate bowl, whisk together the flour, baking powder, baking soda, and salt. In alternating increments, mix the dry ingredients and the buttermilk into the batter.

4. Pour ⅓ of the batter into a greased loaf pan, then spread with ½ cup of the jam. Repeat the layers twice, ending with the jam.

5. Use a fork to swirl the topmost layer of jam and batter across the top of the loaf so that it looks marbled. Sprinkle the almond slivers over the top.

6. Bake in the oven for 45–50 minutes or until a toothpick inserted in the center comes out clean. Cool in pan for 15 minutes before turning out; then cool completely on a rack.

CHAPTER 18

Desserts

Swedish Apple Cake

Swedish apple cake, with its beautiful top layer of apple slices and almonds, is a harbinger of autumn. Serve it warm with vanilla sauce or ice cream.

INGREDIENTS | SERVES 12

¼ cup dry rye bread crumbs

1 cup butter

1 cup white sugar

3 eggs

1 teaspoon baking powder

1¼ cups flour

4 baking apples, pared and sliced into thin wedges

3 tablespoons brown sugar

2 teaspoons ground cinnamon

½ teaspoon nutmeg

⅓ cup coarsely chopped almonds

1. Preheat oven to 350°F. Generously butter a 10" round cake pan. Shake the bread crumbs across the pan so they adhere to both the bottom and sides of the pan.

2. Cream together butter and white sugar, then incorporate eggs into the batter. Sprinkle with baking powder, then add the flour in ⅓-cup increments, mixing well to prevent lumps.

3. In a small bowl toss the apple slices together with the brown sugar, cinnamon, and nutmeg.

4. Transfer the cake batter to the prepared pan, then gently arrange the apple slices in circles on top of the batter, covering it completely. Sprinkle any remaining sugar-spice mixture and the chopped almonds across the top of the cake.

5. Bake cake for 1 hour, then test it for doneness in the center with a toothpick.

Chocolate Sticky Cake (*Kladdkaka*)

*Ready in less time that it takes to whip up a humdrum box of brownies,
Swedish kladdkaka is the ultimate in chocolate decadence.*

INGREDIENTS | SERVES 8

2 eggs

1½ cups sugar

⅛ teaspoon salt

½ cup flour

4 heaping tablespoons unsweetened
cocoa powder

1 teaspoon vanilla extract

½ cup melted butter, cooled to room
temperature

Powdered sugar to garnish

1. Preheat oven to 350°F. In a mixing bowl combine the eggs and sugar. Sprinkle with salt, then beat in the flour.

2. Whisk the cocoa powder and vanilla extract into the melted butter. Vigorously whip the butter into the cake batter to get as much air into it as possible.

3. Butter and flour a 9" round cake pan; pour in the batter. Bake in the oven for 25 minutes. At this point, use a toothpick to test the cake—it needs to come out dry when inserted at the edge of the cake, but should come out sticky with chocolate when placed in the cake's center.

4. Sprinkle top of cake with powdered sugar and serve.

Sandbakkels

*Sandbakkels are equally delicious served alone as cookies (place them on the plate so their "design" side
is showcased) or as delicate tarts filled with fresh berries and whipped cream.*

**INGREDIENTS | MAKES 3 DOZEN
COOKIES**

1 cup salted butter

¾ cup sugar

1 egg

1 teaspoon almond or vanilla extract

2½ cups flour

1. Preheat oven to 350°F. In a large bowl, cream together the butter and sugar, then add egg, almond extract, and flour, beating vigorously into a smooth batter.

2. Use cooking spray to grease your *sandbakkel* tins, then arrange them on a baking sheet. Pinch off small balls of the dough and, using your thumbs, press each ball into a tin so that it thinly covers the bottom and sides (⅛" thick or less).

3. Bake in oven for 12–15 minutes, just until brown (watch closely, for they will burn quickly).

4. Remove from oven, cool, and then carefully remove from tins (it helps to tap the bottom of each tin very lightly on the counter to loosen the tart).

Gluten-Free Norwegian Wet Cake (*Bløtekake*)

*Bløtekake, or "wet cake," moistened by the juice of its crushed-strawberry filling,
is the premier birthday cake of Norway. This gluten-free version will be much appreciated
when made as a surprise for friends with wheat sensitivity.*

INGREDIENTS | SERVES 12

5 eggs

1½ cups sugar

Juice and zest of 1 lemon

1¼ cups Swan's potato starch flour

1 teaspoon gluten-free baking powder

3 cups whipping cream

3 teaspoons vanilla sugar (see sidebar)
  or 3 teaspoons vanilla extract

4 cups crushed strawberries

Extra strawberries, blueberries, other
  colorful fruit, or edible flowers for
  garnish

Vanilla Sugar

Vanilla sugar is more commonly used than vanilla extract in Scandinavian baking. To make it, fill a mason jar with 1 cup of powdered sugar, then split open a vanilla bean. Stick the vanilla bean in the middle of the jar, then pour 1 more cup of powdered sugar on top. Cover and place in the cupboard for 2 weeks, shaking the jar every day or two. This makes a superlative gift for those who enjoy baking the Scandinavian way.

1. Grease and use a small amount of the potato starch flour to prepare 2 (9") round cake pans for baking. Preheat oven to 350°F.

2. Separate the egg whites from the yolks into two separate containers. Mix together the yolks, sugar, lemon juice and zest, then incorporate the potato starch flour.

3. Whip the egg whites until solid peaks arise. Lightly fold ½ of the whites into the cake batter, then pour all of the batter into the remaining egg whites and fold together just until blended.

4. Transfer ⅔ of the batter to 1 cake pan, and ⅓ of the batter to the second pan. Bake in oven for 40 minutes (it's a good idea to check the thinner cake with a toothpick for readiness at 30 minutes). Place both pans on baking racks until cooled.

5. In a separate bowl, combine the cream with the vanilla sugar and whip until peaks form.

6. When ready to assemble the cake, cut the thicker cake evenly in half. Place the bottom portion on a decorative plate and cover with ½ of the crushed strawberries. Frost with enough of the whipped vanilla cream to cover, then top with the next cake layer and repeat: crushed strawberries and then whipped vanilla cream. Use the remaining whipped vanilla cream to frost the entire cake.

7. Garnish with additional berries and/or edible flowers and serve with aplomb. In Norwegian, *Gratulerer med dagen*! ("Happy Birthday!" but also said on other occasions.)

Swedish Strawberry Cake (*Jordgubbstårta*)

Similar in preparation to Norwegian bløtekake, this version of strawberry cake incorporates a luscious almond cream filling and white chocolate icing. Use June's seasonal local strawberries to make this the crowning glory of a Midsummer's Eve bonfire party.

INGREDIENTS | SERVES 12

4 eggs

2 cups plus 2 tablespoons sugar, divided

1 cup flour

¾ cup plus 2 tablespoons Swan's potato starch flour, divided use

1½ teaspoons baking powder

2 teaspoons vanilla sugar or 1 teaspoon vanilla extract

3 cups milk

2 egg yolks

½ cup toasted almonds, ground

6 ounces grated white chocolate

8 ounces cream cheese

¼ cup butter, softened

1–2 cups powdered sugar

2 cups strawberries, sliced or lightly mashed

1. For the cake, beat together 4 eggs and 2 cups regular sugar, then gradually add 1 cup flour, ¾ cup potato starch flour, baking powder, and vanilla sugar. Set aside in the refrigerator to rest while you prepare the cake filling.

2. To make almond cream filling, bring milk almost to a boil in a saucepan over medium heat. Meanwhile, in a large mixing bowl beat together 2 egg yolks and remaining 2 tablespoons sugar, then whisk in remaining 2 tablespoons potato starch flour. Slowly whisk the warm milk into your egg mixture; when all is incorporated, return the cream to the saucepan and cook over medium heat, whisking constantly, until mixture thickens and begins to bubble. Remove from heat, fold in toasted ground almonds, and cool.

3. Preheat oven to 350°F. Butter and flour a 9" springform pan. Pour the cooled batter into the pan and cook for 40 minutes or until done. Remove from oven and cool completely before removing from pan.

4. For icing, melt white chocolate in a double boiler or microwave, then cool slightly. Whip together cream cheese and softened butter, stir in melted white chocolate, then beat in enough powdered sugar to make a fluffy icing. Place in refrigerator for 15 minutes or more to set.

5. To assemble cake, release the cake from its springform pan and cut into two equal halves. Spread the bottom half with almond cream and top with the strawberries. Top with remaining half of cake, then cover the tops and sides with the frosting. Garnish generously with additional strawberries and serve.

Almond Cake

Almond cake is a big seller at Scandinavian-American festivals and fundraisers.
Baked in a grooved metal pan, it is just rich and dense enough to be the superlative coffeecake.

INGREDIENTS | SERVES 18

¾ cup sliced almonds
1 stick butter or margarine
1¼ cups sugar
1 egg
2 teaspoons almond extract
⅔ cup milk
1¼ cups flour
1 teaspoon baking powder
½ teaspoon salt
Powdered sugar for garnish

Cold Cakes and Cookies

It's traditional for Scandinavian and Scandinavian-American bakers to provide a regular potlatch of homemade cookies and cakes (at least 7 varieties) for their loved ones during Advent and Christmas. The secret to doing this without killing themselves: their freezers. Most cakes, cookies, breads, and even lefse freeze beautifully for up to 4 months, so you can begin baking your holiday treats in September (preferably after the kids have returned to school, to avoid shrinkage).

1. Preheat oven to 350°F. On the stovetop, toast sliced almonds in a large, ungreased frying pan over medium heat, stirring constantly, until golden. Remove, cool, and grind in a food processor or nut grinder.

2. Whisk together butter and sugar, then add in egg, almond extract, and milk. Beat in flour, baking powder, and salt to make a smooth batter.

3. Use additional butter to coat all inner sides of an almond cake pan (or substitute a regular bread pan). Drop in the ground almonds and shake pan so they stick to the pan's bottom and sides.

4. Spoon cake batter evenly into the pan.

5. Bake in oven for up to 50 minutes, checking for doneness at 40 minutes. When done, remove cake from oven and cool in the pan (if you remove the cake from the pan while it's warm, it will break). Sprinkle cooled cake with powdered sugar before serving.

Icelandic Prune Cake (*Vinarterta*)

Vinarterta, also known as randalín ("striped lady cake"), is sometimes topped with an almond or butter icing. But, the cake is so incredibly rich that it is perhaps best when served unfrosted, glorified by its stripes alone.

INGREDIENTS | SERVES 40

2 pounds pitted prunes

3½ cups sugar, divided use

1 teaspoon cinnamon

2½ teaspoons freshly ground cardamom, divided use

1 cup butter

3 eggs

1 teaspoon vanilla extract

1½ teaspoons almond extract

6 cups flour

2 teaspoons baking powder

1 teaspoon salt

¼ cup whipping cream

1. For prune filling, place prunes in a saucepan and add just enough water to cover. Bring pot to a low boil over medium heat and simmer until the prunes are soft, about 20 minutes. Drain the prunes, reserving 1 cup prune juice.

2. After prunes have cooled, purée them in a blender or food processor. Transfer to a bowl and stir in the reserved prune juice, 1½ cups of the sugar, cinnamon, and ½ teaspoon of the cardamom. Return to the saucepan and heat, stirring steadily, until mixture thickens to the consistency of lemon curd. Remove from heat and allow to cool.

3. For cake, mix together the butter and remaining 2 cups sugar in a heavy mixer. Add the eggs one at a time, then stir in the vanilla and almond extracts.

4. In a separate bowl, sift together the flour, baking powder, remaining 2 teaspoons of the cardamom, and the salt.

5. Alternate adding the dry ingredients and the cream to the cake batter. The dough will be heavy and dense.

6. Preheat oven to 375°F. Divide dough evenly into 8 portions. On a floured counter, roll each portion into a ⅛"-thick round, about 10" in diameter. Line a large baking sheet with parchment paper, place one round on it, and bake just until golden, about 10 minutes. Cool on a cake rack; repeat for the remaining 7 layers.

7. To assemble, place the least attractive layer of cake on a plate and spread with a thin layer of prune filling. Repeat the layers, ending with the prettiest layer. Place in an airtight container and allow to sit for 48 hours (the prune filling will soak into and soften the cake layers).

8. Dust with powdered sugar and cut into very thin slices.

Apple Pie with *Gjetost* Cheese

*The spelt flour used in this flavorful apple pie lends a special nutty flavor to the crust.
Look for it in organic food stores.*

INGREDIENTS | SERVES 10

2 cups plus 1 tablespoon spelt flour, divided use

1 teaspoon salt

⅔ cup unsalted butter, chilled and diced

6–7 tablespoons ice water

6 baking apples (like Granny Smith)

½ cup sugar

1 teaspoon cardamom, freshly ground

½ teaspoon cinnamon

4½ ounces Ski Queen *gjetost* cheese

1 egg beaten together with 2 teaspoons water as egg wash

1 tablespoon sparkling sugar

Sifting Flour

You don't need a fancy sifter to mix together today's flours and spices for baking. Simply use a large balloon whisk to fluff the dry ingredients together for 30 seconds before incorporating them into your batter or dough. It's a lot faster than a sifter and less likely to scatter flour all over your kitchen.

1. Sift 2 cups of the spelt flour and the salt into a chilled mixing bowl, then use a pastry blender or 2 knives to cut the butter into the flour until the mixture has the texture of small dried peas. Add the ice water, 2 tablespoons at a time, and blend into the mixture with a fork until the dough pulls away from the sides of the bowl in a soft mass (you don't want to add too much water).

2. On a lightly floured counter, gently knead the dough 3 times, then return it to its bowl, cover, and refrigerate for at least 30 minutes.

3. After the spelt pastry dough has rested, divide it in half and roll each half into rounds. Place one round in the bottom of a 9" pie plate and pierce the bottoms and sides with a fork.

4. Preheat oven to 350°F. Peel, pare, and thinly slice the apples, then toss together with the sugar, remaining tablespoon of spelt flour, cardamom, and cinnamon.

5. Coarsely grate the *gjetost* cheese, then sprinkle half of it on the bottom pie crust. Spoon in the apple mixture, then top with the remaining grated *gjetost*. Cover with the second pie crust, sealing the edges together; crimp the sides and cut a few slits in the top.

6. Shield the edges of the pie with aluminum foil, then bake in center of oven for 30 minutes. Remove the foil, brush the top of the pie with the egg wash, then sprinkle with sparkling sugar. Return to the oven and cook for 15 more minutes.

7. Serve warm, accompanied by cardamom or rye bread ice cream.

Almond Rusks

Whether you call them biscotti, rusks, kavring, zweiback, or mandelskorpor, these twice-baked cookies should be considered mandatory whenever a Scandinavian-style coffee table is hosted.

INGREDIENTS | MAKES 4 DOZEN

2 eggs

1 cup sugar

1 cup canola oil

1 teaspoon almond extract

3 cups spelt flour (or substitute all-purpose)

1 teaspoon baking powder

½ teaspoon baking soda

½ teaspoon salt

¾ cup coarsely chopped almonds, toasted

Be Creative

In the spirit of Swedish cookbook author Kasja Warg's credo, "Use what you have" available to jazz up this basic almond rusk recipe—dried cranberries, apricots, chocolate chips, dates—the possibilities are limited only by what's on hand in your baking cupboard.

1. Preheat oven to 375°F. In a mixing bowl, whisk together the eggs, sugar, canola oil, and almond extract.

2. In a separate bowl, use a balloon whisk to stir together the flour, baking powder, baking soda, salt, and toasted almonds. Add to the batter in ½-cup increments until all of the flour is incorporated into a soft dough.

3. Line two jellyroll or other large baking sheets with parchment paper, then divide the batter between the two, using a spatula to spread the batter into long, 1½"-wide lengths.

4. Bake for 10–15 minutes until golden brown. Remove pans from the oven and reduce the heat to 275°F.

5. Cut each length into ½-inch diagonal slices, then place the slices, cut-side down, back on the baking sheets. Return to oven and bake for 10 more minutes, then turn the heat off completely and allow the rusks to remain in oven for an additional 20 minutes.

Rye Cookies

In Finland and Sweden, rye cookies are often strung with a ribbon on one's Christmas tree, available as a festive snack for guests.

INGREDIENTS | MAKES 4 DOZEN

1 cup butter

½ cup sugar

1 egg

1 cup all-purpose flour

½ cup light rye flour

½ teaspoon salt

1 teaspoon ginger

1 teaspoon cinnamon

1 teaspoon hornsalt (or 2 teaspoons baking powder)

1 egg white

3 tablespoons sparkling white sugar

Hornsalt

Hornsalt, also known as baker's ammonia, is the secret to achieving cookies with an unparalleled crispness—and without the metallic aftertaste that can accompany baking powder. Although you'll catch a whiff of ammonia as your cookies bake (don't be tempted to taste the raw cookie dough), the ammonia completely bakes off, leaving cookies with the most delicate of textures.

1. Using a stand mixer or large mixing bowl, cream together the butter and sugar, then beat the egg into the batter.

2. Sift together the flours, salt, spices, and hornsalt, then incorporate into the batter in ⅓-cup increments. Once the dough has pulled together, place it on a floured counter and divide it in half. Flour your hands and gently roll each half into a 2"-thick cylinder. Wrap in cling wrap and refrigerate for at least 3 hours.

3. Preheat oven to 350°F. Cut the cooled dough into ⅛"-thick slices, then use a thimble to cut the center out of each slice. Place on a cookie sheet lined with a silpat or parchment paper. Brush each cookie with egg wash and sprinkle sparkling sugar on top.

4. Bake until browned, about 10 to 15 minutes.

Danish Pepper Nuts (*Pebernødder*)

Tuck these tiny ginger-scented jewels into woven paper baskets as treats for children and adults alike.

INGREDIENTS | MAKES AROUND 300

1 cup butter or margarine, at room temperature

½ cup packed brown sugar

½ cup white sugar

1 egg

3 cups all-purpose flour (or use 1½ cup spelt flour and 1½ cup all-purpose flour)

1 teaspoon baking powder

½ teaspoon baking soda

1 teaspoon ground cardamom

1 teaspoon ground cinnamon

½ teaspoon ground ginger

½ teaspoon ground cloves

1. Preheat oven to 375°F. Cream together the butter, brown sugar, and white sugar, then beat in the egg.

2. In a separate bowl, use a balloon whisk to mix together the remaining ingredients.

3. Beat the flour into the creamed butter to form a stiff dough.

4. On a floured counter, roll the dough into ½"-thick "snakes." Use cooking shears or a knife to cut the snakes into pieces the size of hazelnuts.

5. Place on a parchment paper–lined baking sheet and place in preheated oven; bake for 8 minutes or until browned (watch to make sure peppernuts don't burn).

6. Remove from oven and cool on rack. Peppernuts, like most Scandinavian cookies, freeze beautifully for later enjoyment.

Frozen Lingonberry Yogurt

Pleasantly tart, frozen lingonberry yogurt is a delightful finish for a summer supper. Here's how to make it without an ice-cream maker; you can, of course, use an ice-cream maker for similar results with less work.

INGREDIENTS | MAKES 2½ CUPS

18 ounces heavy whipping cream

18 ounces plain *skyr* or nonfat Greek yogurt

2 cups Lingonberry Jam (see Chapter 7)

½ cup sugar

1. Whisk together the whipping cream, yogurt, jam, and sugar.

2. Pour mixture into a bowl and freeze for 45 minutes.

3. After 45 minutes, remove bowl from freezer and whisk ingredients strongly to break up the crystals. Return to freezer.

4. Repeat this process every 20 minutes for up to 3 hours, until the mixture is solid. Cover and freeze until serving.

Norwegian Troll Cream (*Trollkrem*)

Although traditionally made by beating together egg whites, sugar, and fresh lingonberries into a foam, Norwegian troll cream can be made even more easily by substituting pasteurized meringue powder (available in craft stores and from cake decorating suppliers) for the raw egg whites.

INGREDIENTS | SERVES 6

2 teaspoons meringue powder

2 tablespoons warm water

½ cup Lingonberry Jam (see Chapter 7)

1. In a mixing bowl, whisk together the meringue powder and warm water until dissolved, then stir in the jam.

2. Using a hand mixer or the whisk attachment of a stand mixer, whip the liquid vigorously at a high speed for 15 minutes, until the mixture expands into a thick foam.

3. Spoon the *trollkrem* into serving bowls and serve immediately.

Cardamom Ice Cream

Cardamom and vanilla ice cream are a match made in heaven—while wonderful served on its own, this easily prepared cardamom ice cream is phenomenal as an accompaniment to warm fruit pies or fruit crumbles.

INGREDIENTS | MAKES 1 PINT

8 egg yolks, room temperature

1 cup Superfine sugar

2 cups milk

2 cups whipping cream

1 (2") piece vanilla bean

1 tablespoon cardamom, freshly ground

No Ice Cream Maker?

No worries. To make ice cream without a machine or salt, simply place the custard in a pan and place it in the freezer. Remove it at 20-minute intervals and stir vigorously with a whisk, until it has frozen to the desired consistency. Allow it to freeze an additional 24 hours before serving.

1. Beat together the egg yolks and Superfine sugar until creamy.

2. In a saucepan, combine the milk and whipping cream. Scrape the seeds of the vanilla bean into the liquid, then add the bean halves and the cardamom.

3. Heat the milk over medium-high heat just until it reaches a low scald. Remove from heat and very slowly whisk the warm milk in a steady stream into the egg yolks. After the custard is thoroughly combined, remove the vanilla bean halves and return the custard to the saucepan.

4. Bring the custard to a simmer over medium heat and cook for 8 minutes, stirring constantly, until the mixture is thick enough to coat the back of a spoon. Remove from heat, cover, and refrigerate for at least 1 hour.

5. Prepare the ice cream in an ice-cream maker according to the manufacturer's directions.

Rye Bread Ice Cream

It's hard to say exactly where rye bread ice cream originated, since it is now popular across northern Europe. In Iceland, it is the hallmark dessert served at Reykjavik's trendy Café Loki.

INGREDIENTS | SERVES 8

4 thick slices rye bread (spicy Swedish limpa bread also works beautifully)

4 tablespoons butter

½ cup brown sugar

1 teaspoon cinnamon

2 cups heavy whipping cream

1 (14-ounce) can sweetened condensed milk

1 teaspoon vanilla or cardamom extract

1 tablespoon toasted caraway seeds (optional)

1. Cut the rye bread into coarse bread crumbs. Toast the crumbs in a large frying pan until they start to brown, then mix in the butter, sugar, and cinnamon. Fry until the crumbs have caramelized, stirring constantly. Remove from heat and cool.

2. Using a mixer, whip the heavy whipping cream until soft peaks form. Add the sweetened condensed milk and vanilla or cardamom extract, and beat a minute or so until combined. Fold in the caramelized rye bread crumbs and pour into a freezer container. Cover and freeze overnight.

3. Top with toasted caraway seeds, if desired, when serving.

Veiled Country Lass (*Bondepige med Slør*)

Scandinavia's take on trifle, Veiled Country Lass gets its name from the snowy mantle of sweetened whipped cream that crowns layers of rustic rye bread crumbs and slightly spiced applesauce.

INGREDIENTS | SERVES 6

½ cup water

2 tablespoons lemon juice

1 tablespoon white or brown sugar plus 1 tablespoon brown sugar, divided

½ teaspoon ground cardamom

¼ teaspoon ground cinnamon

8 large apples, peeled, cored, and coarsely chopped

4 tablespoons butter

2 cups rye bread crumbs

¼ cup walnuts or pecans, finely chopped

1 cup whipping cream, chilled

1 tablespoon vanilla sugar

½ cup raspberry, lingonberry, or red currant preserves

1. In a microwave-safe bowl, combine the water, lemon juice, 1 tablespoon white or brown sugar, cardamom, cinnamon, and apples. Cover and microwave on high for 5 minutes. Stir, return to microwave, and cook on high for 5 more minutes.

2. Melt the butter in a frying pan over medium heat until frothy. Add the bread crumbs, nuts, and remaining 1 tablespoon brown sugar, and fry until the crumbs are crisp, golden brown, and caramelized, about 5 minutes. Remove from heat.

3. Whip the cream and vanilla sugar together until stiff peaks form.

4. To assemble the dessert, place a layer of the crumbs in the bottom of dessert glasses. Top with a layer of apples, raspberry jam, and whipped cream; repeat the layers once.

CHAPTER 19

Beverages and Cordials

Lingonberry Cordial

Slightly less sharp than cranberries, tangy low-bush lingonberries yield a refreshing drink. Use either fresh or frozen lingonberries to enjoy their health benefits throughout the year.

INGREDIENTS | MAKES 1½ QUARTS

6½ pounds fresh or frozen lingonberries
1½ quarts water
1½ tablespoons lemon juice
3–4½ cups sugar

Easy Stirred Lingonberries

Lingonberries, hard enough to come by in America, should never be wasted. Stir sugar or honey into the mashed berries strained from Lingonberry Cordial and enjoy them either as a spread or as an accompaniment for meat dishes.

1. Wash and pick through the lingonberries, discarding any bad ones.

2. Place lingonberries in a large pitcher and crush with a potato masher to release juices. Stir in water and lemon juice, cover, and allow to sit in the refrigerator for 2 days, stirring every 12 hours.

3. Strain the lingonberry mixture, then stir sugar into the cordial in 1-cup increments until the concentrate reaches the desired sweetness.

4. To serve as lingonberry juice, add chilled plain or sparkling water to taste and serve over ice.

Icy Wolf's Paw

To truly experience this popular Nordic cocktail, pull on your mittens and sip it like they do at the world's first permanent icebar, Icebar Stockholm—in a glass made of ice!

INGREDIENTS | SERVES 4

3½ cups tap water
40 lingonberries or halved cranberries
4 (9-ounce) paper or plastic cups
4 (3-ounce) paper or plastic cups
Masking tape, as needed
8 ounces (1 cup) vodka
8 ounces (1 cup) sparkling water
½ cup Lingonberry Cordial (see recipe in this chapter)

1. Fill the 9-ounce cups ¾ of the way up with tap water; drop in 10 whole lingonberries or cranberry halves in each one.

2. Push the smaller 3-ounce cups into the larger ones until their lids are parallel; place a piece of masking tape across the top of the cups to keep the smaller one centered and in place. Freeze for 4 hours or more, then remove and unmold by running the cups under warm water.

3. Stir together the vodka, sparkling water, and Lingonberry Cordial.

4. Pour into the ice glasses and enjoy—*Skål!* ("Cheers!")

Rhubarb Cordial

Fresh rhubarb isn't just for pies—combine it with just enough sugar to make this sweetly tart summer refresher.

INGREDIENTS | MAKES 2 QUARTS

4 pounds fresh rhubarb stalks
2 quarts water
5 cloves
1 cinnamon stick
½ vanilla bean, split
1 cup sugar

1. Clean and cut the rhubarb into 1"-long slices. Combine in a large nonreactive pot with the water, cloves, cinnamon stick, and vanilla bean; bring to a boil, then reduce to a steady simmer. Cook until the rhubarb becomes mushy, about 15 minutes. Remove from heat and cool slightly.

2. Strain the mixture and return the juice to the pot; add the sugar and simmer for an additional 5 minutes, stirring steadily, until sugar dissolves.

3. Remove from heat and transfer to sterilized bottles.

4. To serve, dilute with water or sparkling water to taste and add ice.

Blueberry Cordial

This concentrated Blueberry Cordial is remarkably versatile—mix it with 3–4 parts sparkling water to make a refreshing summer drink, or use it as a base for blueberry cocktails by adding vodka and water to taste.

INGREDIENTS | MAKES 1 QUART

5 pounds fresh blueberries
1 quart water
3 cups sugar

1. Rinse blueberries and remove stems. Place in a nonreactive pot with the sugar and enough water to cover by 1".

2. Bring blueberries to a steady simmer over medium heat; cook 30 minutes or until berries have broken down.

3. Remove from heat and crush the berries with a potato masher. Cool.

4. Line a colander with cheesecloth; place the berry mixture in it and press down with the potato masher to release and strain all the juice.

5. Freeze the concentrated cordial in ice-cube trays or in plastic containers until needed.

Elderflower-Orange Cordial

To catch spring's elderflowers at the height of their freshness and flavor, be sure to pick them as soon as the buds open—from trees well away from roadsides. Elderflowers favor wet areas like streambanks.

INGREDIENTS | MAKES 1½ QUARTS

6 cups water

5 cups sugar

Zest of 1 lemon

Zest of 3 oranges

2 ounces citric acid

30 elderflower clusters

Citric Acid

Citric acid is an additive that enhances the flavor of citrus fruits like lemons, oranges, limes, and grapefruit when they are added to cordials, candies, or other foods. You generally can find it in the pharmacy section of big-box stores, in ethnic stores, or in specialty candy, canning, or brewing supply stores.

1. In a large nonreactive pot or glass bowl, bring the water to a boil. Sprinkle the sugar into the boiling water, stirring until sugar is dissolved.

2. Grate the zest of the lemon and the oranges into the sugar water, then slice the fruit and add these as well. Stir in the citric acid until dissolved.

3. Wash the elderflower clusters well in order to remove any insects, then add to the sugar water.

4. Cover the bowl and leave on the counter for 2 days, stirring occasionally.

5. After 48 hours, strain through a cheesecloth-lined colander to remove all solids. Pour the cordial into sterilized bottles, seal, and store in a cool cupboard.

6. To use, dilute the cordial with water or sparkling water to taste (Elderflower-Orange Cordial and SodaStreams are a match made in heaven).

Elderflower Cocktail (*Fläderbål*)

If you're not a fan of hard spirits, substitute 4 cups of sparkling white wine for the vodka and sparkling water used here.

INGREDIENTS | SERVES 4

⅔ cup Elderflower-Orange Cordial (see recipe in this chapter)

Juice of 2 limes

⅔ cup vodka or gin

4 cups sparkling water

Fresh fruit (strawberries, peaches, or plums) for garnish

1. Mix together the Elderberry-Orange Cordial and the lime juice.

2. Stir this mixture into the vodka, then combine with the sparkling water.

3. Fill 4 glasses with ice cubes, then add the cocktail mixture.

4. Garnish with fresh fruit and serve.

White *Glögg* (*Valkoinen Glögi*)

Those who prefer white wine to red will love this fruity version of mulled wine.

INGREDIENTS | SERVES 4

1 lemon

1 bottle white wine

1" piece fresh ginger, coarsely chopped

10 cloves

1 teaspoon cardamom seeds

½ cup sugar

1. Peel the lemon, taking care not to remove the bitter white pith with the peel. Scrape the pith off the lemon and discard, then slice the lemon.

2. In a nonreactive pot, stir together the white wine, lemon peel, ginger, cloves, cardamom seeds, and sugar; bring to a slow simmer over medium heat and cook for 10 minutes, stirring to dissolve the sugar.

3. Strain the warm *glögg* to remove the solids, pour into mugs, and crown with a lemon slice.

Mulled Wine (*Glögg*)

Christmas couldn't come in Scandinavia without glögg—
mulled wine that, when enjoyed with friends, warms the heart and soul.

INGREDIENTS | SERVES 6

1 bottle red wine

2 cups brandy

Peel of 1 orange, coarsely chopped

Peel of 1 lemon, coarsely chopped

2 cinnamon sticks

6 cardamom pods, crushed to open

10 cloves

1 cup raisins

1 cup pitted prunes, coarsely chopped

½ cup dates, coarsely chopped

20 whole blanched almonds

10 sugar cubes

Glögg Cake

For an easy and festive holiday cake, stir the fruit strained from your Christmas *glögg* making into a packaged spice-cake mix. Bake as directed on the package, then drizzle with a light lemon glaze.

1. Pour the wine and 1 cup of the brandy into a large nonreactive pot.

2. Tie the spices and citrus peels in a cheesecloth bag and immerse in the wine; add the dried fruit and almonds. Bring to a boil, then reduce heat to a slow and steady simmer.

3. Combine the sugar cubes and remaining cup of brandy into a small pan and heat over medium-low for about 15 minutes, stirring constantly, until sugar has dissolved and the syrup begins to bubble.

4. Add the sugar syrup to the *glögg*, cover, and cook for 30 minutes.

5. To serve, strain the mixture, reserving the dried fruit and almonds for other uses. Serve the *glögg* warm, accompanied by a few raisins and almonds in each glass.

Black Currant/Blackberry Cordial

If you aren't lucky enough to have access to black currants, blackberries are equally delectable in this fruit concentrate—just be sure to strain the mixture after cooking to remove the seeds.

INGREDIENTS | MAKES 1 QUART

4 cups black currants or blackberries
1½ cups brown sugar
4 cups water
Juice and peel of 1 orange

1. Wash the berries well, removing all stems.

2. Place berries with brown sugar and water in a nonreactive pot. Bring contents to a low and steady simmer, stirring constantly to dissolve the sugar. Simmer until the berries begin to pop, about 10 minutes.

3. Add the orange juice and peel; simmer for 10 more minutes.

4. Taste the cordial and if you find it too tangy, sweeten with more sugar. Remove from heat and cool for 20 minutes, then press the mixture through a cheesecloth-lined sieve to separate the juice from the pulp. Discard pulp.

5. Pour the concentrated juice into a sterilized bottle, cover, and refrigerate for up to 4 weeks. To use, dilute with water or sparkling water to taste.

Black Currant *Glögg* (*Mustaherukkaglögi*)

This is a great glögg to make when families gather—you can serve the basic nonalcoholic glögg to children and people who dislike spirits, or add crème de cassis (black currant liqueur) to the steaming mugs to give it some punch.

INGREDIENTS | SERVES 6

1 cup brown sugar

1 teaspoon whole cardamom seeds

5 whole cloves

1 cinnamon stick

Juice and peel of 1 naval orange

4 cups water

2 cups Black Currant/Blackberry Cordial (see recipe in this chapter)

Raisins and blanched whole almonds, to taste

Crème de cassis (optional) to taste

1. Combine the brown sugar, spices, and orange juice and peel in a pot. Add enough of the water to cover by 1". Bring the mixture to a low boil, reduce heat to medium, and simmer for 15 minutes.

2. Add the remaining water and cordial; simmer for an additional 15 minutes.

3. Strain the warm *glögg* through a cheesecloth-lined sieve into cups and serve immediately, accompanied by a few raisins and almonds in each mug.

4. For alcoholic black currant *glögg*, add a jigger of *crème de cassis* to each mug.

Caraway Aquavit

There are as many versions of aquavit in Scandinavia as there are families who make it; the only common element is that it must contain either caraway seed or dill. It's great fun to experiment with what you choose to infuse into the vodka.

INGREDIENTS | MAKES .75 LITER

2 teaspoons caraway seeds

1 (.75 liter) bottle potato vodka

2 star anise

1 orange, unpeeled, thinly sliced

Dill Aquavit

Looking for a great aquavit to accompany seafood? Instead of caraway seeds, infuse the vodka with a bunch of dill and a sliced lemon and/or lime.

1. Toast the caraway seeds lightly in a dry frying pan over medium heat to release their oils, about 5 minutes.

2. Combine the toasted caraway with the remaining ingredients in a glass container and cover.

3. Place in a cold, dark cupboard for at least 2 weeks, then sample. If you prefer a spicier blend, allow to rest for another week or two.

4. Transfer the aquavit to clean, sanitized bottles and store in the freezer.

5. Serve ice cold in chilled glasses.

Finnish Spring Mead (*Sima*)

The Finns celebrate the return of spring on Walpurgis Night (Walpurgisnacht) with sima, lemony spring mead, accompanied by fried "bird's nest" pastries—tippaleivät.

INGREDIENTS | MAKES 1 GALLON

2 large lemons
1 cup granulated white sugar
1 cup brown sugar
1 gallon water
½ teaspoon yeast
Raisins and additional sugar for bottles
Plastic bottles, 1 quart size or smaller

Fermentation Safety

Walpurgis bonfires are all fine and good, but it's best to avoid adding exploding sima bottles to the celebration. To prevent making your celebration more exciting than it needs to be, use plastic rather than glass bottles for your sima, and make sure you either consume it within the week that the raisins float or—if you want to brave fermenting it longer—that you loosen then retighten the caps every few days to allow excess carbon dioxide to escape.

1. Wash all the equipment you will be using (pot, spoon, knife/peeler, plastic bottles, lids) and rinse with boiling water to sanitize.

2. Wash the lemons well and use a potato peeler or sharp knife to peel the zest into long, thin strips. Cut away the bitter white rind and discard. Slice the lemons and place in a large, nonreactive container (heat-proof Pyrex or enamel is best). Add the peels and the white and brown sugars.

3. Bring the water to a roaring boil and pour over the lemon slices; stir to dissolve the sugar. Allow to sit undisturbed until lukewarm, then add the yeast and stir again to dissolve.

4. Cover the container loosely with a lid (so the carbon dioxide can escape). Allow to sit at room temperature for 24 hours.

5. Fill each sanitized plastic bottle with 1 teaspoon white sugar and 4 or 5 raisins. Strain the *sima* into the bottles, leaving 1" of air space at the top for expansion. Cover loosely and allow bottles to sit in a cool, dark place at room temperature for 24 more hours.

6. Tighten the lids on the bottles and transfer to the refrigerator for 2–5 days. The yeast will bond to the raisins during the fermentation process, producing carbon dioxide that eventually makes the raisins rise to the top of the bottles.

7. Once the raisins have risen, be sure to consume the lightly fermented *sima* within a week; keeping it longer will increase the alcoholic potency and you risk the bottles exploding.

Egg Coffee

Open any Scandinavian-American church cookbook from the early twentieth century, and chances are you will encounter a recipe for egg coffee. The egg clarifies the coffee, producing a virtually bitter-free brew requiring neither cream nor sugar to make it palatable for coffee-lovers with sensitive stomachs.

INGREDIENTS | SERVES 10

10¼ cups cold water, divided use
¾ cup ground coffee, medium grind
1 egg

1. Pour 9 cups of the water into a large pot and heat to boiling.

2. In a small bowl, combine the ground coffee, ¼ cup of the water, and the egg.

3. Once the water boils, turn down the heat to medium and gently drop in the coffee mixture. Bring the water back to a boil and cook for exactly 3 minutes. At this point the coffee grounds will clump together at the top of the liquid.

4. Immediately remove the pot from the burner and pour in the remaining cup of cold water. Allow the pot to simmer over low heat for at least 10 minutes or until the coffee grounds settle to the bottom of the pot. The coffee will become stronger the longer that it simmers.

5. To serve, strain the coffee through a sieve lined with cheesecloth or a coffee filter into cups.

Swedish Christmas Beer (*Julmumma*)

With its snowy head of froth, julmumma is a favorite Christmas tipple in Sweden.

INGREDIENTS | SERVES 6

2 bottles dark beer
3 bottles light beer
1½ cups sparkling lemonade
½ cup sherry, Madeira, or port wine
1 teaspoon cardamom, finely ground
Additional cardamom for garnish

1. Chill the beer and sparkling lemonade in the refrigerator for a few hours.

2. Combine the lemonade, Madeira wine, and ground cardamom in the bottom of a pitcher.

3. Carefully pour the beer into the pitcher so that a generous head of froth forms.

4. Pour the mixture into glasses, sprinkling a pinch of cardamom, if desired, on top of the froth in each glass.

Trøndelag Karsk for Wimps

The strong and hearty people of Trøndelag, Norway, are famous for the way they drink coffee—cut with equal amounts of moonshine. The Norwegians call this karsk (or kaffedoktor, "coffee doctor," good for what ails you). Here's a less potent version for the rest of us.

INGREDIENTS | SERVES 1

1 sugar cube
1 cup of hot coffee
1½ ounces potato vodka or brandy

1. Drop the sugar cube in the bottom of a mug, then pour in the coffee.

2. Add the potato vodka or brandy.

3. Sip slowly and enjoy.

Don't Try This at Home

Still longing to try Trøndelag karsk? Intrepid Norwegians place a copper penny in the bottom of a coffee cup, then pour in enough strong coffee that they can't see the coin, followed by enough moonshine (just as illegal in Norway as it is in the United States) to dilute the drink enough that they can see the coin again. It's hard to say which is greater—the choking hazard or the risk of alcohol poisoning.

Greenlandic Coffee

Create your very own "northern lights" with Greenland's take on Irish coffee.

INGREDIENTS | SERVES 1

1 tablespoon whisky
½ cup strong, hot coffee
1 tablespoon coffee-flavored Kahlúa
⅓ cup whipped cream
1 tablespoon Grand Marnier

1. Pour the whisky in a stemmed wine glass, then warm the glass carefully over a candle flame or spirit burner before setting the whisky alight. Allow it to flame for a few seconds, then pour in the coffee and Kahlúa.

2. Spoon the whipped cream on top of the coffee (this represents Greenland's ice).

3. Pour the Grand Marnier into a spoon and set it alight in the candle flame, then pour the burning blue liquid onto the layer of whipped cream (to represent the blue fire of the northern lights).

CHAPTER 20

Recipes for a Nordic Christmas (*Julbord*)

Saint Lucia Cats (*Lussekatter*)

Serve these sweet saffron buns on December 13, Saint Lucia Day in Scandinavia.

INGREDIENTS | SERVES 20

½ teaspoon saffron threads, crumbled (or 1 teaspoon powdered saffron)

1 cup melted butter

1 cup milk

½ cup sugar

1 teaspoon salt

2 packages dry active yeast (4½ teaspoons)

2 eggs, beaten, plus one egg white

6½ cups all-purpose flour

40 raisins, plumped in warm water

1. In a bowl or measuring cup, stir the saffron threads into the melted butter and allow to sit 30 minutes–1 hour.

2. In a saucepan, bring the milk to scalding over medium heat. Stir in the melted butter-saffron mixure, sugar, and salt. Transfer to the bowl of a stand mixer equipped with a paddle attachment, and allow to cool until finger-warm. Stir in the yeast and allow to sit for 10 minutes.

3. Stir the eggs into the liquid, then gradually add 3½ cups of the flour. Replace the paddle with the dough hook, then add enough of the remaining flour to form a soft dough (you've added enough when the dough pulls away from the side of the bowl).

4. Transfer the dough to a greased bowl, turn to coat, cover with a tea towel, and allow to rise until doubled, about 1 hour.

5. Punch down the dough, then knead it by hand 3–4 times on a floured counter. Pinch off egg-sized pieces of dough and roll them into ¾"-thick ropes. Shape the ropes into *S*-shaped buns. Place on a lightly oiled baking sheet, cover with the towel, and let rise for 1 more hour. Preheat oven to 375°F.

6. When the "cats" have doubled in size, brush them with the egg white and decorate with raisins (place raisins in the loops of the *S*). Bake for 15 minutes until golden.

Icelandic Leafbread (*Laufabrauð*)

Making laufabrauð, also called "snowflake bread," Scandinavia's most beautiful flatbread, is a not-to-be-missed ritual in Iceland during Advent. Families gather to prepare and cut intricate designs into each circle of bread using penknives or specially made laufabraudsjárn cutters.

INGREDIENTS | MAKES 50

2 cups all-purpose flour

2 cups rye flour (or wheat or all-purpose)

1 tablespoon sugar

1 teaspoon hornsalt (or substitute baking powder)

1 teaspoon salt

¼ cup butter, diced and chilled

1 cup milk, finger-warm

Canola oil or vegetable shortening for frying

Classic *Laufabrauð* Designs

As intricate as their knitting patterns, Icelanders use both traditional and family patterns to decorate their leaf bread, patterns with names like "Winter Sun," "The Star of Bethlehem," "Light of Wise Men," "Northern Lights," and "Winter Flower." For a great description of these designs, along with video tutorials demonstrating how to make laufabrauð, check out Esther Martin's blog, "Why'd You Eat That?" (*http://whydyoueatthat.wordpress.com*)

1. Use a balloon whisk to sift together the flours, sugar, hornsalt (or baking powder), and salt in a large bowl. Cut the butter into the dry ingredients with a pastry blender (as you would pie crust). Gradually add the warm milk to form a soft dough; transfer to a lightly floured counter and knead a few times, until dough is smooth and glossy. Divide the dough into 2 equal parts and roll into thick cylinders, then wrap these in a moist tea towel as you continue to make individual *laufabrauð* (this dough dries out very quickly).

2. Cut off a small slice of the dough—the size of a large walnut—from one of the cylinders and roll it into a circle 8⅛" in diameter. Place an 8" plate on the round and trim around the outside edges to make a perfect circle; set the trimmings aside to fry later as a separate snack. (The trimmings will be too dry to knead back into the dough. Instead, fry them as you would potato chips.)

3. Use a sharp knife to decorate the bread by cutting rows of diamond shapes into it (you could probably cheat and use a small, perhaps leaf-shaped, cookie cutter). Store each sheet between moist towels to prevent their drying out until you can fry them.

4. To fry, heat 2" of oil or shortening in a frying pan to 395°F. Prick the bread all over with a fork, lower into the oil, and fry for a mere second or two. Flip the bread over with a fork, as soon as it rises to the top of the oil, to fry the opposite side. As soon as the bread is golden, lift it out and place it on paper towels to drain. Repeat with the remaining dough.

5. Allow bread to cool, then store in an airtight container (it will keep for weeks). Serve it spread with butter, if desired.

Swedish *Knäck*

Once you get the "knack" of making Sweden's Christmas toffee, you'll find it becomes a seasonal tradition!

INGREDIENTS | SERVES 40

½ cup sugar

½ cup Swedish light syrup (or substitute golden syrup)

½ cup whipping cream

3 tablespoons finely chopped almonds or hazelnuts

Tiny paper cupcake wrappers, as needed

Anne's Food

Probably the best blog on Swedish cooking on the Internet is the gorgeously photographed Anne's Food. Anne not only publicizes traditional Swedish foods, she improves upon them and then shares her secrets with you (in English!). For her delicious variations on knäck, visit her blog (*http://annesfood.blogspot.com*).

1. In a 4-cup Pyrex measuring cup (or a high-sided, microwave-safe bowl), combine the sugar, light syrup, and whipping cream.

2. Place the mixture in the microwave and cook on high for 7 minutes, but check it at 5 to make sure it isn't boiling over. (*Use caution: you're dealing with scalding-hot sugar syrup here.*)

3. When the syrup reaches the soft ball stage (235°F on a candy thermometer, or when it forms a ball when dropped into ice water), remove syrup mix from the microwave, stir, and fold it together with the nuts. (If you boil it less, the syrup will have the consistency of fudge; if you boil it more, it will be rock solid. Tastes differ regarding densities.)

4. Very carefully pour the hot mixture into the wrappers; place in the refrigerator to set.

Herring and Beet Salad

To keep this classic Christmas salad from becoming a shocking shade of pink (unless, of course, you like pink food), arrange the ingredients on a platter, offer the sour cream dressing on the side, and allow your guests to mix their own salads to taste.

INGREDIENTS | SERVES 8

2 cups pickled herring tidbits

2 potatoes, peeled, cooked, and diced

1 red apple, cored and diced

1 green apple, cored and diced

2 cups pickled beets, diced

2 dill pickles, diced

½ cup sour cream

1 tablespoon lemon juice

1 teaspoon beet juice (optional; use if you like a bright pink salad)

1 teaspoon sugar

¼ teaspoon white pepper

Lemon zest to taste

1. Arrange the pickled herring, potatoes, diced apples, beets, and dill pickles in a colorful pattern on a serving platter, leaving room for the dressing bowl in the middle of the plate.

2. To make the dressing, whisk together the sour cream, lemon juice, beet juice (if you want pink dressing), sugar, and white pepper.

3. Transfer the dressing to a separate serving bowl and sprinkle with the lemon zest. Place in the middle of the salad platter and serve.

Dip in the Kettle (*Dopp i Grytan*)

Dopp i grytan is a traditional Christmas Eve dinner in Sweden. If you've made ham, simply strain the broth to remove the fat and spices, heat it up, and serve with thick slices of limpa or your other favorite rye bread. If, however, the in-laws are insisting upon turkey, here's an alternate method.

INGREDIENTS | MAKES 6 CUPS

1½ pounds pork (your choice: short ribs, ham hocks, spare ribs, pork shoulder)

6 cups water

1 bay leaf

1 large onion, peeled and studded with 3–4 whole cloves

1 teaspoon ground allspice

1 teaspoon ground pepper

Chunks of homemade rye bread to taste

1. Stir all the ingredients except the rye bread in a large soup pot. Bring the pot to a boil, reduce heat to low, cover, and simmer for 1–3 hours, skimming off the fat occasionally (the flavor will intensify the longer it cooks).

2. Strain the broth through a cheesecloth-lined colander into a soup tureen; you can serve the pork in a separate dish or reserve for other uses.

3. Place the tureen on the table, hand the rye bread around, and dunk the bread in the soup, fondue-style.

Mock Lutefisk

Although much beloved as an Advent pastime (or penance, depending on one's opinion), lutefisk dinners are more common today in Wisconsin than in Norway. Offer this "mock" version as an alternative to the traditional lye-cured lutefisk—while it won't taste exactly like fish Jell-o, it's healthier than meatballs.

INGREDIENTS | SERVES 4–6

1 pound dried codfish

8 ounces bacon or pancetta, chopped

1 medium onion, peeled and thinly sliced

2 teaspoons salt

3 tablespoons butter

3 tablespoons flour

4 cups milk

½ teaspoon nutmeg

Salt and pepper to taste

Lutefisk Declared Nontoxic . . .

By the state of Wisconsin, which firmly exempts lutefisk from classification as a toxic substance in Section 101.58(2)(j)(f) of the state's laws governing workplace safety.

1. Immerse the dried cod in enough water to cover and allow to soak for 36 hours, changing the water every 8 hours. Remove from water, pat dry, and remove the skin and any bones. Cut into serving-size pieces.

2. Fry the bacon or pancetta together with the onion until crisp; transfer to paper towels to drain.

3. Place the cod in a frying pan and add the salt and enough water to cover. Bring to a boil, reduce heat to low, and simmer until the fish flakes easily, about 8 minutes. Remove from the pan and drain.

4. Melt the butter in a saucepan over medium-high heat and stir in the flour, whisking constantly, until the roux bubbles. Gradually whisk in the milk, stirring, until it thickens to sauce consistency. Season with the nutmeg and with salt and pepper to taste.

5. To serve, transfer the fish to plates, pour the sauce over them, and crown with the bacon and onions.

Swedish Christmas Ham (*Julskinka*)

Cook this ham a day or two ahead of time, reserve the broth for Christmas Eve "Dip in the Kettle" and then do the final browning with the bread crumbs right before serving.

INGREDIENTS | MAKES 1 CHRISTMAS HAM

1 (9-pound) salt-cured, fresh ham (not smoked or dried)

2 onions, peeled and chopped

1 large carrot, peeled and chopped

3 quarts water

2 bay leaves

10 peppercorns

10 allspice berries

5 whole cloves

2 egg whites

1 tablespoon brown sugar

½ cup Swedish mustard

¾ cup fine bread crumbs

1. Preheat oven to 250°F. Place the ham in a Dutch oven or high-sided, oven-proof pot with the onions, carrot, water, bay leaves, peppercorns, allspice berries, and cloves.

2. Bake for 1–1½ hours until a thermometer inserted in the thickest part reads 167°F. Remove from the oven and allow the ham and broth to cool completely. The ham can be refrigerated overnight or completed immediately.

3. For your glaze, combine the egg whites, brown sugar, and mustard. Preheat the oven to 450°F. Cut the rind and most of the fat off the ham, then brush the ham well all over with the mustard mixture. Press the bread crumbs into the mustard and place the ham in a roasting pan. Bake for 10 minutes or until the ham is golden brown.

Norwegian Christmas Pork Ribs (*Juleribbe*)

In Norway, the traditional Christmas Eve dinner is ribs—either juleribbe, pork ribs, *or* pinnekjøtt, *dried and salted lamb ribs that are steamed over birch branches. It's difficult to find* pinnekjøtt *ribs in the United States. Christmas Pork Ribs, more easily obtainable, are a delicious and authentic option.*

INGREDIENTS | SERVES 8–10

8 pounds French-trimmed, bone-in pork loin

Salt and pepper to taste

1 cup water

But I Really Prefer Lamb . . .

If you still long for the *pinnekjøtt* experience, the salt-dried ribs are often offered seasonally by stores including: Scandinavian Specialties in Seattle (*www.scanspecialties .com*); historic Ingebretsen's in Minneapolis (*www.ingebretsens.com*); Scandinavian Food Store (Willy's Products) in Lauderhill, Florida (*www.willysproducts.com*); Nordic House in Berkeley, California (*www.nordichouse.com*); and Nordic Delicacies in Brooklyn, New York (*www.nordicdeli.com*). Be sure to place your order well ahead of time; most suppliers sell out quickly, especially in areas that still have large Norwegian-American populations.

1. Forty-eight hours before serving, score the skin side of the roast in a cross-hatch pattern with a sharp knife. Generously rub salt and pepper all over the loin, making sure to push them down into the scored skin.

2. Preheat oven to 450°F. Place the loin on a rack, skin-side down, and pour 1 cup of water in the bottom of the roasting pan. Cover the pan with heavy-duty aluminum foil, sealing the edges tightly. Place on the center rack of the oven and allow to steam-cook for 40 minutes.

3. Remove the foil from the pan, turn the loin over, and return the pan, uncovered, to the second-highest rack in the oven. Reduce heat to 390°F. Roast for 1½– 2 hours more, until the skin is crispy (but not blackened) and a digital thermometer registers between 145°F and 150°F. If the internal temperature is reached before the crackling is bubbly, you can increase the heat to 485°F for 5–10 minutes to crisp the skin (watch closely to prevent burning).

4. Remove meat from the oven, tent with foil, and allow to rest for 20 minutes before slicing and serving.

Smoked Lamb Ribs (*Pinnekjøtt*) with Rutabaga Mash (*Kålrabistappe*)

Now you can make Norway's own beloved pinnekjøtt, steamed over birch twigs and served with rutabaga mash (see sidebar for recipe).

INGREDIENTS | SERVES 10

8 pounds pinnekjøtt

A handful of birch twigs, peeled of all bark

5 rutabagas for Rutabaga Mash (see sidebar recipe)

Kålrabistappa

Kålrabistappa (rutabaga mash) is a traditional side dish served with *pinnekjøtt* on Christmas Eve. To make: peel, coarsely chop, and simmer a rutabaga, in enough water to cover, over medium-high heat until tender (30 minutes); drain, and mash together with some of the liquid from the *pinnekjøtt* pot into a chunky purée. Season with salt, pepper, nutmeg, and butter to taste.

1. Three days ahead of time, cut the meat into individual ribs and place in enough cold water to cover; change the water every 12 hours.

2. Crisscross the peeled birch twigs on the bottom of a large pot, then add enough water to surround, but not immerse, the twigs. Place the ribs on the birch twig rack, cover, and cook over low heat for 2–3 hours or until the meat falls off the bone (check the pot occasionally and add more water if necessary).

3. If desired, crisp the steamed ribs quickly under the broiler or on a grill before serving with the rutabaga mash.

Red Christmas Cabbage

For the best flavor, make this special spiced cabbage a few days ahead of time, refrigerate, and warm before serving.

INGREDIENTS | SERVES 6

1 head red cabbage

3 tablespoons butter

1 large onion, peeled and thinly sliced

1 large apple, peeled and thinly sliced

Zest and juice of 1 orange

½ teaspoon ground nutmeg

½ teaspoon ground cardamom

½ teaspoon ground cloves

3 tablespoons red wine vinegar

4 tablespoons currant or Lingonberry Jam (see Chapter 7)

½ teaspoon salt

¼ teaspoon pepper

1. Wash the cabbage well and chop into a fine julienne dice, either by hand or with a food processor.

2. In a heavy pot, melt the butter over medium heat. Add the onion and stir-fry until opaque.

3. Add the chopped cabbage and sliced apple, and cook until the cabbage begins to release its juices. Add the remaining ingredients, tossing well. Reduce heat to low, cover, and allow to simmer for 1 hour, checking occasionally and adding a little water (if necessary) throughout the cooking process.

4. Remove from heat, cool, and refrigerate overnight. Reheat prior to serving.

Danish Roast Duck with Apples and Prunes

Far less expensive but just as elegant as Christmas goose, this juicy duck, roasted with fragrant apples and prunes, is sure to be a crowd-pleaser.

INGREDIENTS | SERVES 4

1 (5-pound) duck

1 large yellow onion, peeled and quartered

10 baby carrots

2 celery stalks, cut in 1" lengths

2 bay leaves

10 peppercorns

Salt and pepper to taste

1 apple, peeled, cored, and cut into wedges

Pitted prunes (enough to stuff the duck, about 10)

3 tablespoons flour

1. With a sharp knife, prick the skin only (not the meat) of the duck on all sides.

2. Place the duck in a large stockpot and add enough water to cover it by 2". Remove the duck from the water, then place the onion, carrots, celery, bay leaves, and peppercorns in the water. Bring the pot to boiling over high heat. Gently lower the duck into the boiling water. Return to a boil, then immediately reduce heat to medium-low. Place a weight (a plate or two) on the duck to keep it from rising. Simmer for 45 minutes, skimming off any foam. Remove duck from the water, pat dry with paper towels, and cool to room temperature.

3. While the duck rests, skim the fat that has arisen in the stock and place it in a separate container. Strain the stock through a cheesecloth-lined colander to remove the solids. Reserve the stock to make gravy.

4. Preheat oven to 500°F. Season the duck inside and out with salt and pepper. Stuff the cavity of the duck with the apple slices and as many of the prunes as it will hold.

5. Place the duck on a rack in a roasting pan and cook for 15 minutes. Rotate the pan, then roast for an additional 15 minutes. Remove from the oven; carefully spoon out the stuffing onto a cutting board and chop it coarsely. Strain the pan drippings, removing and reserving the fat that rises to the top. Allow the duck to rest for 15 minutes before carving.

6. To make your gravy, melt 2 tablespoons of the reserved fat in a saucepan over medium heat, then whisk in flour. Add the pan drippings and 3 cups of the strained broth. Reduce heat to medium-low and simmer until the gravy thickens, about 10 minutes, whisking often. Fold in the chopped prunes and apples, season with salt and pepper to taste, then transfer to a gravy boat to serve alongside the carved duck.

Nordic Christmas Cake (*Julekake*)

Actually more of a yeasted bread than a cake,
julekake *is the perfect fruited bread for those who dislike heavy fruitcakes.*

INGREDIENTS | MAKES 2 LOAVES

1 package active dry yeast (2¼ teaspoons)

¼ cup warm water

1 cup milk, scalded then cooled until finger-warm

¼ cup softened butter

½ cup white sugar

1 teaspoon salt

2 eggs, beaten

½ teaspoon freshly ground cardamom

4–4½ cups all-purpose or bread flour

1 cup mixed raisins (dark and golden)

1 cup citron

¼ cup slivered almonds

Milk for basting loaves

Pearl or sparkling sugar to taste

A Norwegian Christmas

For beautiful illustrations of how to celebrate Christmas like a Norwegian, check out two of the best books ever written on the subject: Astrid Karlsen Scott's *Authentic Norwegian Cooking* (Nordic Adventures: 2002; Skyhorse Publishing: 2011) and its companion volume, *Traditional Norwegian Christmas* ("Ekte Norsk Jul"; Nordic Adventures: 2002).

1. Stir the yeast into the warm water and allow to proof for 15 minutes until it becomes foamy (if it doesn't start to bubble, buy new yeast and try again).

2. Combine the milk, butter, sugar, salt, beaten eggs, and cardamom in the bowl of a stand mixer. Stir in the yeast mixture and 2 cups of the flour. Equip the mixer with its paddle blade, turn it on low, and gradually increase the speed to medium as the flour incorporates into the liquid. Beat until smooth. Add the raisins, citron, and slivered almonds; beat on low speed just until incorporated, then scrape down the sides of the bowl.

3. Replace the paddle with the dough hook, and add enough of the remaining 2½ cups of flour to make a slightly stiff dough that pulls away from the side of the mixer. Increase the speed to medium-high to high (depending on the strength/capacity of your mixer), and knead the dough until it is smooth and glossy.

4. Turn the dough out onto a lightly floured counter and knead 2–3 times, then place it in a greased bowl and roll it over once, bringing the greased side up. Cover with a tea towel and place in a warm spot to rise until doubled, about 1 hour (this may take as long as 1½ hours, depending on the heat in your kitchen). Punch the dough down.

5. Divide the dough into 2 equal halves, and then form these into circular loaves. Place on a greased cookie sheet, cover with the tea towel, and allow to rise until doubled.

6. Preheat oven to 350°F. Brush the loaves with milk, sprinkle with the pearl or sparkling sugar, and bake for 15–20 minutes until golden.

Finnish Yule Bread *(Joululimppu)*

Finnish Yule Bread is quite similar to Swedish vörtlimpa *("wort loaf"), but is slightly sweeter and typically doesn't incorporate beer or brewer's wort. Use dried bitter (Seville) orange peel if you can get it; otherwise dried orange peel is fine.*

INGREDIENTS | MAKES 2 LOAVES

- ½ cup plus 1 tablespoon molasses or golden syrup, divided use
- 3 cups buttermilk, room temperature
- ¼ cup butter, softened
- 1 teaspoon fennel seeds
- 1 teaspoon anise seeds
- 2 packages active dry yeast (4½ teaspoons)
- 2 teaspoons dried orange peel, finely minced
- 1 teaspoon salt
- 2½ cups rye flour
- 3–3½ all-purpose or spelt flour
- ¼ cup warm water

1. In a saucepan, combine the ½ cup molasses, buttermilk, butter, fennel seeds, and anise seeds. Bring to a low boil and cook for 5 minutes, stirring occasionally to dissolve the molasses and butter. Remove from heat and cool until the mixture is lukewarm.

2. Sift the dry yeast, orange peel, salt, and rye flour into the bowl of a large mixer equipped with a paddle.

3. Set the mixer on low and gradually incorporate the liquid into the flour. Scrape down the sides of the bowl and swap the paddle for a dough hook.

4. At low speed, incorporate 3 cups of the all-purpose flour into the dough; increase speed to medium-high and beat for 7 minutes or so, until the dough begins to pull away from the sides of the bowl (add more flour, if needed, until the dough is workable). Allow the dough to rest in the bowl for 20 minutes. As the dough rests, preheat oven to 300°F, then turn it off immediately.

5. After the dough has rested, knead it lightly, until it is stiff and smooth, about 5 minutes.

6. Place dough in a lightly buttered bowl, flipping once to coat with butter. Cover with a clean tea towel, place in the warmed oven, and let rise until double, 1–2 hours.

7. Punch down the dough, divide it into even halves, and shape each half into a round loaf. Place on a lightly floured baking pan or a wooden paddle if you use a bread stone in your oven. Cover with the tea towel and let the loaves rise until doubled, 1–1½ hours.

8. Preheat oven to 390°F. Place a cake pan on the lowest shelf in the oven; position the bread stone (if using) on the shelf above.

9. Prick each loaf well with a fork. Transfer to the oven and place 2–3 ice cubes in the lower pan, shutting the door immediately. Bake for 30 minutes, then whisk together the remaining tablespoon of molasses in the warm water and baste the loaves. Bake for an additional 15 minutes or until the bread sounds hollow when you tap the bottom. Cool completely on a wire rack.

Finnish Prune Jam Pastries

Take the labor—but not the love—out of making Finland's "windmill" prune pastries by using puff pastry instead of homemade pastry dough.

INGREDIENTS | MAKES 30

2 sheets frozen puff pastry, thawed

1 egg, beaten with 1 tablespoon water into an egg wash

10 tablespoons prune jam or Prune Filling (see sidebar recipe)

Warm milk to glaze

Sparkling sugar to taste

Prune Filling

To make homemade prune filling, place 2 pounds of prunes in a saucepan with just enough water to cover. Simmer until prunes are soft, about 20 minutes; drain and cool the prunes, reserving 1 cup juice, then purée prunes in a blender or food processor. In a saucepan, combine the purée with the reserved juice, 1½ cup sugar, 1 teaspoon cinnamon, and ½ teaspoon ground cardamom. Simmer over medium heat, stirring constantly, until the mixture thickens to the consistency of lemon curd. Cool.

1. Preheat oven to 400°F. Cut each of the pastry sheets into 15 squares (about 3¼" each).

2. Use a sharp knife to make a diagonal cut from the corners toward the center of each square, stopping within ½" of the center. With a pastry brush, coat all four sides of each square well with the egg wash. Place a teaspoon of prune jam in the center of each square, then fold the left-hand side of each corner down to meet in the center, forming a windmill. Push each corner down slightly to secure.

3. Baste each pastry with the warm milk, then sprinkle with the sparkling sugar.

4. Bake in oven for 8–10 minutes until light golden brown.

Rice Pudding with Almonds and Warm Cherry Sauce

In Denmark, rice porridge left over from Christmas Eve is used to make this favorite Christmas dessert.

INGREDIENTS | SERVES 6

1 cup short-grained glutinous rice

1½ cups water

1 tablespoon butter

½ teaspoon salt

4½ cups milk

1½ cups heavy cream

1 tablespoon vanilla sugar or 1 teaspoon vanilla extract

1 cup sugar, divided use

1 teaspoon freshly ground cardamom

½ cup chopped almonds, toasted

1 (16-ounce) package frozen pitted cherries, thawed

1 tablespoon lemon juice

1 tablespoon potato starch flour or cornstarch plus 1 tablespoon water

1. Wash and drain the rice well. Combine water, butter, and salt in a saucepan and bring to a boil over high heat. Pour in the rice, reduce heat to low, and stir until the boiling is reduced to a steady simmer. Cover the pot and simmer for 10–15 minutes until most of the water has been absorbed. Stir in the milk, return pot to a boil, then reduce heat again to low. Cover pot and cook until the milk has been absorbed, about 45 minutes. Cool completely.

2. Whip together the cream, vanilla sugar (or vanilla extract), ½ cup of the sugar, and the cardamom until stiff peaks form. Gently fold the whipped cream and toasted almonds into the rice porridge. Cover and refrigerate for at least 3 hours (or up to overnight).

3. In a saucepan, combine the frozen cherries, lemon juice, and remaining ½ cup sugar; cook over medium heat, stirring, until the sugar has dissolved and the cherries begin to soften, about 7 minutes. Whisk together the potato starch flour and water into a slurry, then stir into the cherry sauce to thicken slightly.

4. To serve, spoon the chilled rice pudding into individual bowls and top with the warm cherry sauce.

Nordic Cookbooks, Culinary Websites, and Blogs

Cookbooks

Adlerbert, Elna. *Cooking the Scandinavian Way* (London: Spring Books, 1961)

Blomquist, Torsten, and Werner Vögeli. *A Gastronomic Tour of the Scandinavian Arctic* (New York: Bergh Publishing, 1987)

Brown, Dale. *The Cooking of Scandinavia* (Alexandria, VA: Time-Life Books, 1968)

Doub, Siri Lise. *Tastes & Tales of Norway* (New York: Hippocrene Books, 2002)

Favish, Melody, trans. *Swedish Cakes and Cookies* (New York: Skyhorse Publishing, 2008)

Gillespie-Lewis, Anne. *Ingebretsen's Saga: A Family, A Store, A Legacy in Food* (Minneapolis, MN: Ingebretsen's Gift Shop, 2011)

Hahnemann, Trina. *The Nordic Diet* (London: Quadrille Publishing Ltd, 2010; New York: Skyhorse Publishing: 2011)

Hahnemann, Trina. *The Scandinavian Cookbook* (Riverside, NJ: Andrews McMeel Publishing, 2009)

Hazelton, Nika Standen. *Classic Scandinavian Cooking* (New York: Charles Scribner's Sons, 1965, repr. 1987)

Hedh, Jan. *Swedish Breads and Pastries* (New York: Skyhorse Publishing, 2010)

Henderson, Helene. *The Swedish Table* (Minneapolis, MN: University of Minnesota Press, 2005)

Hill, Anja. *The Food & Cooking of Finland* (London: Aquamarine, Anness Publishing Ltd., 2008)

International Book Automation. *Kajsa Wargs Kokbok* (Uddevala: ICA, 1969)

Jensen, Ingeborg Dahl. *Wonderful, Wonderful Danish Cooking: 500 Specialties That Americans Love to Eat* (New York: Simon and Schuster, 1965)

Käkönen, Ulla. *Natural Cooking the Finnish Way* (New York: Quadrangle, New York Times Book Co., 1974)

Martin, Janet Letnes, and Ilene Letnes Lorenz. *Our Beloved Sweden: Food, Faith, Flowers & Festivals* (Hastings, MN: Sentel Publishing, 1996)

Nellie Gerdrum, Lodge #41, Daughters of Norway. *Skandinaviske Oppskrifter* ("*Scandinavian Recipes*")(Bellingham, WA: 2005)

Ojakangas, Beatrice. *The Finnish Cookbook* (New York: Crown Publishers, 1964, repr. 1989)

Ojakangas, Beatrice. *The Great Scandinavian Baking Book* (Minneapolis, MN: University of Minnesota Press, 1999)

Ojakangas, Beatrice. *Scandinavian Cooking* (Minneapolis, MN: University of Minnesota Press, 2003)

Ojakangas, Beatrice. *Scandinavian Feasts: Celebrating Traditions Throughout the Year* (Minneapolis, MN: University of Minnesota Press, 2001)

Redzepi, René. *Noma: Time and Place in Nordic Cuisine* (London: Phaidon Press, Har/Map edition, 2010)

Rögnvaldardóttir, Nanna. *Icelandic Food & Cookery* (New York: Hippocrene Books, 2002)

Samuelsson, Marcus. *Aquavit: And the New Scandinavian Cuisine* (New York: Houghton Mifflin Co., 2003)

Scott, Astrid Karlsen. *Authentic Norwegian Cooking* (Olympia, WA: Nordic Adventures, 2002; New York: Skyhorse Publishing, 2011)

Scott, Astrid Karlsen. *Traditional Norwegian Christmas ("Ekte Norsk Jul")* (Olympia, WA: Nordic Adventures, 2002)

Shaw, Hank. *Hunt, Gather, Cook: Finding the Forgotten Feast* (Emmaus, PA: Rodale Books, 2011)

Viestad, Andreas. *Kitchen of Light: The New Scandinavian Cooking* (New York: Artisan, 2003)

Viola, Pauline, and Knud Ravnkilde. *Cooking with a Danish Flavour* (London: Elm Tree Books, 1978)

Culinary Websites and Blogs

ABOUT.COM: GUIDE TO SCANDINAVIAN FOOD

A website and accompanying blog about traditional Scandinavian, New Nordic, and fusion recipes. Written, photographed, and managed by Kari Schoening Diehl.
http://scandinavianfood.about.com

CLAUS MEYER

The homepage of one of the two chief architects of the New Nordic Cuisine Movement.
www.clausmeyer.dk/en

NEW SCANDINAVIAN COOKING

The online presence of public television's best cooking show.
www.newscancook.com

ANDREAS VIESTAD

Norwegian chef and cookbook author Andreas Viestad's personal website.
www.andreasviestad.com

TRINE HAHNEMANN

The website of cookbook author and chef extraordinaire, Trine (spelled "Trina" on her book jackets) Hahnemann.
http://trinehahnemann.com/en

BEATRICE OJAKANGAS

Recipes from America's own greatest Scandinavian chef and cookbook author.
http://beatrice-ojakangas.com

MARCUS SAMUELSSON

Home site of world-famous Chef Marcus Samuelsson, of Aquavit and Red Rooster fame.
http://marcussamuelsson.com

ANNE'S FOOD

One of the best blogs running about Swedish food.

http://annesfood.blogspot.com

ICELANDIC RECIPES, COOKING, AND FOOD

Jo's Icelandic Recipes, one of the premier websites on Icelandic cuisine.

http://icecook.blogspot.com

HUNTER ANGLER GARDENER COOK

Although not focused on Nordic food *per se*, Hank Shaw's website is unparalleled in its great descriptions of the value of foraging, fishing, and hunting; in short, to "Find the Forgotten Feast." Twice nominated for a James Beard Foundation Award and winner of the 2010 and 2011 International Association of Culinary Professionals awards for Best Blog.

http://honest-food.net

ALLT OM MAT ("ALL ABOUT FOOD" MAGAZINE)

The website of what for forty years has been Sweden's most popular food magazine. It is *the* go-to resource for learning about what's hot on Sweden's food scene.

www.alltommat.se

ALLETIDERS KOKEBOG ("ALLETIDERS COOKBOOK")

An interactive cookbook with literally hundreds of user-submitted recipes; in Danish.

www.dk-kogebogen.dk

Storefront and Online Nordic Food Suppliers

AUNT ELSE'S ÆBLESKIVER
2010 East Hennepin Avenue #20
Minneapolis, MN 55413
www.auntelse.com

A very cool, family-owned company that manufactures different varieties of *æbleskiver* mix as well as everything you need to make these Danish delicacies like a pro. Check out the website video for a great demonstration of how to do the "*æbleskiver* flip."

BETHANY HOUSEWARES
431 2nd Avenue SW, P.O. Box 199
Cresco, IA 52136-0199
563-547-5873
www.bethanyhousewares.com

An established manufacturer and distributor of quality Scandinavian/Norwegian housewares.

IKEA
www.ikea.com/us/en

It's IKEA. Lingonberry jam, *matjes* herring, Scandinavian chocolate. Never mind the furniture—go there for the food market. 'Nuff said.

INGEBRETSEN'S
1601 East Lake Street
Minneapolis, MN 55407
612-729-9333; Toll-Free: 1-800-279-9333
www.ingebretsens.com

Minneapolis' historical Scandinavian meat market and store, first opened in 1921 and still going strong!

KING ARTHUR FLOUR
135 U.S. Route 5 South
Norwich, VT 05055
802-649-3361; Toll-Free: 1-800-827-6836
www.kingarthurflour.com

Excellent store, café, and online provider of a wide range of whole grains—including different varieties of rye flour and other hard-to-source ingredients like diastatic malt powder. Shipping can be pricey, so order in bulk when possible.

LEFSE TIME
115 North Shore, P.O. Box 222
Fountain City, WI 54629
Toll-Free: 1-800-687-2058
www.lefsetime.com

A retail and online store specializing in lefse-making accessories and other Scandinavian bakeware.

MARINA MARKET
Street Address: 18882 Front Street
Poulsbo, WA 98370
Toll-Free: 1-888-728-0837
www.marinamarket.com

A jewel in the center of Norwegian-American Poulsbo, Washington—and one of the few places you can order frozen lingonberries online. At last count, Marina Market also had the largest collection of European licorice available in the United States. Visit Poulsbo's "Viking Days" in May, witness the lutefisk eating contest, then go to Marina Market, wave at owner Andrea Rowe, and stock up on hard-to-find Scandinavian foods and ingredients.

NIELSEN'S MARKET

608 Alamo Pintado Road
Solvang, CA 93463
805-688-3236
www.nielsensmarket.com

Even older than Minneapolis' Ingebretsen's, Nielsen's Market has been a fixture in the Danish-American community of Solvang, California, since 1911—more than 100 years! Visit the store for its Scandinavian specialties and full-service deli, or check out its online market.

NORDIC DELICACIES

6909 Third Avenue
Brooklyn, NY 11209
718-748-1874
www.nordicdeli.com

Scandinavian deli and importers of food and chocolate; online orders accepted.

NORDIC HOUSE

2709 San Pablo Avenue
Berkeley, CA 94702
1-800-854-6435
www.nordichouse.com

Storefront and online provider of Nordic foods, cookware, and gifts.

NORDIC WARE

5005 Highway 7
Minneapolis, MN 55416-2274
Toll-Free: 1-877-466-7342

www.nordicware.com

Distributor of "Made in America" aluminum cookware, bakeware, and kitchenware.

SCANDINAVIAN SPECIALTIES

6719 - 15th Avenue NW
Seattle, WA 98117
206-784-7020 / Toll-Free: 1-877-784-7020
www.scanspecialties.com

Seattle-based café/deli and importer of Scandinavian foods and goods.

SIGGI'S (A.K.A. THE ICELANDIC MILK AND SKYR CORPORATION)

135 West 26th Street, 11th floor
New York, NY 10001
Distribution: 212-966-6950
http://skyr.com

Home site of America's premier producer of Icelandic *skyr*. Read about how Siggi Hilmarsson single-handedly introduced Iceland's wonderful *skyr* to U.S. markets—it bodes well to replace Greek yogurt in popularity!

SCANDINAVIAN FOOD STORE (WILLY'S PRODUCTS)

1601 NW 38th Avenue
Lauderhill, FL 33311
954-316-1350
www.willysproducts.com

Online distributor of Norwegian, Swedish, Danish, and Finnish foods.

Standard U.S./Metric Measurement Conversions

VOLUME CONVERSIONS

U.S. Volume Measure	Metric Equivalent
⅛ teaspoon	0.5 milliliters
¼ teaspoon	1 milliliters
½ teaspoon	2 milliliters
1 teaspoon	5 milliliters
½ tablespoon	7 milliliters
1 tablespoon (3 teaspoons)	15 milliliters
2 tablespoons (1 fluid ounce)	30 milliliters
¼ cup (4 tablespoons)	60 milliliters
⅓ cup	90 milliliters
½ cup (4 fluid ounces)	125 milliliters
⅔ cup	160 milliliters
¾ cup (6 fluid ounces)	180 milliliters
1 cup (16 tablespoons)	250 milliliters
1 pint (2 cups)	500 milliliters
1 quart (4 cups)	1 liter (about)

WEIGHT CONVERSIONS

U.S. Weight Measure	Metric Equivalent
½ ounce	15 grams
1 ounce	30 grams
2 ounces	60 grams
3 ounces	85 grams
¼ pound (4 ounces)	115 grams
½ pound (8 ounces)	225 grams
¾ pound (12 ounces)	340 grams
1 pound (16 ounces)	454 grams

OVEN TEMPERATURE CONVERSIONS

Degrees Fahrenheit	Degrees Celsius
200 degrees F	95 degrees C
250 degrees F	120 degrees C
275 degrees F	135 degrees C
300 degrees F	150 degrees C
325 degrees F	160 degrees C
350 degrees F	180 degrees C
375 degrees F	190 degrees C
400 degrees F	205 degrees C
425 degrees F	220 degrees C
450 degrees F	230 degrees C

BAKING PAN SIZES

American	Metric
8 x 1½ inch round baking pan	20 x 4 cm cake tin
9 x 1½ inch round baking pan	23 x 3.5 cm cake tin
1 x 7 x 1½ inch baking pan	28 x 18 x 4 cm baking tin
13 x 9 x 2 inch baking pan	30 x 20 x 5 cm baking tin
2 quart rectangular baking dish	30 x 20 x 3 cm baking tin
15 x 10 x 2 inch baking pan	30 x 25 x 2 cm baking tin (Swiss roll tin)
9 inch pie plate	22 x 4 or 23 x 4 cm pie plate
7 or 8 inch springform pan	18 or 20 cm springform or loose bottom cake tin
9 x 5 x 3 inch loaf pan	23 x 13 x 7 cm or 2 lb narrow loaf or pate tin
1½ quart casserole	1.5 litre casserole
2 quart casserole	2 litre casserole

Index

Note: Page numbers in **bold** indicate recipe category lists.

We Have

EVERYTHING

on Anything!

With more than 19 million copies sold, the Everything® series has become one of America's favorite resources for solving problems, learning new skills, and organizing lives. Our brand is not only recognizable—it's also welcomed.

The series is a hand-in-hand partner for people who are ready to tackle new subjects—like you!

For more information on the Everything® series, please visit *www.adamsmedia.com*

The Everything® list spans a wide range of subjects, with more than 500 titles covering 25 different categories:

Business	History	Reference
Careers	Home Improvement	Religion
Children's Storybooks	Everything Kids	Self-Help
Computers	Languages	Sports & Fitness
Cooking	Music	Travel
Crafts and Hobbies	New Age	Wedding
Education/Schools	Parenting	Writing
Games and Puzzles	Personal Finance	
Health	Pets	